The Song Remains the Same

The Song Remains the Same

*800 Years of Love Songs,
Laments and Lullabies*

Andrew Ford
& Anni Heino

Published by La Trobe University Press in conjunction with Black Inc.
Level 1, 221 Drummond Street
Carlton VIC 3053, Australia
enquiries@blackincbooks.com
www.blackincbooks.com
www.latrobeuniversitypress.com.au

La Trobe University plays an integral role in Australia's public intellectual life, and is recognised globally for its research excellence and commitment to ideas and debate. La Trobe University Press publishes books of high intellectual quality, aimed at general readers. Titles range across the humanities and sciences, and are written by distinguished and innovative scholars. La Trobe University Press books are produced in conjunction with Black Inc., an independent Australian publishing house. The members of the LTUP Editorial Board are Vice-Chancellor's Fellows Emeritus Professor Robert Manne and Dr Elizabeth Finkel, and Morry Schwartz and Chris Feik of Black Inc.

9781760640118 (paperback)
9781743821060 (ebook)

 A catalogue record for this book is available from the National Library of Australia

Cover design by Regine Abos
Cover image © Dome Studio/Shutterstock
Text design and typesetting by Akiko Chan

Contents

To Anon.

Introduction

This tune was composèd by Spencer the Rover,
As valiant a man as ever left home
He had been much reducèd,
Which caused great confusion,
And that was the reason he started to roam.

In Yorkshire, near Rotherham, he had been on the ramble;
Weary of travelling, he sat down to rest.
At the foot of a mountain
There's a clear crystal fountain:
With bread and cold water he himself did refresh.

With the night time approaching, to the woods he resorted,
With woodbine and ivy his bed for to make,
But he dreamt about sighing
Lamenting and crying:
Go home to your family and rambling forsake.

'Twas the fifth day of November, I have reason to remember,
When first he came home to his family and wife.
They did stand so astounded
Amazed and dumbfounded
To see such a stranger once more in their sight.

His children come around him with their prittle-prattling stories,
With their prittle-prattling stories to drive cares away.
He's as happy as those
As have thousands of riches.
At home he'll remain, and not ramble away.

> This tune was composèd by Spencer the Rover,
> As valiant a man as ever left home
> He had been much reducèd,
> Which caused great confusion,
> And that was the reason he started to roam.

Is 'Spencer the Rover' the only song signed by its composer?

Other songwriters have mentioned themselves. Bo Diddley was the named hero of a number of his own songs, Elton John's 'Your Song' is one of dozens that describes the process of songwriting (not that he wrote the words), and since the troubadours and trouvères of medieval France, there have been thousands of songs addressed, in the Beatles' words, 'From Me to You'.

But Spencer identifies himself in the first line, laying claim to his story and to the words and music that tell it. 'This tune was *composèd*' by him. In some versions it's 'This song' or 'These words'. Whatever. It's his song, on loan to the singer for the duration of a performance. Perhaps that's true of any song – the songwriter lends it to the singer – but in Spencer's case, it's poignant: as a vagrant, he would have had few other possessions.

Of course, the song is credited to 'Anon.' It is anonymous, traditional. Who knows if there was a real Spencer? Probably there were dozens of them. Certainly, there are multiple versions of the song to be found throughout the island of Great Britain. In many of them, including one sung for centuries by the Copper Family of Rottingdean in Sussex, Spencer had 'travelled through Britain and most parts of Wales'; but between versions the differences aren't great, the song fleshed out here or there, an extra verse of contentment added to celebrate Spencer's eventual homecoming.

One thing that most versions of 'Spencer the Rover' share is the reference to the Yorkshire town of Rotherham. Even the Coppers' south-coast version mentions the place, leading some writers to speculate that the song itself must have originated there. Perhaps it did, although given Spencer is 'on the ramble' near Rotherham, he quite likely set out from somewhere else.

The element of the song that all versions seem to include is the prittle-prattle of Spencer's children, who crowd eagerly around this 'stranger' upon his return. It is a piercingly exact image, which the song repeats – a detail that summons the singer and listener into the children's clamour. Whatever it was that had 'reducèd' him in the first place – industrialisation, the enclosure of farming land, economic hard times, mental illness – it was the thought of his family 'lamenting and crying' that brought him home. And now here they are, all talking at once.

Perhaps this affirmation of family life is what endeared the song to our small daughter, for whom it became an oft-requested 'lullaby' (that's our version given here, derived largely from the version sung by John Martyn on his album *Sunday's Child*). In the nearly nightly performances at our place the song quickly took on some of the qualities of musical theatre, as Elsie would sit up in bed at the end of verse two to take a sip of cold water at the same moment as Spencer.

The point of the bedtime song is to unite child and parent in a special and important way. Whether or not the child understands the words of a lullaby, she certainly understands the tone of the voice singing it. A lullaby is the day's final moment of parent–child bonding. It makes sleep easier, if not inevitable.

One aspect of the lullaby ritual, as with all rituals, is repetition: it is essential that each time it's sung, the song remains the same. Mistakes will be spotted. It is, for example, not unknown for the singer of a lullaby to doze off mid-song (this is exactly what happens in Modest Musorgsky's song 'S kukloy' from *The Nursery*, in which a child sings a bedtime song to her doll), but any slip-ups in the performance will be seized upon by the possibly less drowsy audience and pointed out to the singer. Lyrics become fixed in the child's mind, even when they are the *wrong* lyrics. When one of Elsie's parents discovered he had been singing the words 'And weeping' instead of 'Lamenting' in the third verse of 'Spencer the Rover', his regular attempts to use the correct word in his night-time performance were greeted with protests from the would-be sleeper. 'Weeping, Daddy. It's weeping.'

Repetition is also the key to songs in a more fundamental sense. In the two- to five-minute structure of the average song, repetition is inherent. Songs are self-contained packages of words and music, sometimes working together and sometimes in opposition, more often than not bound by a structure that is bipartite. In this structure there are verses (in a fixed format) that make a case or advance a story, punctuated by a chorus that repeats most, if not all, of its features. Sometimes the music of the verse and the chorus is more or less the same ('Tutti Frutti', 'You Are My Sunshine', 'The Battle Hymn of the Republic' and 'The Holly and the Ivy' are examples from the present volume where a single tune fits both parts of the song); sometimes there are other elements such as a bridge – often called the 'middle eight', because it is frequently eight bars long. There are plenty of exceptions to this model – and there are plenty considered in this book – but alternating verses and choruses is the most common structure of a song.

The relationship between words and music may exist on the surface of the song, and so can be rather obvious. For example, the babbling brook or millwheel or galloping horse piano accompaniments in some of Schubert's songs serve to illustrate the story being sung. But the relationship can operate in more subtle ways. Michel Legrand's 'Windmills of Your Mind' (with words by Alan and Marilyn Bergman), has a harmonic scheme that whirls off through the circle of fifths. It only gets halfway before swinging back to where it started, but it's a pleasing musical metaphor for the windmill.

One of the slickest songwriters of the late twentieth (and early twenty-first) century was Nick Lowe. Wordplay was his particular talent, and in 'All Men Are Liars' he memorably rhymed 'Rick Astley' with 'ghastly'. But it is another line in the song's lyrics that subtly connects with its music. 'There stands the naked ape in a monkey suit,' sings Lowe, the melody obliging him to allocate three notes to the final word 'suit', thus creating the monkey-like melisma 'oo-oo-oo', with a little staccato attack for each 'oo'. For a moment we hear and see this dressed-up ape.

Songs are written in different ways. Art songs (and what an unfortunate phrase that is!) tend to be a matter of a composer putting an existing text to music. The text is generally a poem – words that have been worked and reworked and have a strict form (and music) of their own – and the poet may be long dead. The composer's job is to make the poem sing, perhaps in a way that never crossed the poet's mind. Heinrich Heine might have thought he was writing a simple poem about burgeoning love in 'Im wunderschönen Monat Mai', but Robert Schumann found in the words an opportunity for a song about love that was doomed. The words are unchanged, the doom all in the music. That's the composer's prerogative. And even when the musical setting seems at odds with the structure or tone or meaning of the original text, the poet's work remains to be read in its original form. We can, for instance, listen to Andrea Keller's setting of Dylan Thomas's 'Do not go gentle into that good night', then return to the poem on the page. And, like Keller herself, we may also wish to listen to the poet's recorded performance of the poem. These are three separate experiences.

Words are hardly ever fitted to existing tunes in classical music, but this was the standard approach on Broadway and in Hollywood. George and Ira Gershwin, Jerome Kern and Dorothy Fields, Harold Arlen and Johnny Mercer, Richard Rodgers and Lorenz Hart: they all worked that way round. When we detect a symbiotic closeness between words and music in a song from the so-called 'Great American Songbook', it's generally down to the skill of the lyricist. Mitchell Parish's words for Hoagy Carmichael's 'Stardust' are a good example; likewise, Dorothy Fields's lyrics for 'I'm in the Mood for Love'. Another – slightly extreme – instance is Annie Ross's fitting of words to Wardell Gray's 'Twisted'.

Irving Berlin and Cole Porter were two composers of the musical comedy genre who wrote both words and music, and in pop music from the 1960s this practice has become increasingly standard. Not only that, but nowadays the songwriter and the singer are likely to be one and the same. And yet, while the songwriting process might involve a good deal of toing and froing, words and music are seldom invented simultaneously. When they are, the results might be exciting music, but the words will sometimes make little sense. Brian Eno has explained that, as a producer, part of his job is to make sure that the singer-songwriter's desire to refine a lyric doesn't result in musical stultification. Often it's better to stick with the nonsense that emerged with an initial burst of musical originality rather than risk losing the latter in an attempt to produce a profound and well-wrought set of words, because if you're trying to have a hit, the most important aspect of a record is how it sounds.

This is true of nearly all meetings of music and words. We probably won't notice a great lyric in a song if we're not first attracted by its music.

It's the music that fixes songs in the memory, and if the music is strong enough – in the context of pop, if it's catchy enough – the words, too, might stick. This is not to say there are no exceptions. 'Strange Fruit' has a rather weak and unmemorable tune, yet an unforgettable set of words, but even here, it is Billie Holiday's (or Nina Simone's) delivery of those words – the singer's articulation and placing of the words in time – that helps lodge them in our minds.

That lodging is important. It's a large part of what songs are for. A successful song is (in some way) a memorable song. Few of us are capable of carrying a whole symphony around in our heads, but most of us know some songs, and know them from start to finish. We carry them through our lives. We hold them close; they become part of us. We may even share them: in a choir, in a classroom, a pub, a car. Sharing a song is like sharing a meal. And even when the experience of songs and singing isn't communal, it's still participatory.

Songs require singers. When we listen to a song, as opposed to singing one, we are hearing another voice or other voices addressing us in music, telling us a story or an episode from life, real or imagined. The music not only carries the words, it colours them, and the words tell us about the music. The singer might be standing in front of us or the voice might be coming from a radio. We might be listening to a recording made last week or early last century. Perhaps the singer wrote the song; perhaps it's a song that has been recorded by hundreds of others and sung by millions. In a way, it's all the same. When we sing a song, we make it ours, at least for the duration of the singing. When we listen to someone else sing a song we still make it ours, because we take it into our imagination and, in so doing, participate in the performance. And if we find a connection to the song – it may be a wholly involuntary 'earworm' – it will remain with us for a few minutes, for a morning, or for the rest of our lives.

The songs in this book haven't been chosen because they are the authors' favourites, and neither do we consider them the best songs we know. Some of the songs are extremely simple in structure, some complex. We've tried to include as many types of song as possible – as the book's subtitle points out, there are love songs, laments and lullabies, but there are also protest songs, novelty songs, a prison song, a national anthem and a Christmas carol. We thought about genres, as well, so you'll find art songs and pop songs, Broadway songs and blues, reggae and bossa nova, jazz standards, gospel, country music and medieval chant. We only had two rules: no operatic arias (because we didn't want to cut them adrift from their dramatic contexts) and only one song per composer. Even so, the list of omissions is long and painful to consider, and it includes many of our favourite songwriters: John Dowland, Claudio Monteverdi, Barbara Strozzi, Hugo Wolf, Gabriel Fauré, Claude Debussy, Richard Strauss, Charles Ives, Irving Berlin, Jerome Kern, Kurt Weill, Blind Willie Johnson, Francis Poulenc, Benjamin Britten, Frank Loesser, Charles Trenet, Mikis Theodorakis, Jerry Leiber and Mike Stoller, Burt Bacharach and Hal David, Mick Jagger and Keith Richards, Pete Townshend, Smokey Robinson, Jimmy Webb, Brian Wilson, David Bowie, Randy Newman, Carly Simon, Joan Armatrading, Elvis Costello, Sting, Michael Jackson, Cyndi Lauper, Tom Waits, Rickie Lee Jones, Prince, Tupac Shakur and Gillian Welch. We had songs by each of them on our original list, and we wish there'd been room for them all.

Still, we believe the songs we have chosen represent most of the facets and functions of the song form. Songs are unlike other musical types. These small packages of words and music – even if they began in song cycles, musicals or concept albums – cut loose, tunnel their way into our lives and stay there. In structure and purpose, Schubert's 'Ständchen' has more in common with Amy Winehouse's 'Love Is a Losing Game' than with one of Schubert's piano sonatas or string quartets or symphonies. For whatever the function of a song, whatever the style, a song is still a song, as Led Zeppelin conveyed so successfully in the song that gives this book its title. Whether in 'California sunlight' or 'Sweet Calcutta rain', as Robert Plant sings, 'the song remains the same'.

1

I Heard It Through the Grapevine

music by Norman Whitfield
words by Barrett Strong

A FLICK OF A TAMBOURINE over a snare-drum rimshot. It may not be the luminous opening chord to 'A Hard Day's Night' or the pair of staccato guitar chords that start 'Brown Sugar' or even the wa-wa pedal that introduces Jimi Hendrix's 'Voodoo Child (Slight Return)', but in its way this percussive upbeat is every bit as distinctive. And it heralds the keyboard's ominous, slow march – a trudge into despair that every lover of sixties pop will instantly recognise as the beginning of 'I Heard It Through the Grapevine'. Or at least Marvin Gaye's account of the song.

In fact, Gaye's was not the first recording. The song was written in 1966 by a pair who together would become one of the crack creative teams associated with Berry Gordy's decade-defining Motown record label. Barrett Strong had been the singer on Gordy's first hit, 'Money (That's What I Want)' – later made more famous by the Beatles – and had the idea for a song that used the expression 'heard it through the grapevine'. He took it to composer and producer Norman Whitfield and together they finished it.

Whitfield produced a recording of the song that same year with Smokey Robinson and the Miracles, but Gordy felt it wasn't strong enough to be released as a single. The following year, it was recorded by Marvin Gaye, but again Gordy was unimpressed. The first release of the song was the version by Gladys Knight & the Pips in September 1967, and it sold well. Motown eventually released Gaye's album *In the Groove* nearly a year later, including his version of the song, and when radio stations began to play it Gordy was prompted finally to put it out as a single. It became a worldwide hit – so much so that the album itself had to be re-released, its title changed to *I Heard It Through the Grapevine*.

Gordy's complaints seem to have hinged on the song's tempo – he wanted a dance number (in spite of the lyrics about a doomed relationship) – and Gladys Knight's radically different recording delivered that. Knight's version is pure call-and-response soul, the trudge replaced with funky percussion licks, and while Whitfield couldn't bring himself to dispense with the piano figure altogether, it is relegated to a lesser role, appearing at the end of each verse and taking us from C major, briefly to C minor, even as the soul-funk rhythms continue all around it. The record is clearly an attempt to cash in on the success of Aretha Franklin's 'Respect', but while the performance is fine, it is totally unsuited to the material.

Like the Miracles' recording, Gaye's is slow and sultry. Both are performed in E flat minor – a key with six flats that allows a pianist to use mostly black notes – and both make much use of that inexorable trudge. There is so much to admire on Gaye's recording. Take the first twenty seconds alone. Following the percussive anacrusis and piano, the production gradually adds bass guitar and bass drum (b-boom, b-boom, like a nervous heartbeat), then hi-hat, a shaken tambourine, an electric guitar, a horn section, and finally tom-toms as Gaye's voice enters, at first wordlessly, like the final instrument in the build-up: 'Oo-oo, I bet you're wonderin' how I knew ...'.

Now it's down to Gaye himself, joined by a string section from the Detroit Symphony Orchestra, and there, in the second line of the song, is a masterstroke. In the line 'With some other guy that you knew before', he places the word 'guy' on a high, falsetto E flat. He's trying to remain cool, this man, as he confronts his faithless woman, but this abrupt jump up an octave is like a window to his grief. Beneath the calm exterior he is beside himself – in vocal terms, literally so. He repeats the effect in the second verse on 'you' in the line 'Losin' *you* would end my life you see' and again in the third verse on 'help' – it's always on a key word – and each time it's like a cry of pain.

This isn't the only aspect of the song that is coloured by vocal tessitura. Falsetto is one thing, but the entire song is high in Gaye's voice – too high, in fact. It may, of course, simply have been that this was the key that suited Smokey Robinson and Whitfield failed to transpose it for Gaye. But he was too canny a producer for that. On this record, Whitfield takes Gaye out of his vocal comfort zone. If he is a man in distress, so he should sound like one.

The effect is expressive and powerful, and together Whitfield and Gaye created a pop masterpiece. When Creedence Clearwater Revival included an eleven-minute version of the song on their 1970 album *Cosmo's Factory*, they retained most of the basic features of Gaye's record: a semitone lower, John Fogerty recreates both the high tessitura and the falsetto wails. In their otherwise quite different versions, both the Slits (in 1979) and the Flying Pickets (in 1984) did the same.

We haven't even mentioned Ike and Tina Turner's up-tempo version, or Human Nature's faithful (if hi-tech) copy, or Bill Frisell's typically deconstructive approach, or Jessica Mauboy's performance in the film *The Sapphires*, which takes us back to Gladys Knight. There are plenty of others, too, and so the question arises: what and where is the song itself? Which is the authoritative version? What is the song's provenance?

It's easy enough to answer this question in the context of the classical tradition. There are dozens of recordings of most of Schubert's songs and there must have been many thousands of performances of them. Had Schubert composed 'I Heard It Through the Grapevine', any tenor or soprano could turn to the sheet music to check their interpretation against the composer's wishes. Had Mahler composed a symphonic movement entitled 'What the Grapevine Tells Me', a conductor would find the authority for his or her performance in the full score. In classical music, a text is a text, maybe even an urtext. But in pop music, as in jazz, each recording is a new text. Marvin Gaye's 'I Heard It Through the Grapevine' may have more currency than other texts of the same name, but unlike a score by Schubert or Mahler, it doesn't tell the next performer what to do. A recording stamps a vocal personality on a song (to say nothing of the producer's personality), and the ebb and flow of sonic details – the timbre of voice and instruments, the mix, the added reverb – become a part of these texts as much as the words and the music.

2

Lili Marleen

music by Norbert Schultze
words by Hans Leip

THE SURPRISING THING ABOUT 'Lili Marleen', which has music written by a card-carrying Nazi, is that it should have been the most popular song of World War II, not only in Germany but also among the Allies – especially British soldiers. In wartime you might expect songs to be partisan – after all, the 'Horst-Wessel-Lied' is not 'There'll Always Be an England' – but soldiers are soldiers and in the 1940s, it seems, they all liked to imagine meeting a woman in the lamplight outside their barrack gates.

Songs of war have a long history, and they fall into several categories. There are, for one, all the anti-war songs, from the traditional spiritual 'Down by the Riverside' to 'War (What Is It Good For?)'. But there are many more songs that are either in some sense pro-war, or at least fall into the category of 'grin and bear it', packing up 'your troubles in your old kit bag'.

Among these are the victory songs. 'Owre Kynge went forth to Normandy / With grace and myght of chyvalry' sang fifteenth-century English yeomen of Henry V in 'The Agincourt Song' (sometimes called 'The Agincourt Carol'). Then there are the songs of military encouragement. In the American Civil War, which produced dozens of popular songs, 'Marching Through Georgia' is a good example. And then there's what we might call the song of personal encouragement, such as 'It's a Long Way to Tipperary', which was easily the most popular song of World War I, at least on the Allied side. Yes, it was a long way to Tipperary, and yes, that's where the singer's girl was, but the swift marching metre and bright diatonic tune left no one in any doubt that it was not long before the two would be reunited. Something worth fighting for, then.

There are plenty of other songs in which the soldier thinks more generally of home ('Keep the Home Fires Burning', 'You'd Be So Nice to Come Home To'), or in which either the soldier or the one left behind thinks of the other ('I'll Be Seeing You', 'We'll Meet Again', 'A Nightingale Sang in Berkeley Square'). There are also songs about how good it will be when the war is won. A particularly poignant line in '(There'll Be Bluebirds over) The White Cliffs of Dover' is 'And Jimmy will go to sleep / In his own little room again' – poignant because Jimmy is currently in his mum's bed, something they both doubtless find reassuring while Jimmy's dad is away at the war.

There are plenty of war songs about women. 'Goodbye, Dolly Gray', written by two American songwriters during the Spanish–American War of 1898, became popular among British troops during the Second Boer War, a couple of years later. (This is also an example of a war song going on to have a new and unrelated use – with different words, of course – as the club song of Collingwood Football Club in the Australian Football League: 'Goodbye, Dolly, I must leave you' transformed into 'Good old Collingwood forever'.

'Lili Marleen' is a song about a woman – like Dolly Gray, she's right there in the title – but in reality, she was *two* women, the one the poet Hans Leip left behind when he was called up to serve in the German army in 1915, and the one who used to wave to him on sentry duty. The first was called Lili, the second Marleen,

> Vor der Kaserne
>
> Vor dem grossen Tor
>
> Stand eine Laterne
>
> Und steht sie noch davor
>
> So woll'n wir uns da wieder seh'n
>
> Bei der Laterne wollen wir steh'n
>
> Wie einst Lili Marleen.

'In front of the barracks, before its large gate, stood a lantern and it stands there still. Let's meet there again in the lamplight, like before, Lili Marleen.'

'Das Lied eines jungen Soldaten auf der Wacht' ('The Song of a Young Soldier on Watch'), remained a poem for the next twenty-three years until

Norbert Schultze put it to music. It was recorded by Lale Andersen as 'Das Mädchen unter der Laterne' ('The Girl beneath the Lamp') in 1939.

It opens with a trumpet call. Then, to the accompaniment of an accordion, a small body of strings, plucked bass, military drum and possibly, further back in the mix, a piano (it's hard to be sure), Andersen sings, with the merest hint of Sprechstimme – a semi-spoken singing style – the familiar tune. She's backed by a small male choir, or it might be just a quartet. It's a touching tune, quite simple but well made. Characterised by mostly stepwise movement, a single rising fifth and descending sequences of notes, until, in the final two lines ('Wie einst, Lili Marleen') the tune steps out of the octave first to the tone above, then to the semitone below, both times on the first syllable of 'Marleen'.

There is a great deal of anecdotal information (and probably misinformation) about 'Lili Marleen', as the song was soon known. One story has it that the German propaganda minister, Joseph Goebbels, banned Andersen's recording shortly after its release due to its insufficient patriotism. It's true there's more than a tinge of regret about the lyrics, and yet the tune is a march – something emphasised by the drum – and it's hardly an anti-war song. In another version of the same story, it was Radio Belgrade's broadcasting of the song that Goebbels attempted to ban. Whatever the truth of these stories, the song certainly put out tendrils in many directions, with versions in several other languages. There was an Italian recording by Lina Termini in 1942, and Anne Shelton made the first commercial recording in English in 1944 – the first *commercial* recording, but not the first in English.

The latter had been by Lale Andersen again, and she did it at Goebbels' request. The song was already popular with British troops – especially the Eighth Army fighting Rommel in North Africa – from the original recording, and getting wind of this, Goebbels decided it might well be used as propaganda. So, in 1942, he had Andersen record it again in English with a more prominent and ominous bass drum.

> Then I heard the bugle calling me away
> By the gate I kissed her, kissed her tears away
> And by the flickering lantern's light

I held her tight, 'twas out last night
My last night with Marleen,
My last night with Marleen.

In this version the tempo slows considerably at the start of the penultimate verse, when the bugle calls and the soldier must kiss away his girlfriend's tears on his 'last night with Marleen'. The message to Allied troops was clear: it's time to go home to your women. This new recording became as popular as the first.

Not to be outdone, in 1944 the US Office of Strategic Services (the wartime equivalent of the CIA), through its Morale Operations Branch, asked Marlene Dietrich to record the song in German, with a poignant accordion accompaniment by Charles Magnante in the hope of demoralising German troops. German soldiers loved it as much as the British troops had loved both of Lale Andersen's recordings.

At the end of the war an English language version was released by Dietrich, again with Magnante, and in recognition of the now universal popularity of both song and singer – in German and English – the record label renamed the song, in the singer's honour, 'Lili Marlene'.

3

Milord

music by Marguerite Monnot
words by Georges Moustaki

'MILORD' WAS ONE OF THE last hits for the French chanteuse Edith Piaf. But is it even a song?

Structurally, it's more like an operatic scena with recitatives, both sung and, finally, spoken. The 'Milord' of the title is an English gent, complete with a stiff upper lip, whose emotional mask slips when the woman who has been observing him (and singing about him to us) raises the topic of love. He weeps, she comforts him, and the two of them end up laughing and dancing to the final chorus.

Marguerite Monnot (1903–1961) composed much of Edith Piaf's staple repertoire with a variety of lyricists, many of whom were Piaf's lovers, and occasionally with Piaf herself. 'Hymne à l'amour' is the two women's most famous song together. Monnot's talent was sustained by strong, formal technique, developed under her impressive roster of conservatoire teachers, including the great pedagogue Nadia Boulanger and the composer Vincent d'Indy. She also studied piano with Alfred Cortot. At first writing popular songs was a sideline, but, following her success with Piaf, songwriting became Monnot's career. 'Milord', with lyrics by another of Piaf's lovers, Georges Moustaki, was their last hit together, and like so many of Piaf's most famous songs it presents the air of autobiography: in the recording studio and particularly on stage, Piaf became the woman from whose point of view she sang.

Piaf's own life was the stuff of legends – literally so, since some of the details are disputed and others certainly exaggerated. Born in 1915, she was abandoned by her mother and raised for a time in a brothel. In some accounts she was also blind for these years. She started singing in the 1930s and by the outbreak of World War II was already famous – indeed notorious, having been implicated in the murder of her manager. In the 1940s, in Nazi-occupied Paris, Piaf became more famous still and also wealthy, but her success was tainted by accusations of collaboration. It all seemed grist to the mill for the chanteuse, whose fame simply rose above it. Her health had never been especially good, but after a series of car accidents later in her life she became addicted to morphine, then other drugs, as well as alcohol. And then there were the men, the number and unsuitability of whom she blamed on a childhood surrounded by prostitution.

In 'Milord', the singer addressing the English gent calls herself only 'une fille du port' (a girl from the docks) and 'une ombre de la rue' (a shadow of the street), so possibly a prostitute. She has been observing 'Milord', but he has never noticed her – 'l'ombre' also implies obscurity. Now he enters a bar or cafe and she invites him to sit at her table and warm himself. He was a dandy, and he was happy. She spotted him walking proudly on the arm of a woman so beautiful it made her heart freeze. But now the woman has gone and he is sad and alone.

Piaf, the 'shadow', consoles him, but he begins to weep.

Mais vous pleurez, Milord?
Ça je l'aurais jamais cru!

'But are you crying, Milord?' She asks. 'That's unbelievable!' And then she sets about cheering him up, this previously inscrutable gent.

Allez, riez, Milord!
Allez, chantez, Milord!

'Go on, laugh, Milord! Go on, sing, Milord!' And this is where the words run out, and perhaps the alcohol kicks in, as she begins to sing the final chorus over and over to 'la-la-la', interjecting only for one last exhortation:

Mais oui, dansez, Milord!

'Yes, dance, Milord!'

In live performances, Piaf would, at this point, enlist the help of the audience with the chorus, in a singalong finale as calculated as the one that ends 'Hey Jude'. The more they sing, the more the gent laughs and dances. The operatic scene has a happy ending, a musical catharsis for all involved – and we are all involved. There's no other song quite like it.

A historical postscript: in January 1963, Charles de Gaulle, the French president, vetoed Britain's attempt to join the European Economic Community or European Union, as it ultimately became known. Asked later what he had said to his British counterpart, the aristocratic prime minister Harold Macmillan, the next time they met, de Gaulle replied, 'Ne pleurez pas, Milord' – 'Don't cry, Milord'.

4

Tutti Frutti

music by Little Richard
words by Little Richard and Dorothy LaBostrie

A-wop-bop-a-lu-mop, a lop bam bam

FEW PEOPLE AGREE ON how to spell the phrase, but with something like these sounds, Little Richard launched one of the most important musical recordings in history. 'Tutti Frutti' might not have been a great song, but there had been nothing like it before, and music would never be quite the same after it. It was 1955, and with 'Tutti Frutti', rock'n'roll was properly launched.

In 1954, Bill Haley & His Comets had released 'Rock Around the Clock' and hardly anyone had noticed. It was only the B side of the now largely forgotten novelty song, 'Thirteen Women (and Only One Man in Town)'. But early the following year, 'Rock Around the Clock' was heard over the opening credits of Richard Brooks's controversial film set in an interracial school, *The Blackboard Jungle*, and the song was thus provided with a dangerous context. Juvenile delinquency had arrived at a cinema near you, and rock'n'roll was the noise it made. Except Bill Haley still wasn't enough. Six months later, with 'Tutti Frutti', Little Richard made Haley sound as harmless as Perry Como.

Richard Penniman was outrageous. His voice and stage persona were just this side of out of control. He was unprecedentedly raucous (was he in ecstasy or in pain?), had bouffant hair, wore make-up and affected a mincing walk. His showmanship might raise eyebrows even today, but this was a black man flaunting his homosexuality in the segregated Deep South of the United States in 1955. It's remarkable that he survived to 1956.

So what was 'Tutti Frutti' about? Well, sex, of course – although Dorothy LaBostrie did her best to disguise the fact. LaBostrie was a young song-writer, engaged to clean up Little Richard's original lyrics. She came up with the familiar chorus.

> Tutti frutti, aw rutti
> Tutti frutti, woooh!
> Tutti frutti, aw rutti
> Tutti frutti, aw rutti
> Tutti frutti, aw rutti
> A-wop-bop-a-lu-mop, a lop bam bam

'Tutti frutti' is a type of ice-cream, and 'aw rutti' – 'all righty' – implies that it is good ice-cream. LaBostrie did such a good job of bowdlerising the song that 'Tutti Frutti' could later be safely covered by Pat Boone, that emblem of pop piety, his version of the single climbing higher on the charts than Little Richard's own.

Euphemisms were nothing new to song, of course. We can go back 400 years and find them in Elizabethan England. 'It was a lover and his lass / With a hey and a ho and a hey-nonny-no,' sing the two pages in Shakespeare's *As You Like It*, and we have a fair idea of what they mean. In the case of 'Tutti Frutti', however, we know exactly what Little Richard meant, because in 2015 his drummer, Charles Connor, told the BBC about the original lyrics:

> Tutti Frutti, good booty,
> If it's tight, it's all right,
> If it's greasy, makes it easy.

You can see why the producer called in LaBostrie.

The record company was Art Rupe's Specialty Records. Disappointed with his existing label, Richard had sent Rupe a demo and Rupe had been impressed enough to line up a recording session for him in New Orleans, with Fats Domino's band. Richard recorded his new material, but the song that most excited the producer, Robert 'Bumps' Blackwell, was 'Tutti Frutti', which wasn't on the official song list. Since Blackwell knew at once he could never release it with Richard's lyrics, it must have been the sound of Richard's performance that impressed him.

That's still what's impressive about it. Even with its euphemistic lyrics, there's no denying the raw power of the record. The song has the structure of a twelve-bar blues. There are two verses, which have the same music as the chorus, telling of a girl called Sue who 'knows just what to do', and another named Daisy 'who always drives me crazy'. Domino's band consists of two saxophones, piano, drums and double bass, with a guitar so far back in the mix you're barely aware of it. It's hardly a rock'n'roll line-up – there was already more of that on 'Rock Around the Clock' – but there can be no doubt that it is rock'n'roll we're hearing. We are also hearing the future.

The steady rock beat of Chuck Berry, the gravelly soul voice of Wilson Pickett, Paul McCartney's falsetto 'woooh', laden with vibrato, the excited squeaks of Michael Jackson: they are all on this 2½-minute record.

5

Born to Run

music and words by Bruce Springsteen

ONE OF THE MOST NOTABLE ASPECTS of Bruce Springsteen's music is the glorious sound of the E Street Band. The personnel have changed a little over the years, but across the band's classic period from the mid-1970s its constants were Clarence Clemons's enormous tone on saxophone (generally a baritone), at least two guitars, bass, drums and two keyboard players – one on piano, one organ. A veritable wall of sound. Danny Federici was the organist and he often also played glockenspiel.

The glockenspiel – two and a half octaves of tiny metal bars – is a fairly common orchestral instrument, and a miniature version of it may be found in the toy boxes of small children. Although it is rare – and, you might think, unlikely– in rock music, that tinkling, high-frequency sonority can register above the noise of a rock band as surely as it can cut through a symphony orchestra. That's what it does on 'Born to Run', doubling the famous guitar riff that is the song's principal hook.

According to Springsteen, 'Born to Run' is the 'wide-screen rumble' that opens side two of his album of the same name, released in 1975. In many ways it's the most typical Springsteen song of them all: urgent, anthemic and grand – grandiloquent even. It's addressed, in part at least, to 'Wendy', a typical Springsteen girl (others include Rosie, Sandy, Candy, Sherry and Mary, the last named in both 'The River' and 'Thunder Road', the song that begins side one of *Born to Run*). Like most of these girls, Wendy is being invited to join the singer in his car (or is it a motorbike?), on a quest for something like salvation.

It isn't Springsteen, of course, it's everyman – at least every young New Jersey man – and while this escape-from-quotidian-drudgery-in-a-fast-car trope is now most strongly associated with Springsteen, it was born with rock'n'roll. Bo Diddley and Eddie Cochrane, Smokey Robinson and Wilson Pickett, Chuck Berry and the Beach Boys: they all sang about the freedom that comes with wheels, but no one did it more often or with more belief than Springsteen.

The guitar riff is the first thing you hear in 'Born to Run' and it's the first thing you remember. Harmonically, it's a progression from the tonic E major to the subdominant A major (chord IV), then the dominant B major (V, at first with the E suspended), then back to E major. Nothing special there. But over that first tonic chord (pumping away) the lead guitar goes from E to the B below, then leaps a minor seventh up to dissonant A, descending stepwise via G sharp to C sharp on the A major chord. So that melodic A is now 'justified' by the subdominant chord.

The chord pattern of the guitar riff is now applied to the verse (there's no chorus as such in this song), which will later enable the two to be combined in the ecstatic final verse. But let's not get ahead of ourselves.

The first line of the lyric has all the quotidian drudgery you could wish for, while the second embodies the noble danger of the highway. 'In the day we sweat it out on the streets of a runaway American dream / At night we ride through the mansions of glory in suicide machines.' The imagery is something of a blur. There are 'chrome wheeled' cars and 'fuel injected' bikes (later there will be 'velvet rims' and 'rear-view mirrors'). Cars or bikes, they are 'suicide machines', but then staying on the job is itself 'a suicide rap'. Once sprung from their cages, the denizens of Highway 9 are no less at risk, just freer.

Melodically, the verse consists of that same dissonant A we heard in the guitar riff, again falling to G sharp (then F sharp, then the tonic E). Vocally the song lies low in Springsteen's range, creating a tone of a pure reason for his petition to Wendy in verse two.

> Wendy let me in I wanna be your friend,
> I want to guard your dreams and visions.
> Just wrap your legs 'round these velvet rims
> And strap your hands 'cross my engines

As he has already admitted to Mary on 'Thunder Road', 'the ride, it ain't free', but he hopes it may be worth it. The singer of 'Born to Run', this 'scared and lonely rider', wants 'to know if love is wild' and 'real' and he's asking Wendy to help him find out.

Now comes the more harmonically adventurous bridge, starting, rather remotely, on the supertonic chord of D major, rising through G and A to C. These are not clean chords, but carry with them pitches suspended from previous chords, smudged like the trails of headlights on a highway at night. More blurring.

Here are the escapees – on the boulevard, in the amusement park and on the beach 'in a mist' – and here is the climax of the singer's offer:

> I wanna die with you, Wendy, on the streets tonight
> In an everlasting kiss.

It is a Wagnerian moment, Springsteen proposing nothing less than a *Liebestod*, a love-death – orgasm as obliteration – and it takes us to the song's climax. As the band returns us chromatically to the home key, Springsteen counts us in and we arrive at the final verse.

> The highway's jammed with broken heroes on a last-chance power
>> drive
> Everybody's out on the run tonight
> But there's no place left to hide

And indeed there isn't. Suddenly Springsteen sounds like Springsteen, because he's singing much higher. In fact he's a minor seventh higher than in the first two verses. It's the minor seventh from the guitar riff, the key interval of the song, and here too the riff is blazing away, guitar and glockenspiel together. In a moment of supreme rock'n'roll jubilation, everything fits.

There's a moment of introspection, perhaps even reality, in the line 'Together, Wendy, we can live with the sadness', but there's no turning back. One day they may 'walk in the sun', but until that happens 'tramps like us / Baby, we were born to run'.

So off they run, into the darkness, bound, if not for glory or salvation, then at least for hope, the glockenspiel twinkling above them like the stars in the night sky.

24

6

Fast Car

music and words by Tracy Chapman

THE CAR IN ROCK MUSIC represents freedom from work (or school) and privacy from parental eyes, a means of escape, even if there is no clear destination.

The car song is a male construct. There are practically no similar songs by women, and those that present a woman's point of view tend to be by men. In the Pointer Sisters' 'Fire', for example, the woman is 'riding in your car' while acting out a male fantasy ('You're pulling me close / I just say no / I say I don't like it / But you know I'm a liar'). The song, in fact, is by Bruce Springsteen and when he sings it and the point of view shifts ('You just say no / ... / But I know you're a liar'), the effect is unsettling.

Tracy Chapman's 'Fast Car' was that rarity, a car song by a woman (there are later examples). The first single from her eponymous first album, it romanticises the passenger seat while staring down reality.

When Tracy Chapman first appeared in 1988 and 'Fast Car' climbed the charts, it was part of the mythology surrounding the singer that she was from a poor background and had been discovered busking. Photos showed her in a big overcoat with a turned-up collar, eyes downcast. It wasn't pure media hype, there was some truth to it. Chapman was indeed from a working-class home in Cleveland, Ohio, and brought up by her mother, before being offered a scholarship to the Wooster School in Connecticut. She had also been discovered, but singing in a club, not busking. Mind you, she had busked, albeit in Harvard Yard while studying at Boston's neighbouring Tufts University.

What made the mythology easy to believe was the lyrics of the song and the voice, a low-pitched mumble. Chapman never had a high voice, but on 'Fast Car' it was lower than on the album's other tracks, restricting itself, for the most part, to the octave below middle C. There was an emotional catch in her voice, and a hint of vulnerability. It was a sound that matched the turned-up collar and downcast eyes.

The lyrics relate a story of disappointment. If 'Fast Car' resembles a Springsteen song, it is not 'Born to Run' or 'Thunder Road' but 'The River'. The relationship was always doomed, but for a time there was hope of redemption in the car or the river. But Chapman's structure is more complex than Springsteen's, for while 'The River', a song set in the past tense, wears regret on its sleeve, Chapman's present-tense song narrative begins hopefully. 'You've got a fast car', she sings, 'Maybe together we can get somewhere'; 'I got a plan to get us out of here'.

'Here', it turns out, is where she looks after a father who 'lives with the bottle, that's the way it is', and who has been abandoned by his wife. Perhaps the 'fast car' will be the daughter's means of escape. 'Any place is better'.

But as the story moves on, still in the present tense, the optimism fades: 'You still ain't got a job …'; 'You stay out drinking late at the bar …' In the end, things have not improved. They have children, but he's rarely home to see them. Perhaps the best solution for everyone is that he 'take [his] fast car and keep on driving'.

Interspersed with the present-tense narrative of the verses, is a past-tense memory of riding in the fast car itself with 'your arm … wrapped round my shoulder'. Is it a chorus or a middle eight, a bridge?

Musically, 'Fast Car' has three layers. There's Chapman's voice; a wistful guitar line that echoes it, playing a variation of the first two lines of the vocal melody; and the harmony, just four chords: D major, A major, F sharp minor and E major (IV–I–vi–V), which go round and around. Each time the harmony rises hopefully, then sinks back to the beginning; a bar of IV–I, a bar of vi–V, line after line, verse after verse. Like the singer at the end of the song, the chords 'ain't going nowhere', and even when the words suggest the possibility of escape, the harmony makes it clear the singer is trapped.

After three and a half verses – two minutes into the song – comes that chorus/middle eight. As the singer remembers 'driving in your car', the drums kick in and we feel a momentary sense of exhilaration. For the first four bars, the melodic line seems to mimic the Doppler effect of traffic speeding by, a string of As with the occasional flick of a G sharp.

Then, at '*I* had a feeling that I belonged / *I* had a feeling I could be someone', we hear the first melisma of the song. It is only three notes long ('I–yee–hi'), but it involves the melody leaving the constraining octave, and because of the song's previous monotony, this is a big moment. The step is just a whole tone, however, and there ends the melodic adventure. The flourish returns each time this line is sung, but it is always the same and soon the thrill is gone.

The exhilaration that comes with the arrival of the chorus/middle eight is enhanced by a change to the harmony. Instead of chord IV moving to I in the first bar, the music stays on chord IV. Like the brief melisma and the whole-tone step out of the octave, it is a small matter, but after two minutes of IV–I, followed by VI–V, it's a relief. But then you realise the IV–I–IV–V pattern hasn't gone away at all, only slowed down. The pattern is exactly the same, but now occurring at half speed. The words describe 'Speed so fast I felt like I was drunk', while the slower harmonic rhythm suggests the memory may be just a dream.

As the dream fades ('be someone, be someone, be someone'), we're wide awake and no better off. If that was a bridge rather than a chorus, then it was a bridge to nowhere, a bridge back to the start, to the original opening line, the original chord pattern. The 'fast car' is now just for 'cruising to entertain ourselves'. He remains unemployed while she works 'in the market as a checkout girl'. Still, hope hasn't been extinguished. Things 'will get better', he'll 'find work', she'll 'get promoted', they'll move to the suburbs. The chorus/bridge/memory/dream comes again and it's the same as before. It's always the same. That's the point. This time when it fades and we're back at the start once more ('You've got a fast car'), it's evident the relationship hasn't worked. The song ends with another half verse. 'You gotta make a decision,' she tells him. 'Leave tonight or live and die this way.' Then the chords just keep going, round and round until they stop.

Is it a depressing song? Yes and no. The singer claims she might have 'been someone, been someone', but in truth she is someone. She has looked after her abandoned, drunken father, she's maintained a steady job while bringing up children, and by the end of the song she is determined enough to send away her dream of escape. Meanwhile the low mumble that began the song has transformed in our minds into a voice that has a quiet strength, that is dignified. If not triumphant, there is nonetheless something heroic about it.

There have been quite a few cover versions of this song in the decades since its release, adding folksy violins or techno beats. But embellishing this song only reduces its impact. Its strength is its simplicity, its repetitious logic unforgiving and complete.

7

Goldfinger

music by John Barry
words by Leslie Bricusse and Anthony Newley

THE NAME JOHN BARRY is so closely associated with the James Bond franchise that many people assume he composed the famous 007 theme. He didn't – that was Monty Norman – although at some point Barry seems to have come to believe the fiction himself, and he was eventually sued by Norman over the false claim.

There is little else in movie history that resembles this chain of films that has run for more than half a century, and music has been central to its success. The theme is instantly recognisable and evocative, the films are always tightly scored and most of the songs have been hits. Most composers would be content to have written the score for eleven of the Bond films, as well as ten of their famous songs, but for Barry, perhaps, the world was not enough.

In 1962, Barry worked on the first Bond film, *Dr No*, as Norman's arranger, but when it came to the follow-up, the producers, who were dissatisfied with Norman's music, engaged Barry to compose the second score. He also added big, brassy power chords to the front of the James Bond theme and these would live on along with the theme itself. *From Russia with Love* (1963) was the first in the series to have a title song, though this wasn't by Barry. Written by Lionel Bart, the composer of *Oliver!* (1960), 'From Russia with Love' is a slow ballad, sung by Matt Monro, an early-sixties pop crooner. He doesn't sing it over the opening titles, where it appears in an up-tempo orchestral arrangement, but in the diegetic world of the film where it's played on a radio, and then reprised over the closing credits.

It was the third film in the series where everything came together, at least from a musical point of view. *Goldfinger* (1964) established the convention of playing the big hit song over the titles. And because Barry was the composer of both the song and the score, he was able to work one smoothly into the other – the song remains part of the action throughout. A particular singing style was also established with *Goldfinger*, with the choice of Shirley Bassey – a powerful voice from South Wales, associated with moody, melodramatic torch songs such as 'I Who Have Nothing' – who considerably ramped up the voltage after Monro's rather anodyne effort. This was to be the first of three Bond songs sung by Bassey, and the selection later of Bassey's compatriot Tom Jones for the fourth film, *Thunderball* (1965), and numerous other big voices, including Tina Turner, Gladys Knight, Rita Coolidge and Adele, consolidated just one among many Bond clichés.

'Goldfinger' is probably the most famous of the lot, so it's surprising that in a couple of ways it's also the least typical. The concept of the Bond song, released a month or two before the film appears in cinemas, is partly to garner advance publicity. Consequently, nearly all the songs share the title of their respective films. 'Goldfinger' is no exception, but it's the only film in the series to be named after its villain, leaving the lyricists, Leslie Bricusse and Anthony Newley, little choice but to write a song about him. There are later songs that use the personal pronoun 'he' – in the *Thunderball* theme song, for instance, we're told, somewhat prosaically, that 'He always runs while others walk' and, more enigmatically, 'His needs are more so he gives less'. These lines were presumably also intended to conjure Agent 007 himself. But a song about a villain presented special challenges.

It was suggested to Bricusse and Newley that they take 'The Ballad of Mack the Knife' from *The Threepenny Opera* (1928) by Kurt Weill and Bertolt Brecht as a template. In that eponymous ballad, the knife-wielding Macheath is glamorised, and Bricusse and Newley achieve something similar with 'Goldfinger'. They also borrowed Brecht and Weill's structure – unique among Bond songs, the ballad form is used to (fore)tell the story. Long before we meet the man himself, we have been warned that Auric Goldfinger – he of the 'Midas touch' and the 'cold finger' – is capable of delivering 'the kiss of death' to 'a golden girl'. In other words, we know what to expect.

In spite of these unique qualities, 'Goldfinger' remains the ur-Bond song and this goes beyond Bassey's voice. The song starts with its title sung to a rising perfect fifth, followed by a whole-tone step down to the fourth: 'Gold–FIN–ger'. These are common intervals, of course, and would be unremarkable if they did not establish a sort of thematic DNA for Bond songs, especially the rising fifth. These fifths appear everywhere: 'Diamonds are for e–VER'; 'The spy who LOVED me'; 'Sky–FALL'. And when they're not rising, they're falling, as in 'For your eyes on–LY'. Michael Giacchino's music for *The Incredibles*, which draws heavily on the gestures of Bond music, has a rising fifth at the start of its main theme.

The Bond musical DNA can be traced back to Monty Norman's original theme, which begins with a chromatic four-note motto, starting on the fifth note of the scale. In the key of E, this is B–C–C sharp–C, and this motto worms its way into a good many of the songs. Again, it was inaugurated in 'Goldfinger', appearing in the orchestra at the end of the verse (after the words 'But don't go in'), and then resurfaces in many of the subsequent songs. We should never forget that Bond – James Bond – is a brand, and instant recognition is vital. In this regard, the sound of the music is as important as all the other recurrent features in the films, from the way Bond treats his women to the way he prefers his martinis.

8

When You Wish upon a Star

music by Leigh Harline
words by Ned Washington

THIS IS THE SONG OF hope par excellence: 'When you wish upon a star … your dreams come true.' In time, it would come to stand for the entire Disney franchise, but it was first heard in *Pinocchio* (1940), sung by Cliff Edwards as Jiminy Cricket.

The two songwriters would independently go on to become notable Hollywood figures. Leigh Harline (1907–1969), whose Disney apprenticeship had been on *Snow White and the Seven Dwarfs* (1937) as an assistant to composer Frank Churchill, left Disney soon after *Pinocchio* to work on a broad range of movie genres, from light comedies to noir thrillers. Ned Washington (1901–1976) was already established as a lyricist at the time of *Pinocchio*, having worked with Victor Young, and with Hoagy Carmichael ('The Nearness of You'). His later successes would include 'Stella by Starlight' and 'My Foolish Heart' (both with Young), before he finally came to specialise in theme songs for Westerns, the best known of which are 'The Ballad of High Noon' and 'Rawhide', both with Dimitri Tiomkin.

But what of Cliff Edwards? His singing is incredibly touching, even before you know his story. As Jiminy Cricket, he is kindly and wise, an insect elder; and his voice certainly sounds elderly, though Edwards was just forty-five at the time of recording. It is the miraculous flexibility of his singing that is so affecting, the ease of his falsetto that is one of the song's greatest listening pleasures. He sings 'When You Wish upon a Star' in the key of E major, beginning on a baritone's low B. Two minutes later, he ends the song on the B, two octaves higher, in the middle of the soprano range. It's like a musical embodiment of those dreams coming true – surely he can't go any higher, you think, he's an old man (or, at least, an old cricket), but on he floats, up and up.

In the 1920s and 1930s, Edwards had been a star of vaudeville. A big star. As 'Ukulele Ike', he did as much as anyone to popularise his eponymous instrument. In 1929 he had a hit record with the first recording of 'Singin' in the Rain', which he performed in one of the earliest movie musicals, *The Hollywood Revue of 1929*. By the time of *Pinocchio*, however, his career was already in decline, and not only because the ukulele was going out of fashion.

To employ the parlance of the time, Edwards was a wastrel. He made a lot of money and squandered it on booze. The same year as *Pinocchio*, he appeared in Howard Hawks's romantic comedy *His Girl Friday*, playing a shabby newspaper reporter alongside Cary Grant and Rosalind Russell, his big sad eyes reminiscent of Peter Lorre. The following year he voiced Jim Crow in *Dumbo*, singing 'When I See an Elephant Fly'. But opportunities were thinning out for him and he was reduced to hanging around the studio in the hope of picking up work wherever he could. When he died, penniless, in 1971, his body lay unclaimed for some days in the morgue at Hollywood's Virgil Convalescent Hospital, until it was finally sent to the UCLA medical school. Learning of Edwards' fate, Disney offered to buy back his remains and pay for a funeral, but the Actors' Fund of America had already taken care of the matter. Disney paid for the stone.

'When You Wish upon a Star' is a homily, its structure befittingly simple. The melody spells out the lesson in even crotchets, each phrase beginning with an octave, before stepping out of it.

> When you wish upon a star,
> Makes no difference who you are,
> Anything your heart desires
> Will come to you.

'When you' is the first octave leap, rising from B to B, before moving stepwise, though chromatically (an E sharp on '–pon'), to the C sharp above (on chord ii, the relative minor of IV). 'Makes no' is the next octave, from D sharp to D sharp, this time rising to the tonic E. Then, for 'Anything your heart desires / Will', there's a descending E major scale, though it begins and ends on F sharp (another octave), still in simple, even crotchets, and 'come to you' takes us squarely to the dominant.

The second verse does what you would expect, which is to repeat the structure and most of the notes of the first, but to land us back on the tonic. Then the middle eight bars, beginning with the words 'Fate is kind', take us to darker territory, their diminished chords sung by a choir as the top line – almost Wagnerian in its winding chromaticism up to a sighing cadence on 'secret longing' – returning us to E major and Edwards singing the final chorus.

> Like a bolt out of the blue,
> Fate steps in and sees you through.
> When you wish upon a star
> Your dreams come true.

The melody and chords are as before until the final syllable of the second line, where Edwards takes a high G sharp instead of the expected tonic E (and it *does* come out of the blue). But it gets better, Edwards affecting a gorgeous portamento down to F sharp for the start of the descending scale, before rising back up to the G sharp again, this time topping it off with that soprano B to complete the phrase 'Your dreams come true'. Just for that moment, it seems they will.

9

Rainbow

music and words by Sia Furler,
Jesse Shatkin and Victor Notorleva

IT BEGAN WITH A MODEL some twenty-five centimetres high and made out of hard plastic. This was in 1981, it was called My Pretty Pony and it didn't go well. But Hasbro, the toy manufacturer, persisted, releasing six smaller ponies the following year. Nearly four decades on, the My Little Pony annual turnover is more than a billion dollars, and in addition to models of various sizes, the franchise includes books, comics, a TV series and feature films.

The TV show contains music that references the classics (Tchaikovsky is a favourite) as well as original songs by Daniel Ingram that occasionally borrow, musically and lyrically, from the likes of Stephen Sondheim. 'Art of the Dress', Rarity's dressmaking song from the TV episode 'Suited for Success', is Ingram's homage to 'Putting it Together' from *Sunday in the Park with George*. Sondheim's song begins:

> Ounce by ounce, putting it together
> Small amounts, adding up to make a work of art ...

Rarity sings:

> Thread by thread, stitching it together
> Twilight's dress, cutting out the pattern snip by snip ...

Clearly, *My Little Pony* is not aimed solely at small girls.

In addition to new material by Ingram himself, *My Little Pony: The Movie* (2017) features songs from rapper CL, pop bands DNCE and Lukas

Graham, and the Australian singer-songwriter Sia, who also had a role in the film – you could call it an alter ego – in the form of Songbird Serenade, a pop star Pegasus. (In the land of Equestria, ponies come in many varieties. A Pegasus can fly.)

Her song 'Rainbow' embodies the My Little Pony ethos, which is that a mixture of self-belief and friendship will get you pretty much anything you want in life. Like 'When You Wish upon a Star', 'Rainbow' is a song of hope; Songbird Serenade first sings it to her fellow ponies who have been captured and caged by the evil Storm King. At the end of the film, after the ponies' inevitable victory over these dark forces, she performs it on stage at the Friendship Festival to an audience that includes pretty much the whole of Canterlot, with the six 'mane ponies' in the front row.

'Rainbow' employs just three chords – D, G and A – yet while the song is nominally in D major, the other chords (IV and V) are more important. The verse begins in A (chord V), moving to G (chord IV), with the tonic just a means to get there. The chorus is really in the subdominant G (IV). Only the song's bridge, which cheekily borrows the line 'Here comes the sun', is in the home key.

Sia has a rich mezzo-soprano voice that easily takes in a low A in the verse and could, you feel, go lower. It's slightly breathy but with vibrato, a soulful sound.

> I know you, you're a special one
> Some see crazy where I see love
> You fall so low, but shoot so high
> Big dreamers shoot for open sky

Musically, the verse is rather static. Over a distorted electric keyboard, the first two lines are rhythmically four-square, and melodically tame. They depend on Sia's voice to animate them (the portamento on 'special', for example, and another on 'love'). In the third line ('You fall so low, but shoot so high') she momentarily floats an ornamental line, returning to the melodic shape of the first two lines for the fourth. Then the bass and drums arrive, but melodically the next verse mirrors the first. Harmonically, too

(V–I–IV), line after line. We're ready for the chorus, complete with swirling backing vocals.

Though the chorus is no more harmonically adventurous than the verse IV–I–V–IV (three times), the melody now moves out of the octave, and while it's only a whole-tone step, up to B, it seems much more. And it gives the melody further to fall, because the chorus is all about sinking. Tears 'fall on down' and 'hit the ground', and Sia's voice drops expressively down to the low B on both 'down' and 'ground' – a low note for low words. Yet for all that, she 'can see a rainbow' in the tears, and can see 'your soul grow'. The song is not addressed to any pony in particular – it's a generic 'you' – and the hope of which it speaks keeps going as the simple chord progression continues, refusing ever to do more than lightly touch the song's home key.

A word about image. When Sia had her first big hit in 2014 with 'Chandelier', she was thirty-nine – unthinkably ancient for a pop musician's breakthrough to stardom. The video that accompanied the song starred a child dancer called Maddie Ziegler, her bobbed hair and fringe underlining the fact that she was a surrogate for the retiring singer. More hits followed – including 'Cheap Thrills' and 'The Greatest' in 2016 – both with Ziegler's dancing. In *My Little Pony: The Movie*, Songbird Serenade has the same hairstyle, though purple and white, and when the video of the song was released (ahead of the film) there was Maddie Ziegler, her two-tone bob matching Songbird's, dancing and splashing in a pool of tears, somewhere between Lewis Carroll's Alice and Gene Kelly.

10

No Woman, No Cry

music and words by Bob Marley

THE SUMMER OF 1975 WAS relentlessly hot in the United Kingdom, the hottest since 1947. In the south of England, the temperature was exacerbated by high humidity, the nights scarcely less oppressive than the days. On 17 July, the Lyceum Theatre in London was packed to the rafters – literally so, as some people climbed onto the roof in an attempt to gain entry. The heat inside the auditorium was such that steam rising from the crowd condensed on the ceiling until it began to drop like rain. The people in the crowd being rained on were there to hear Bob Marley and the Wailers, and, although they didn't yet know it, to participate in Marley's most famous recording.

It's hard to overstate the almost messianic figure the Jamaican Marley cut in 1970s London, riven, as it was, with racial tension. The following summer – which was hotter still – the Notting Hill Carnival, created as a celebration of Caribbean music and culture after the Notting Hill riots of 1958, itself ended in rioting. In 1958, it had been 'Teddy Boys' – white youths with dandyish clothes and violent temperaments – that had attacked black neighbourhoods. In 1976 the fighting was between black youths and the police, the latter using stop-and-search powers on a community affected by unemployment at three to four times the rate of the British population at large. The young men and women who now found themselves fighting with police were descended from a generation that had been encouraged to come to the UK in the postwar years – the so-called 'Windrush generation' – specifically to take jobs in a country depleted of able-bodied workers. Some of those who came had fought alongside British troops and felt themselves to be returning home. But three decades on, the jobs simply didn't exist.

For these young people, bound together by their shared experience of racism, Bob Marley – and reggae in general – symbolised a Caribbean they had been told so much about, but in most cases, never visited. In Marley's music, they heard a soundtrack of resistance.

On stage at the Lyceum, Marley sang songs such as 'Burnin' and Lootin'', 'Them Belly Full (but We Hungry)' and 'Get up, Stand Up'. And he sang a song from his more recent album, *Natty Dread*, that, in spite of its unusually slow tempo, the crowd quickly recognised, and immediately began singing along to. The album version of 'No Woman, No Cry' is up-tempo and synthetic. Driven by a drum machine, Marley doesn't seem especially engaged. But at the Lyceum, it was different. The organ leads off, ushering us into the song almost as though we're entering a church. A cheer goes up and, by the second line of the introduction, the audience has joined the backing singers: 'No woman, nuh cry'. The two-line introduction repeats three times, before Marley himself begins to sing, and by now the crowd is as much a part of the song as the singer himself.

The structure of the song is almost a passacaglia, which is to say the chord structure repeats throughout, with only a slight variation. It runs through all the verses, the chords sinking from the tonic C sharp major through G sharp and A sharp minor to F sharp major (I–V–vi–IV), and it runs through the interpolated call and response: 'Everything's gonna be all right'. The only line that has slightly different chords (I–IV–I–V) is the tagline 'No woman, no cry'. So the crowd has no problem becoming a 2000-voice chorus, singing mostly wordlessly under Marley.

Marley himself performs with such feeling – passionately, affectionately, even humorously – that the song is barely recognisable as the track on *Natty Dread*. At more than seven minutes, the performance is nearly twice as long as on the studio album, though this isn't entirely a function of the slower tempo. Perhaps it continued as long as it did because of the audience participation; perhaps the Wailers didn't want it to end. The following month, Chris Blackwell of Island Records, Marley's label, wrote to the singer informing him that the recording of this performance would be a single in the UK. It was released in September, reaching number twenty-two in the British charts, with the album of the concert – simply called

Live! – following in December. In 1981, on Marley's death, it was re-released as a UK single, this time going to number eight. The live version is the definitive one – the version everyone knows.

Perhaps the lasting popularity of the song lies in the style of its performance. In contrast to the defiance and anger one hears in much of Marley's material, 'No Woman, No Cry' is all consolation. The slow tempo, with its relaxed reggae beat, is better suited to the material than the original drum machine, and it allows Marley to luxuriate in his vocals. The Jamaican patois is a part of this, and Marley relishes it, the phrase 'Observing the hypocrites' becoming 'Oba–oba–serving the *'eepocrits'*. The crowd at the Lyceum takes the song and turns it into a community anthem that speaks of shared identity, shared struggle, pride, hope and optimism. But there is also nostalgia – you can hear the smile in Marley's voice – which, for young black kids in 1970s Britain, must have helped yoke together a sense of community, summoning a past in a country they had never seen, yet felt they belonged to.

A sense of community is also reflected in the song's credits. Marley ascribed its authorship to one Vincent Ford. Five years older than Marley, the Jamaican songwriter, like the singer, grew up in the poor Kingston neighbourhood of Trench Town. As a young man, Ford had both legs amputated and used a wheelchair. It seems unlikely that Ford did write the song, though it is possible he and Marley collaborated on the words, which reminisce about their shared experience sitting round a fire 'in the government yard in Trench Town'. Marley probably gave Ford the credit, the royalties helping him run his Trench Town soup kitchen, while Marley was able to avoid any contractual obligation to his former record label, Cayman Music.

Was there a woman whom Marley told not to cry? There must have been a few. When he died at the age of thirty-six, he left behind at least eleven children, four with his wife, Rita, one that Rita had by someone else but whom Marley called his own, and six more that Marley had, each with a different mother. Still, 'No Woman, No Cry' is probably not about a specific woman. The comfort and reassurance he offers is to us all.

11

Jolene

music and words by Dolly Parton

'DON'T MESS WITH MY MAN,' sang Irma Thomas on her first single in 1959, and she sounded defiant. Still, the 'Soul Queen of New Orleans', as Thomas would soon become known, was prepared to be reasonable. The song was by Dorothy LaBostrie, co-writer of 'Tutti Frutti', and its full title was '(You Can Have My Husband, but Please) Don't Mess with My Man'.

Well, that's soul. Country singers aren't so phlegmatic.

'Jolene, Jolene, Jolene, Jo–LENE!' Dolly Parton's delivery is controlled enough – there's no pleading in the voice – but the music tells a different story. The rising urgency is in the rising pitch, which reaches the top of the octave on that final '–LENE', tumbling down despairingly via the flattened seventh to the fifth. 'I'm begging of you please don't take my man.'

Up we go again: 'Jolene, Jolene, Jolene, Jo–LENE!' The same notes and the same effect, but here comes the song's great twist: 'Please don't take him, *even though you can.*' So this man is without agency: Jolene has the pathetic fellow twisted round her beautiful little finger. Surely, you think, Dolly can do better than this lump.

The song came out in 1973, and it seems there was something in the air. A few years earlier, Dolly's singing partner Kenny Rogers had had a hit with 'Ruby (Don't Take Your Love to Town)' in which a disabled veteran from 'that crazy Asian war' watches his wife apply her make-up before heading downtown. A few years later came 'Lucille', also sung by Rogers, in which a heart-broken farmer finds his wife drunk in a bar with a stranger (the singer) and tells her 'it's a fine time' to be leaving him, what with 'four hungry children and a crop in the field'. The singer and the woman get a room, but he can't get the farmer's words out of his head and, decent fellow that he is, nothing happens. So faithless women abound, but Jolene, cool as a cucumber, is pure predator.

She is also beautiful, and the first part of this song consists of a catalogue of Jolene's gorgeous features: her 'auburn hair', 'ivory skin' and emerald-green eyes, her smile, her voice. It might be a twelfth-century troubadour praising the qualities of his haughty beloved; there is deference in Dolly's voice at the end of the verse, when she adds 'I cannot compete with you, Jolene', and we hear the respectful comma.

But Dolly doesn't sound pathetic, even as she begs, even as she admits that her future happiness depends on whatever Jolene decides to do with Dolly's man.

> And I can easily understand
> How you could easily take my man,
> But you don't know what he means to me, Jolene.

The repetition of 'easily' is striking. The first use sets up and reinforces the second, but it also adds to the apparent insouciance of the music, the ease with which Dolly understands how easily Jolene can take her man, reflected in the flow of the song. The key is C sharp minor, but there's nothing mournful about it. The song is pure diatonic happiness, skipping along at a swift tempo with Chip Young's spritely, thumb-picked guitar, backed by a continuous drum pattern reminiscent of an Irish bodhrán – and perhaps that's what it is. Certainly there is something Celtic about Dolly's use of ornamentation in the vocal line.

The only hint of something darker, however, comes with one of those ornaments – the modal turn that extends the final word of the chorus: 'Please don't take him just because you *can*' (C sharp–D sharp–C sharp–B–C sharp). In the context of a song that employs just three chords in the same pattern for verses and chorus, this is exotic, and made more so by its duplication a fifth higher (another whiff of medievalism). At the very end of the song, this ornament is sung one last time, now attached to Jolene's name, but it's an octave higher, at half speed, and there's a note change. The flattened seventh of B natural that we've heard throughout the song is raised to an eerie B sharp and, as the song fades from our hearing, we are left with the uneasy feeling that we don't know quite what is happening.

12

You've Lost That Lovin' Feelin'

music by Barry Mann and Phil Spector
words by Cynthia Weil

THE BARITONE VOICE IN POPULAR MUSIC was once associated with mid-twentieth-century crooners such as Bing Crosby and Frank Sinatra. Crosby was a bass-baritone, Sinatra a lighter baritone, and their voices weren't only deep but smooth. The sound had been made possible by the invention of the microphone, allowing quieter and more intimate singing. Before Crosby's time, the likes of Al Jolson had to be belters in order to be heard. And to belt successfully, male singers had required voices in the tenor range. The microphone wrought a significant change in popular music.

But then another change occurred. The advent of rock'n'roll brought belting back – even *with* microphones. Suddenly voices were higher again: Little Richard was a tenor; Chuck Berry was a tenor; Elvis Presley was practically a Heldentenor. Crosby and Sinatra seemed like relics of a bygone era.

It's in this context that we must consider the return of the baritone voice, only a few years later, as rock music learned to make use of the crooner's sound and the element of sophistication and nostalgia it invoked. P.J. Proby, Scott Walker, Tom Jones and Long John Baldry could all croon, but none of them quite like Bill Medley of the Righteous Brothers at the start of 'You've Lost that Lovin' Feelin''.

The song was among the biggest hits of 1965, and Medley's voice, though only one element among many, is what people remember. Dark and wistful, full of regret, the effect was not only down to him. It was every bit as much the achievement of the producer Phil Spector and his ear for musical timbres, in this case a vocal timbre. Isolating Medley from his musical partner – the other Righteous Brother, Bobby Hatfield – Spector gave the opening of the song to the baritone. For the first couple of notes, Medley is literally all that we hear. There are no instruments, just his voice, dark and moping, with lashings of reverb. It's said that when the composer Barry Mann first heard the finished record down a phone line, he thought Spector was playing it at the wrong speed.

'You never close your eyes anymore when I kiss your lips,' Medley sings. 'There's no tenderness like before in your fingertips.' Seldom has a song begun with such a statement of foreboding, a tolling bell (possibly a low vibraphone) joining the voice on 'close'. The ensuing three and a half minutes are a progression from darkness to light, from hopelessness to something like redemption, but it's all in the performance and the production. By the end of the song the words are still pleading ('Bring back that lovin' feelin''), but the sound of the music suggests the lovin' feelin' is already back.

How much of this song Spector actually wrote is a moot point. He took a writing credit and seems to have added the whoa-whoahs, a small, yet significant, contribution. But the fact that we hear despairing words in a musical context that represents a kind of triumph of the spirit is surely Spector's doing, and his masterstroke on this occasion was to keep Bobby Hatfield's voice in reserve. Hatfield, who was used to duetting with Medley, wasn't pleased about having to spend most of the song on the bench, but Spector made brilliant use of his high voice, and especially his falsetto.

Medley sings the verses minus Hatfield, but with distant wordless voices filling out the sonic backdrop. His lugubrious tone remains in place for the first two lines in the tonic key of C sharp major, regularly dipping down to B (chord VII). In the third line a bit of passion is heard in Medley's voice ('You're trying hard not to show it', the backing voices interjecting 'Baby!') as the harmony moves to D sharp minor, rising through E sharp minor and F sharp major ('But baby, baby I know it'), building to the dominant G sharp and the first chorus in the tonic C sharp.

This is where Hatfield sings for the first time, a third higher than Medley, but his voice is further back in the mix so we hardly register it. The effect is more that Medley's voice has gained a new colour. As the chorus ends, C sharp major turns to C sharp minor and stays there while the melody droops disconsolately, reality kicking in: 'Now it's gone, gone, gone, whoa-whoah'.

In the second verse, violins provide a slow descant to Medley's singing, picking up speed for the final ascent to the second chorus, the backing choir and drums more prominent. But suddenly Spector's carefully constructed wall of sound collapses, leaving a slow walking bass, answered by individual notes from a vibraphone. This is where in a lot of songs there would be a middle eight, but in the case of this extended interlude, it's a middle forty-eight, all taking place over the same repeating bass patterns and the same three chords.

'Baby, baby, I'd get down on my knees for you,' Medley sings, the choir re-entering on the final word, together with (of all things) a harpsichord. And then, more than halfway through the song, we hear Hatfield alone and, after all that baritone, strikingly high: 'If you would only love me like you used to do.' A bongo adds a dotted rhythm as, together and equally, the Righteous Brothers sing the next two lines, finally breaking into gospel call and response.

> Baby, baby, baby, baby
> I beg you please, please, please, please
> I need your love, need your love
> I need your love, I need your love
> So bring it on back, so bring it on back
> Bring it on back, bring it on back

The violins return with a long-held G sharp, the tom-toms and tambourine are working overtime, a horn section has materialised and Bobby Hatfield's voice quickly hits his falsetto register, continuing to climb higher and higher to join the violins on their G sharp. The chorus, when it comes, is defiantly optimistic, and no sooner has it ended with its drooping 'whoa-whoah', than it's back again.

The fade comes suddenly, but you sense that the chorus will keep on going, and that as long as the Righteous Brothers sing it, the lovin' feeling may be rekindled.

13

Love Is a Losing Game

music and words by Amy Winehouse

AMY WINEHOUSE ONCE SAID in an interview that it helped her to write songs about 'stuff' that she couldn't 'get past emotionally'. But songs can only help us so much, even when we write our own. 'Love Is a Losing Game' from her second and final album, *Back to Black*, was the last single released in her lifetime, and, after her death from alcohol poisoning in 2011, it inevitably took on a new significance. Even now it's hard to hear the song without thinking of the singer's fate, but perhaps we should try to hear it is as the singer intended when she wrote and recorded it aged just twenty-two.

'Love Is a Losing Game' is a simple song, sung simply, but with devastating power. Winehouse was a huge talent and to hear her perform is to discover both her wonderful sense of timing and an ability to use the colours in her voice to bring shades of meaning to a song – endless nuance. It's a weary voice – and not only on this song – but it is sophisticated. Many people have compared her singing to that of Billie Holiday, and while Holiday may have been both more prolific and varied, it is not an idle comparison.

The song itself is quite formally constructed. The first, second and final couplet of each verse have the same refrain 'Love is a losing game' (in the second verse it's 'Love is a losing hand'; in the third, 'Love is a fate resigned'). Musically these couplets are identical, the only variation each time provided by the third couplet. Here's the first verse:

> For you I was the flame
> Love is a losing game
> Five story fire as you came
> Love is a losing game

One I wished I never played
Oh, what a mess we made
And now the final frame
Love is a losing game.

The diction is rather informal here. There's even a wry joke in the third line, with the double meaning of 'came'. 'Oh, what a mess we made' is a colloquial, almost throwaway remark. The second verse builds on the card analogy of a losing game – did we even know it was a card-game analogy until 'losing game' became 'losing hand'? – and in the all-important third couplet ('Self-professed profound / Until the chips were down') the diction becomes a little more poetic, especially with the alliteration of 'professed profound'). In the last verse disappointment is complete ('fate resigned'), the diction is more formal, there's more alliteration and the song becomes slightly melodramatic. She 'battled blind', her mind was marred by memories, the odds were 'futile', the gods laughed at them.

Because of the formality of the structure and the increasingly poetic choice of words, Winehouse's performance also requires formality. Lines such as 'Self-professed profound' can't be sung sloppily – there has to be a break before 'profound'. It's the same with the wholly alliterative line, 'Memories mar my mind': a break is required between 'mar' and 'my', simply to avoid the line turning into nonsense.

It's a slow song and always was. There's a recorded demo performed to an artlessly strummed guitar that is as slow as the final product. But in its addition of the rhythm of a slow samba and lush, loungy orchestration befitting one of the more sultry Bond songs, the studio recording also takes something away. The singing on the demo was more emotive, and Winehouse's producer Mick Ronson seems to have realised that the cooler and more detached the singing became, the more heartbreaking the result would be. This is a recording of someone determined not to break down as she carefully enunciates the details of her 'mess'. She will not slur her words. She will be deliberate, staying in control. The slowness of the tempo is crucial, and so is the narrowness of the melodic range, which spans just a major seventh.

Songs about disastrous relationships tend to be dramatic, self-pitying or both. 'Love Is a Losing Game' is neither. But then it's real.

48

14

I Feel Fine

music and words by John Lennon and Paul McCartney

EVERYBODY KNOWS THAT the Beatles' 'I Feel Fine' begins with the first use of feedback in pop music. It was an accident. John Lennon propped his guitar against a speaker, thus provoking an electronic wail that the group decided to use on the record. But there's more to the song than that.

This was the Beatles' eighth single, released late in 1964 with the group at the height of its powers and fame. It was written and recorded quickly on top of a riff John Lennon had 'borrowed' from American blues guitarist Bobby Parker, and it replaced the intended single 'Eight Days a Week' as the band's Christmas record. It went straight to number one in the UK and the US. ('Eight Days a Week' was eventually released as a follow-up single in the US, but in the Beatles' own country it was only ever an album track, on *Beatles For Sale*.)

In Ron Howard's documentary *The Beatles: Eight Days a Week – The Touring Years* (2016), Paul McCartney explains that early Beatles singles were an attempt to establish a 'fan base'. The four young men, moulded by their manager into a single identity with matching suits and haircuts, sang songs from the first-person singular (the Beatle persona) to a second-person singular (the fan). The first five singles were 'Love Me Do', 'Please Please Me', 'From Me to You', 'She Loves You' and 'I Want to Hold Your Hand'. Only 'She Loves You' was a variant on the you-and-me transaction. And though their first two hits of 1964 – 'Can't Buy Me Love' and 'A Hard Day's Night' – might have left the relationship out of the titles, the songs themselves are resolutely first person–second person: 'I'll buy you a diamond ring, my friend / If it makes you feel all right'; 'You know I work all day to get you money to buy you things'.

'I Feel Fine' was the last of the simple love-song singles. From 1965, things became less predictable with 'Ticket to Ride' and 'Day Tripper', which were about thwarted love, followed by songs about a paperback writer and a yellow submarine. By 1967, *Sgt Pepper's Lonely Hearts Club Band* contained no love songs at all.

'I Feel Fine' shows how good the Beatles were when they weren't trying, the song itself almost as accidental as the feedback. In 1964 the two main songwriting members of the group still collaborated on most material, but despite the shared credit here, 'I Feel Fine' seems to have been exclusively the work of Lennon. He'd been playing around in the studio with Parker's riff before suddenly telling the others he thought he could turn it into a song. The makeshift lyrics are a clue to the speed of the song's completion, Lennon not even bothering to disguise his recycling of lines from the Beatles' previous hits of just months before: ' … her baby buys her things … / He buys her diamond rings …'

But if the words are unremarkable, the music is effortlessly brilliant. Parker's syncopated riff – occupying a single four-beat bar – came from his 1961 song 'Watch Your Step', and consisted of an open E string, rising to the E an octave higher then falling to D (the flattened seventh) and B (the fifth), these three notes repeated in various combinations. It's hard to say if the song is in E major or minor, because the third degree of the scale is avoided.

While Parker's riff is contained within the span of a single octave, Lennon's, though beginning the same, jumps out of the octave, rising a minor seventh from the fifth degree to the fourth of the upper octave, then to the major third. It's clearly a borrowing and it fulfils the same function as the riff in 'Watch Your Step', but Lennon's version is both more inventive and more expressive. In 'I Feel Fine', it is also harmonically mobile, its first three appearances (after the feedback on A) are in D, C and then the tonic G, a sequence that turns out to be the harmonic structure of the one-line chorus.

But although we have a clearly stated major third in 'I Feel Fine', the song isn't exactly in G major – well, not to begin with. That flattened seventh in the riff is also in the melody. In fact it's in the first word of the song, 'Ba-by', rising from the fifth note of the scale to the flattened seventh.

This is the mixolydian mode (play the white notes ascending from G to G); it's a major-key blues scale and a Beatles favourite, specifically a Lennon favourite – 'Paperback Writer' and its B side, 'Rain', both use the mixolydian, and there's something about the flattened seventh that suited Lennon's adenoidal tone. Plenty of Beatles songs involve touches of this mode, even if they don't make thoroughgoing use of it, and 'I Feel Fine' is one of these – no sooner is the flattened seventh established than it is sharpened on the first word of the one-line chorus 'I'm in love with her and I feel fine'.

The middle eight bars ('I'm so glad that she's my little girl ...') have a rich, if solidly conventional, harmonic pattern (tonic to dominant via mediant and relative minor chords), with the melodic line sinking to its lowest note on 'She's telling all the world'. This is the sharpened seventh playing its familiar role as leading note, in this case leading us straight back to the mixolydian with its *flattened* seventh.

We might mention Ringo's lighter than usual drumming, with its nifty cymbal work, George's equally light-fingered guitar and Paul's agile, typically melodic bass.

But let's not dismiss the lyrics totally. The choice of words may be lazy, but the way Lennon uses them to create rhythmic tension with the riff is perhaps the most distinctive feature of 'I Feel Fine'.

> Baby's good to me, you know,
> She's happy as can be, you know,
> She said so.

The words are continuous, and because they run on it is not clear if the colloquial filler 'you know' belongs with the words that precede it or the words that follow. It might be 'Baby's good to me, you know'. But it might be 'Baby's good to me. You know she's happy as can be. You know she said so'.

Like the guitar riff, the words of the first two lines each fill a bar, but the third line is truncated, the words and Lennon's voice stopping abruptly on the first beat: 'She said so.' The rest of the third line is given over to the all-important riff.

Finally – or perhaps, when it comes to the Beatles, it should be first – there are the voices. The singers tended to take the lead in the songs to which they'd made the greatest contribution, and since 'I Feel Fine' was almost exclusively a John song, it's almost exclusively a John solo. At that time, in late 1964, Lennon was approaching his vocal zenith, which was arguably 1965 in 'Ticket to Ride' and the other songs on *Help*. This is not to say *Help* produced his best singing, but the voice itself sounds strongest on the recordings; a remarkable thing, given the incessant touring of that period.

On 'I Feel Fine' he seems nonchalant and pleased with himself (after all, he feels fine). Part of that nonchalance – we might call it coolness – comes through his voice from the melody line itself, particularly the flat seventh. Lennon is at one with the song. When Paul and George join in the one-line chorus ('I'm in love with her and I feel fine'), the flat seventh disappears, and the harmonies are sweeter, again matching the sentiments of the lyric. In these three-part harmonies, John's voice is on the bottom, in the middle eight sustaining a pedal point as the other voices have the melodic notes, before making its solo descent to that lowest note, leading us back again to the mixolydian and its flat seventh. It's a near-perfect pop song, and the lyrics serve it well.

15

Águas de Março

music and words by Antônio Carlos Jobim

THE HISTORY OF THE BRAZILIAN BOSSA NOVA is uniquely unconventional. The blues, country and western, jazz, rock'n'roll: all of these American popular music forms had lowly beginnings. Because their origins were humble, we can't be certain of precisely how or when they came into being – their inventors were not the sort of people to write things down. The blues seems to have begun among black sharecroppers in the Mississippi Delta; country music is the Americanisation of European folk music among poor, white rural communities across the Southern states; the first jazz pianists practised in the back parlours of New Orleans brothels; and the first jazz combos played the cast-off instruments of Confederate marching bands (clarinet, trumpet and trombone), combining them with a rhythm section from the plantations (banjo, tea-chest bass and washboard). Rock'n'roll fused all these elements. And in Europe, going right back to the Renaissance, dance crazes had begun with the peasantry, even if they had ended up at court.

Bossa nova was different. Middle-class and modernist, the music was rhythmically complex – an elaboration of the samba, with its strong second beat and syncopation – and the lyrics suave and optimistic. Also, from the outset, the 'new trend' or 'new wave' was design-conscious. And it has a precise starting date.

In the mid-1950s, Brazil had endured a succession of failed governments that had finally led to the election of Juscelino Kubitschek, with his promise of 'fifty years of progress in five' and Oscar Niemeyer's plans for the modernist jungle capital of Brasilia. By 1958 it was boom time in Brazil. This was the year Brazil's football team (starring the brilliant 17-year-old Pelé) won the World Cup. National pride was at its height.

Bossa nova would be the musical embodiment of this optimism, for 1958 was also the year of 'Chega de Saudade' – 'No More Blues' – the first bona-fide bossa-nova hit sung by João Gilberto to his own guitar, with lyrics by Vínicius de Moraes and music by Antônio Carlos 'Tom' Jobim. A mere six years later, as 'The Girl from Ipanema' entered the US charts, there were tanks in the streets of Rio de Janeiro and bossa nova was finished.

Well, not quite: in Brazil, it went underground, but it had already been successfully exported to the rest of the world. The American jazz saxophonist Stan Getz enthusiastically – not to say fanatically – fused bossa nova with his brand of West Coast jazz, and 'The Girl from Ipanema', with words by Jobim and Portuguese lyrics by Moraes, was a collaboration between Getz, Gilberto and Gilberto's wife, Astrud. Indeed, while the album track had João singing in Portuguese and Astrud in English, the hit single featured only Astrud's English lyrics.

So, the fashion for bossa nova went international, and then, like most fashions, it faded. By 1972 it was already partly matter of nostalgia, and yet the appearance that year of Jobim's 'Águas de Março' ('The Waters of March') was surely one of bossa nova's great moments.

'Águas de Março' sums up the state of bossa nova in its lyrics, especially in the differences between the Portuguese and English versions, which are small but telling. The title refers to the fact that in Rio it rains a lot in March (hear those chords descend!), and the Portuguese lyrics are quite specific about Brazilian food and drink, plants and animals. These references are gone from Jobim's English-language version.

'Águas de Março' is an obsessive song, musically and lyrically. Jobim wrote both the Portuguese and English words, and the influence of Michel Legrand's 'The Windmills of Your Mind' seems clear. It's not only the dreamlike stream of consciousness that Jobim's song shares with Alan and Marylin Bergman's lyrics for Legrand, but the fact that both songs develop from a single musical phrase, a motif that unites the entire composition and underlines the obsessive nature of the lyrics.

In 'The Windmills of Your Mind', the phrase is both rhythmic and melodic:

Round
Like a circle in a spiral,
Like a wheel within a wheel
Never ending or beginning
On an ever spinning reel
Like a snowball down a mountain,
Or a carnival balloon
Like a carousel that's turning,
Running rings around the moon …

Each line consists of two phrases made up of eight semiquaver beats ('Like a circle in a spiral'), followed by seven ('like a wheel within a wheel'), and each phrase begins mid-bar, placing its final word ('spiral' and 'wheel') on the next downbeat. Melodically, both phrases are made of pairs of notes. Melodically and harmonically, the opening phrases are similar to those of the slow movement of Mozart's *Sinfonia concertante*, which is also built from a single phrase.

The phrases in 'Águas de Março' are different – for one thing, they're shorter – but there's the same repetitious structure in which the words reinforce the melodic motif and vice versa. This is true in both Portuguese:

É o pau, é a pedra, é o fim do caminho
É um resto de toco, é um pouco sozinho
É um caco de vidro, é a vida, é o sol
É a noite, é a morte, é um laço, é o anzol …

And in English:

A stick, a stone,
It's the end of the road,

It's the rest of the stump
It's a little alone

It's a sliver of glass,
It is life, it's the sun,

It is night, it is death,
It's a trap, it's a gun.

Like the Bergmans' lyrics, Jobim's make use of anaphora, repeating the opening words of each line – 'Like', 'É', 'It's' – for emphasis, syntactic and semantic, rhythmic and melodic. His melody is even more contained than Legrand's, at its start just a falling major third – D, B flat, D, B flat – occasionally filled in with the C.

All of which is true, all of which is germane, but none of which comes immediately to mind when we watch Elis Regina and Tom Jobim in the studio, together at the microphone. They may be miming – you only have to watch Jobim in the later stages of the song to see that they are – but as these Brazilian singing stars trade phrases, the bubbling happiness that radiates from their performance is palpable. It would be hard to see it any other way.

16

Illalle

music by Jean Sibelius
words by August Valdemar Koskimies

IN 1935, THE NEW YORK PHILHARMONIC SOCIETY asked its members to nominate their favourite composer, dead or alive. They named not Beethoven, not Brahms, not Wagner, but the 69-nine-year-old Jean Sibelius. Such was the Finnish composer's fame that two decades later, on his ninetieth birthday, Sibelius received telegrams from many of the world's heads of state and a box of cigars from Winston Churchill. It is hard to imagine today's equivalent of Churchill (if there is one) sending today's equivalent of Sibelius (ditto) so much as a text.

The composer's popularity with New York concertgoers and the British prime minister is significant. English-speaking countries have always warmed to Sibelius's music. Some of his finest interpreters have been English conductors (Thomas Beecham and John Barbirolli, Colin Davis and Simon Rattle), and the composer's symphonies, tone poems and violin concerto have long been favourites in the concert halls of Australia. It seems odd, then, that Sibelius's songs – of which there are rather a lot – are hardly known outside his homeland. In Finland, they are among his best-loved works.

Jean Sibelius (1865–1957) is so much Finland's composer laureate, that it comes as a surprise to learn that in addition to his French given name and his Latin surname, his native tongue was actually Swedish (the country's second language). The vast majority of Sibelius's songs use poems in Swedish, albeit by Finns; 'Illalle', composed in 1898, is an exception, and it's interesting how different it sounds from the other songs. The rhythms of the Finnish language seem to shape its melodic structure just as Russian shaped Modest Musorgsky's vocal lines and Leoš Janáček was influenced by the rhythms of Czech speech.

But there's a difference. Musorgsky and Janáček made conscious decisions to take linguistic characteristics into their music. It was a form of musical nationalism. Sibelius, the composer of *Finlandia*, might have been nationalistic in other ways, but there's no evidence that using language in this manner was one of them.

The Finnish word *ilta* means 'evening', so the title of the song translates as 'To Evening' – the suffix '-lle' being one of those endings the Finnish language has in place of prepositions. But Ilta is also a woman's name – the name, indeed, of the poet's fiancée and later wife, Ilta Bergroth – and so 'Illalle' also means 'To Ilta'. (Koskimies's sonnet is itself untitled.)

There's a certain formality about the poem: its diction is old-fashioned, and many of its words archaic. But the song is impassioned and urgent. The piano part trembles with anticipation, the melodic line seems to be continually toppling forwards, and the whole thing is over in little more than a minute. The Finnish music critic Vesa Sirén reports in his book *Aina poltti sikaria* that Koskimies said the song came like a flash to Sibelius, 'the muse dictating it directly on to the piano as soon as he'd read the words'. It certainly sounds that way.

> Oi, terve! tumma, vieno tähti-ilta,
> Sun haaveellista hartauttas lemmin
> Ja suortuvaisi yötä sorjaa hemmin,
> Mi hulmuaapi kulmais kuulamilta.

'Oh greetings, dark and subtle starlit evening! I love your dreamy devotion and the dark night of your locks fluttering above your pale brow.' Koskimies's poem goes on to speak of the poet's desire to fly to his beloved Ilta/evening at the end of the day's toil and frenzy, and it is this headlong rush the song captures so well.

The Finnish language places the stress on the first syllable of each word, so each line of Koskimies's poem consists of five trochees, preceded by an 'upbeat' – 'Oi' in the first line. So the poem begins thus: oi, TER–ve! TUM–ma, VI'e–no TÄH–ti IL–ta. Each line thereafter is rhythmically similar.

Sibelius's melody follows this rhythm and makes a feature of the unchanging metre. The first line begins on C, the fifth note of the scale, and remains there until the final syllable of 'vieno', when it begins its descent to the tonic F, dipping down to the leading note and back up to the tonic on 'ilta'. Each subsequent line is a variation on this pattern, with variety provided by the song's underlying harmonic shifts, most memorably the sudden and temporary shift to D flat major (against a now dissonant C in the vocal line) on the reference to 'the black-winged night'.

The headlong nature of 'Illalle' continues until the sonnet's final six lines. In the third and last of these, Sibelius goes into dramatic slow motion, and at the very end (after that jarring visitation of D flat major), the longed for ecstasy ('Oi, Ilta armas' – 'Oh, darling Ilta/evening') is reached in the singer's elongated notes and the piano's blaze of F major. The song might only last a minute, but by its end a lot has been achieved.

17

Ständchen

music by Franz Schubert
words by Ludwig Rellstab

IN THE CENTURY THAT INVENTED the song cycle, in the very city in which it was invented, Franz Schubert was Vienna's pre-eminent composer of songs. One of the best known, 'Ständchen' ('Serenade'), comes from his final song cycle, *Schwanengesang* (Swansong), assembled posthumously by his publisher, Tobias Haslinger. Unlike its predecessors, *Die schöne Müllerin* (The Fair Maid of the Mill) and *Winterreise* (The Winter's Journey), it has no narrative arc and is really just a collection of songs. The words aren't even all by the same poet.

Schubert's songs in general are notable for the way in which they not only present the poetry of the composer's day – the good, the bad and, in some cases, the downright ugly – but also often illustrate it. In the most famous examples, this illustration takes the form of a continuous sound effect in the piano accompaniment. For example, in 'Das Wandern' ('The Wanderer'), the first song from *Die schöne Müllerin*, the piano part conjures a purposeful millwheel, clattering away as our hero strides out abroad. In the final song of *Winterreise* we hear a very different wheel – the turning of a plaintive hurdy-gurdy, its music going round and round above a drone as it highlights the mental disintegration of the singer/protagonist. Schubert's piano is a babbling brook in 'Die Forelle' ('The Trout'), a spinning wheel in 'Gretchen am Spinnrade' ('Gretchen at the Spinning Wheel') and, perhaps most famously of all, the galloping hooves of the distraught father's horse in 'Erlkönig' ('The Erl-King' or 'Elf-King').

But 'Ständchen'? It's a simple love song, isn't it? Well, not quite. In fact, 'Ständchen' is two things at once. It's the serenade its title tells us it is, but it's also a song about serenades.

A serenade is an alfresco love song, performed, at night, beneath the beloved's window. Since the singer will be acting alone, any accompaniment for the song will be the singer's own responsibility. The instrument, of course, will have to be portable – not least because a quick getaway may be necessary if things don't go well – and so a guitar is ideal. When, in Edward Lear's poem, 'The Owl and the Pussycat', the Owl sings 'to a small guitar', he is performing a serenade. For he is not only telling the pussycat he loves her ('Oh lovely pussy, oh pussy, my love, what a beautiful pussy you are'), he is doing so outdoors, at night, and while looking up – in this case 'to the stars above'.

Schubert himself played the guitar and composed a few songs for voice and guitar. While 'Ständchen', like the rest of *Schwanengesang*, has a piano accompaniment, the staccato figuration in the right hand is very much that of a delicately plucked guitar. So this, after all, is one of Schubert's sound-effect songs, the composer evoking a guitar as vividly as he does the millwheel and the galloping horse.

Ludwig Rellstab's poem, though addressing his beloved, has an air of detachment. The singer is also singing about his song.

Leise flehen meine Lieder
Durch die nacht zu Dir;
In den stillen Hain hernieder,
Liebchen, komm' zu mir!

'Softly my songs plead to you through the night,' he sings, as though the songs themselves require some advocacy and explanation (and notwithstanding the fact that this *is* one of those songs). 'In the silent grove below, come to me my beloved.' Self-awareness is a standard conceit of songs addressed to a loved one: 'Beautiful dreamer, queen of my song / List, while I woo thee with soft melody'; 'What would you do if I sang out of tune?'

But Schubert's song here has competition from nature. Treetops are whispering and rustling, nightingales are calling. As it turns out these are not distractions so much as exemplars, and Schubert provides harmonic highlighting for the lessons they bring. Yes, that rustling might be a sign that the lovers are being spied upon (the B flat major song moves abruptly to a chord of D minor): but no, not to worry, their secret will not be overheard (D major). The nightingales understand heartache (D minor): but their silvery tone consoles every heart (D major).

Just as the composer's piano accompaniment apes the manner of a guitar, so his vocal line draws on another convention of this musical courting ritual – the tendency on the part of the singer to show off. In general, Schubert was not one to add ornamentation to songs, but 'Ständchen' has lots of it. You could argue that the basic melodic cell that begins the song and each subsequent verse is itself ornamental – a sort of slow, written-out mordent – but in the second part of each verse the embellishments are very clear, and they come, as you might hope, at key moments – with references to moonlight and yearning and trembling.

So did Schubert compose a spoof? Of course not. The song is genuine. If its style is knowing, if the composer gives us the occasional wink, 'Ständchen' is a serenade, nonetheless, with one of his simplest melodies and one of his most touching.

18

Stardust

music by Hoagy Carmichael
words by Mitchell Parish

HOAGY CARMICHAEL, WHO WAS to all intents and purposes the first modern singer-songwriter, once said that he sang the way a shaggy dog looks. 'Stardust' has a lot of shaggy dog in its tune. It lopes along, going this way, going that, running off to strange places, pausing to sniff other dogs. It makes sudden leaps and ranges far and wide, over nearly two octaves on some of Carmichael's own recordings.

Carrmichael said the tune came to him suddenly. He was sitting on a wall on the campus of his alma mater in Bloomington, Indiana, one summer's evening in 1924, when he looked up at the stars and began whistling it. He dashed to the nearest piano and worked it out.

Well, maybe. What seems incontestable is that the shape and manner of the melodic line were inspired by the playing of his great friend and musical hero, the cornet player Bix Beiderbecke. (Following Bix's untimely death in 1931, Carmichael named his own son Hoagy Bix.) Carmichael's biographer, the jazz trumpeter Richard Sudhalter, pointed out that Beiderbecke tended to deliver his discursive solos in short bursts. Phrases of varying lengths, sounding in different parts of his cornet's range – a few notes here, a few more there – would be gradually pulled together so that the whole finally made sense. This is how the chorus of 'Stardust' works, this is its shaggy-dogness. It makes it an unlikely candidate for one of America's favourites because it's simply quite hard to sing.

The chorus of 'Stardust' is thirty-two bars long, which isn't in itself unusual. The 32-bar structure was a twentieth-century standard. 'Over the Rainbow' is thirty-two bars long, so is 'I Got Rhythm', so are a lot of Beatles songs. But these songs have a common feature that 'Stardust' doesn't share.

It's worth a small detour here to explain. At the end of the first eight bars of 'Over the Rainbow', which we'll call A, there's a perfect cadence – a musical full stop – on 'once in a lullaby'. The song could actually end at this point. It would be only a few seconds long and therefore pretty unorthodox, not to say disappointing, but it would make grammatical sense both in terms of its words and music. The next eight bars of 'Over the Rainbow' have the same music – another A section – and there's another perfect cadence on 'really do come true'. The next eight bars ('Someday I'll wish upon a star') are different – we'll call them B – and the line ends with an imperfect cadence (not a full stop) on 'that's where you'll find me'. This kind of cadence leaves us hanging in the air, the music obliged to come back to earth in the final eight bars, which are yet another A, with one last full stop ('why then, oh why can't I?'). We can say the structure is AABA. 'I Got Rhythm' is the same. So are 'From Me to You', 'Eight Days a Week' and 'Hey Jude'.

'Stardust' doesn't follow this familiar pattern and it affects the way the music works. The first eight bars – the A section – of 'Stardust' do not immediately repeat. The music goes right on to the B section. Also, and more significantly, the A bars don't conclude the chorus. This means they have no need of a perfect cadence. With the AABA structure, you get three of these musical full stops. With the ABAC structure of 'Stardust' there's only one, at the very end. This means that the famous 'Stardust melody' (to quote Parish's lyrics) is continuous. The tune flows; it meanders. And what a tune it is!

'Stardust' – or 'Star Dust' as it was known at first – existed as music without words for a couple of years before Mitchell Parish supplied lyrics. In many ways they were the making of the tune – almost an explanation of it – but fitting words to it can't have been easy.

> Sometimes I wonder why I spend the lonely night dreaming of a song:
> The melody haunts my reverie and I am once again with you,
> When our love was new, and each kiss an inspiration;
> But that was long ago, now my consolation is in the stardust of a song.

Taking his cue from the continuous structure of the melody, Parish's words wonder as they wander. At the end of the first eight bars, there's no perfect cadence – no full stop – and so Parish's words trip across the line to match: 'I am once again with you, / When our love was new …' Parish's lyrics are more wistful reminiscence than stream of consciousness, but their loose feel is a perfect match for Carmichael's tune: they function almost like a vocalese, though that term had yet to be invented. The composer certainly agreed. Not only did he sing the song with Parish's lyrics but he called his second autobiography *Sometimes I Wonder* (his first autobiography was *The Stardust Road*).

There are many famous recordings of 'Stardust' besides Carmichael's own. A particularly legendary account was recorded by Louis Armstrong in 1931. Carmichael had first met Armstrong in 1923 – Beiderbecke had introduced them – and here is Satchmo in the studio, the song still new, offering one of the great reinterpretations of the tune. It's a stomp, above which Armstrong's trumpet explores every last cranny of the melody. But when it's time for him to put the instrument down and sing, a wonderful thing happens: he sings most of this wide-ranging tune gleefully on a single note.

Other notable interpretations include Bing Crosby's (also from 1931), Frank Sinatra's (1943), Willie Nelson's (1978) and Nat King Cole's famous recording from 1956, the last including the verse: 'And now the purple dusk of twilight time steals across the meadows of my heart …' That verse is frequently omitted from recordings. It involves another long and discursive set of lyrics, matching an equally long and discursive tune that has little musical connection to the chorus. It's almost like a separate piece of music and when a chorus itself is so rich, such a verse can seem surplus to requirements. But after Cole's recording it caught on to the extent that in 1961 Sinatra went back into the studio with the song and made a new recording of the verse alone, surely one of the few times a famous song has been recorded without its chorus.

19

You Are My Sunshine

music and words by Jimmie Davis and Charles Mitchell
(disputed authorship)

You are my sunshine, my only sunshine;
You make me happy when skies are grey.
You'll never know, dear, how much I love you.
Please don't take my sunshine away.

FOUR SIMPLE LINES OF MUSIC with words of almost equal simplicity, 'You Are My Sunshine' is one of the Western world's best-known songs. It has been performed and recorded by everyone from bluegrass musicians to soul and gospel singers, from children's entertainers to jazz singers, from the singing cowboy Gene Autry to Bryan Ferry. Does the song's appeal lie in its simplicity, its three chords and a chorus that is musically identical to the verse? Or is it the song's ambiguity? For while the chorus is often sung alone as a cheery, up-tempo number, the lyrics in the verses indicate a darker story: by the end of the song the sunshine has been extinguished.

The song is commonly credited to Jimmie Davis and Charles Mitchell. Davis was born in 1899 and lived through the whole of the twentieth century, dying on 5 November 2000. He was not just a popular hillbilly singer, but also the governor of the state of Louisiana between 1944 and 1948 and again between 1960 and 1964. A larger-than-life good old boy, and a segregationist to his core, he would often perform the song at his campaign rallies, in the company of a horse named Sunshine.

But despite a close association with Jimmie Davis, the song's authorship is far from clear. The only thing that seems certain is that Davis was not the one who wrote it. Before his first recording of the song with Mitchell in

1940 it had already been recorded at least twice in 1939, by the Pine Ridge Brothers and the Rice Brothers Gang. On the blue 'Decca' label of the latter, the song is attributed to Paul Rice, who is believed to have sold the rights to Davis, a common practice at the time. But there are also claims that the man behind the music was not in fact Rice, but a former collaborator of his, Oliver Hood, who'd performed the song live at a war veterans' convention in Georgia in 1933.

Perhaps we'll never know for sure, and in a way, the song's authorship is moot. Like 'Happy Birthday to You', another popular number with disputed authorship, 'You Are My Sunshine' belongs to everyone. What continues to remain interesting is the nature of the song. What is it really about?

Mose Allison, who performed the song most of his long career and liked to introduce it by saying, 'This next song was written by the former governor of Louisiana', sang it as a slow blues. He just did the chorus and the first verse, but by the end of that verse the song has already taken a dark turn. While there's none of the original tune in Allison's interpretation, the bluesy quality of his voice fits the words.

> The other night, dear, as I lay sleeping,
> I dreamt I held you by my side.
> When I awoke, dear, I was mistaken,
> So I hung my head and cried.

The more common second line of this first verse is 'held you in my arms', but Allison always sang 'by my side', which at least rhymes with 'cried'. The song was invariably a highlight of his set, and the fact that it could be performed so convincingly as a blues is testament to the song's flexibility. But then that was there from the start.

The early recorded versions are all in different styles, ranging from the gentle hillbilly treatment by the Pine Ridge Brothers, to the Rice Brothers Gang's more animated foxtrot with pedal-steel solos, to Jimmie Davis and the Charles Mitchell Orchestra's Dixieland jazz version featuring a clarinet and muted trumpet. Along with Mitchell's guitar version, those early recordings were almost immediately followed by numerous others, including Autry's in 1941, and the same year one by Bing Crosby. Both were hits, and both sounded cheery enough, even though Autry and Crosby sang all the verses and the story only gets darker.

> I'll always love you and make you happy
> If you will only say the same
> But if you leave me to love another
> You'll regret it all some day.

> You told me once, dear, you really loved me,
> And no one else, dear, could come between.
> But now you've left me and love another
> You have shattered all my dreams.

It's a major key song, employing the three most basic chords in the tool-box. In C major these are C (and C7 if you must), F and G7. The melody is equally simple, its four lines, with a few variants, really adding up to ABBA. It's common to throw a D sharp/E flat into the melody on the first syllable of 'only', but sheet music generally represents the note as a diatonic D natural. Perhaps it's the music's simplicity that makes it so flexible.

In 1962, Ray Charles included it on volume two of *Modern Sounds in Country and Western Music*, and as in Mose Allison's blues version, retained precisely none of the original tune. Aretha Franklin's account of the song on *The Delta Meets Detroit* (1998) is effectively a tribute to Charles.

In 1974, Bryan Ferry, taking time off from Roxy Music to make a second solo album, *Another Time, Another Place*, included a version of 'You Are My Sunshine'. His account employs only two verses but about a dozen repetitions of the chorus and manages to last nearly seven minutes, adding New Orleans brass and gospel singers along the way.

Perhaps the most touching recording of the song is that made by the ageing Johnny Cash for producer Rick Rubin, issued after Cash's death in 2003 on the boxed set *Unearthed*. Like everything else on those recordings, the performance is pared right back. It's a distillation of 'You Are My Sunshine' to the very essence, Cash even conflating the second and third verses.

But through his shaky wreck of a voice, the tune remains intact, and perhaps for the first time, the tune makes sense of the words. It's still major key, still simple – in fact never simpler – and it's definitely not a blues, but it is heartbreaking.

20

Ode to Billie Joe

music and words by Bobbie Gentry

LIKE NOVELS OR POEMS OR FILMS, songs can bring characters to life. In Bobbie Gentry's 'Ode to Billie Joe' we discover very little about the boy in the title, Billie Joe McAllister, except that he's jumped off the Tallahatchie Bridge. But we learn a lot about the unnamed girl singing the song. She presents herself as a detached narrator but, through the revelation of small details and the casual table talk of her family, we discern her character and her pain.

'Ode to Billie Joe' is in the American literary tradition of Southern Gothic. This could be a story by Flannery O'Connor or William Faulkner or Harper Lee, and like their work it is anchored by place names and customs. It is set in Mississippi. It mentions Carroll County and Tupelo, but the story takes place in Panola County to the north, where the Tallahatchie River flows towards the Delta, west of Choctaw Ridge. In Southern Gothic, places are not chosen simply to make a story credible, but also to add colour, and in Gentry's 'Ode', Choctaw Ridge suggests the old Western trope of Indian braves looking down ominously from their perch in the rocks, while the Tallahatchie is a river of shame. This is where they found the body of Emmett Till, the fourteen-year-old African-American boy, lynched by white supremacists only a dozen years before the song was written.

'Seems like nothin' ever comes to no good up on Choctaw Ridge,' says mama to papa in the song, and we have no difficulty believing her.

The conversation takes place at dinner, the main meal served in the middle of the working day on this family farm, where the narrator has been 'chopping cotton' in the early June heat. We're told at the outset that 'it was the third of June'. The hint of police procedural is significant – this is a song about evidence – and Bobbie Gentry's character never betrays emotion as she tells the story.

By the end of verse one, as the family gathers at the table, we learn that Billie Joe has jumped. The second verse is almost entirely domestic: the black-eyed peas and biscuits are passed around, and papa talks about the ploughing still ahead of him. But in the third verse, we begin to learn important information about Billie Joe and the narrator/singer.

> And brother said he recollected when he and Tom and Billie Joe
> Put a frog down my back at the Carroll County picture show.
> And wasn't I talkin' to him after church last Sunday night?
> I'll have another piece o' apple pie. You know, it don't seem right:
> I saw him at the sawmill yesterday on Choctaw Ridge,
> And now ya tell me Billie Joe's jumped off the Tallahatchie Bridge.

And now our eyes are on the narrator. Her mother notices that she hasn't 'touched a single bite' of her meal, and – just by the way – when 'that nice young preacher, Brother Taylor' stopped by earlier, he mentioned something interesting:

> He said he saw a girl that looked a lot like you up on Choctaw Ridge
> And she and Billy Joe was throwing somethin' off the Tallahatchie Bridge.

And that's all we will ever learn. The final verse, set in the present (we now realise that this family dinner happened more than a year ago), ties up a few loose ends. Brother is married, papa is dead from a virus and mama has grown listless without him.

> And me, I spend a lot of time pickin' flowers up on Choctaw Ridge
> And drop them into the muddy water off the Tallahatchie Bridge

So what happened? What was our narrator and Billie Joe throwing off the bridge? A draft card? A ring? A gun? An aborted foetus? A baby? You could waste a lot of time in internet chat groups discussing the possibilities, because the song is endlessly fascinating, and not only because of the story, but the way it's told, the way it's sung.

Bobbie Gentry's attractive, slightly husky voice has us hanging on every word. Her guitar accompaniment – to what is effectively a 24-bar blues – is clipped, repetitive, desensitised. There's also a small string section that comes and goes, a bit like a film score. At first, the sighing glissandi might be distant passing cars. They are heard between verses, then between phrases, then – as the evidence begins to pile up – accompanying the voice. They function a little like a pedal steel, gilding the vocal line.

Gentry's voice drops through a major tenth at the end of each verse on the line that ends with ' … Tallahatchie Bridge', winding all the way down to a low D. At the end of the whole song, the strings too have a long trilling glissando, intended, presumably, to depict the flowers dropping into the Mississippi river. It's an oddly incongruous – almost comic – moment but it fits the mood at the song's end rather well. One of the most important lines comes at the start of that final verse: 'A year has come and gone since we heard the news about Billie Joe'.

The *news* about Billie Joe? There is something final about the line, maybe something defiant. If we had thought we were going to get a confession, we were wrong. She might memorialise him with her dropped flowers, but there's a coldness in the way she reports hearing 'the news'. Now wasn't that a terrible thing? She knew him a little.

There's a rather creepy video of a live television performance by Gentry from the *Smothers Brothers Comedy Hour* in 1967, the year of the song's release. She sings it on a stool, in front of a dining table around which sit three mannequins, representing the other members of the family. Over the applause at the end of her performance, she puts down her guitar, and turns to join her family as the shades come down.

21

The Time of the Preacher

music and words by Willie Nelson

IT'S A HOWL OF PAIN – like a baby's cry or a panther's scream. The lesson has begun. Willie Nelson's voice rises through a minor seventh, from E to D. 'It was the *time...*'

In 1953, the film and theatre critic of Virginia's *Richmond Times-Dispatch* wrote a cowboy song with a local radio announcer in the hope that it might interest Perry Como. This was not quite as quixotic as it sounds. Edith Lindeman and Carl Stutz had written songs before, and the following year had a big hit with Kitty Kallen's recording of 'Little Things Mean a Lot', which sold more than a million copies and spent nine weeks at number one.

Como never saw their cowboy song, 'Red Headed Stranger', but Arthur Smith & His Crackerjacks recorded a rather jaunty version as the flip side of their 1954 single, a version of 'Sobbin' Women' from *Seven Brides for Seven Brothers*. It wasn't a hit, but the song gained some airplay, particularly on radio station KCNC in Fort Worth, Texas, where Willie Nelson, the host of 'The Western Express', took such a liking to it he occasionally sang it as a bedtime song for his daughter. It was not perhaps the most suitable choice of lullaby.

A stranger rides into town on a 'raging black stallion'. He is leading a second horse, 'a bay', once ridden by his dead wife. The scene is set for a song painted in vivid colours. Not only are the horses black and bay, but the stranger, from Blue Rock, Montana, has red hair. He is about to meet and kill a woman with yellow hair.

'Red Headed Stranger' is a picture-book song. It shows us things but tells us very little. It raises questions that it never answers. What happened to the stranger's wife that he should keep her horse with him? Why does he become so enraged by the yellow-haired lady's attempt to take it that he shoots her?

Evidently, the mystery of the song bewildered Nelson, for his 1975 album *Red Headed Stranger* was an elaborate attempt to construct a rationale for it. The album's other tracks are a mixture of existing songs by the likes of Eddy Arnold and Fred Rose, together with an instrumental version of the hymn, 'Just As I Am', and new songs by Nelson himself. To call it a concept album is to understate and undersell it. The LP even came with a strip cartoon narrating the story.

The first thing Nelson does is identify the red-headed stranger as a preacher:

> It was the time of the preacher,
> When the story began,
> Of the choice of a lady
> And the love of a man

In the 1986 BBC television series *Edge of Darkness*, Nelson's song is something of a recurring motif, its brooding violence underscoring the mood of the series. In one scene, the two main characters, Craven and Jedburgh, discuss the song, agreeing that 'the time of the preacher' means 'the time of the gun'. This would appear to be a flight of fancy on the part of the legendary screenwriter Troy Kennedy Martin, because there seems to be no evidence for it. Nelson's preacher is a preacher, and the later appearance of 'Just As I Am' leaves no doubt of it. Which is not to say this preacher doesn't carry a gun or that he is afraid to use it.

Listening to the song, it is hard not to imagine Robert Mitchum as the Reverend Harry Powell in Charles Laughton's film *The Night of the Hunter* (1955), riding his horse and killing women. The film appeared the year after 'Red Headed Stranger' was first released, and it was an adaptation of James Agee's novel, published the year the song was written. Perhaps, in his mind, Nelson conflated the song and the film.

'The Time of the Preacher' begins Nelson's album, but this first track isn't the end of the song. At the lines 'Now the preaching is over, / And the lesson's begun', the song is interrupted. The 'lesson' comes courtesy of Eddy Arnold and Wally Fowler's song 'I Couldn't Believe It Was True', sung from the point of view of a man arriving home to find his wife gone.

Here endeth the lesson, and Nelson's song continues:

> But he could not forgive her
> Though he tried and he tried and he tried.
> In the halls of his memories
> Still echo her lies.

That third 'tried' is a marvellous bit of songwriting: he tried so hard, he broke the metre of the song. And the preacher, too, it seems has reached breaking point, for these fractionally slower verses end with a new twist:

> Now the lesson is over
> And the killing's begun.

Willie Nelson's song, 'Blue Rock, Montana', comes next. Blue Rock is where the preacher's wife and her lover have holed up, and where the preacher now finds them in a tavern and shoots them both dead ('with their smiles on their faces'). It's a short song that doles out the facts of the double murder, then transforms itself into the chorus of 'Red Headed Stranger' ('Don't cross him, don't boss him, / He's wild in his sorrow'). This is followed by 'Blue Eyes Crying in the Rain', a song associated with Roy Acuff, one of the greats of country music, but fully adapted to its new surroundings as part of the preacher's narrative. Then, at last, comes 'Red Headed Stranger' in full.

But Nelson's theme song has one last appearance to make, brief and full of foreboding. This time, there are four lines only, lasting half a minute: but that's not the scary part. What's scary is that the song is suddenly slower, and the pitch has dropped a whole tone to match it like an old record running down. If we are in a bad dream, it just got worse because we've gone into slow motion:

> It was the time of the preacher
> In the year of '01,
> And just when you think it's all over
> It's only begun.

It's one of the most portentous moments in country music; it's worthy of a Schubert or Schumann song cycle. On *Red Headed Stranger*, 'The Time of the Preacher' is finally ended, but the story will continue for eight more songs, the next being that hymn tune, stripped of its religious words.

The stranger is going to somewhere like hell, and we're going with him.

22

The Long Black Veil

music by Marijohn Wilkin
words by Danny Dill and Marijohn Wilkin

MANY PEOPLE HAVE TAKEN 'The Long Black Veil' to be a folk song. It isn't, but there could be no greater compliment, and performances by Sammi Smith and Johnny Cash, Joan Baez and Mick Jagger (with the Chieftains), Nick Cave and Gillian Welch, have only added to the impression of its folkloric origins. In fact, the song was written by a pair of Nashville pros in 1959 and it revived the stalled career of Lefty Frizzell, a pioneering figure in country music. Frizzell's open, honest voice was an influence on the likes of Merle Haggard and Willie Nelson; it was a particularly apt choice for 'The Long Black Veil', a song that unblinkingly stares fate in the face and asks no sympathy of its listeners.

The singer of the song is dead, hanged for a murder he did not commit. He had an alibi but was honour-bound not to produce it, because at the time of the murder he was 'in the arms' of his 'best friend's wife' (were this really a folk song, it would be his brother's wife). The woman in question now visits his grave 'when the night winds wail', disguised in the black veil of the title, and 'nobody knows' but the dead man himself.

Like 'You Are My Sunshine' and 'Red Headed Stranger', the song wraps dark lyrics in a cheerful tune. There's really nothing special about the melody of the verse or the chords that go with it, but the chorus ('She walks these hills in a long black veil') has some distinction, and the yearning tagline ('Nobody knows, nobody sees, / Nobody knows but me') is the clincher, the melodic line rising like those wailing 'night winds' with Frizzell adding a hint of a yodel and Don Helms's pedal steel supplying a tasteful background moan. Perhaps this was the cue for Nick Cave's version of the song with the Bad Seeds, though it seems more likely Cave was responding to The Band's recording on their first album, *Music from Big Pink*, with Rick Danko's quavering, querulous vocals. The Band wasn't taking the song entirely seriously, and neither was Cave. But Johnny Cash was.

Possibly because he was the self-styled 'man in black', Cash staked his claim early to 'The Long Black Veil' and today it is most closely associated with him. He made his first recording for the album *Orange Blossom Special* in 1965 and sang it in 1968 during his concerts at Folsom Prison. On the ensuing album, *Johnny Cash at Folsom Prison*, we hear him get the giggles after the line 'I had been in the arms of my best friend's wife' ('Did I hear someone applaud?' he laughs). The following year, he sang it as a duet with Joni Mitchell on his TV show, and it remained a staple of his repertoire until the end of his career. On Cash's posthumously released *Unearthed* recordings for producer Rick Rubin, it is track one.

Cash's vocal timbre adds all the musical darkness the tune itself lacks, his hollow tones making us believe that 'the scaffold is high and eternity's near'. But there's not a hint of melodrama. This is a hallmark of the folk singer's art and it was Cash's usual approach: let the story tell itself.

Another feature of the song's history that links it to folk tradition is the way it has been sung, unchanged, by so many women. Not only Baez and Welch, but Marianne Faithfull, Roseanne Cash and a swathe of female country singers. Even the avant-garde soprano *sfogato*, Diamanda Galas, has recorded it in a version that makes Nick Cave's seem demure. But they all sang the song from the man's point of view. In commercial music, lyrics are routinely altered to maintain the presumed heterosexuality of the performer: 'And then he kissed me', sang the Crystals; 'And then I kissed her', sang the Beach Boys. But folk song – at least in the Celtic, British and Appalachian traditions – is different. The point of view may be fluid within a song, switching from the third person to the first and back again as readily as it flips from past tense to present. A man may sing from the point of view of a 'maid that's true in love'; a female singer may become a sadistic brute of a ship's captain.

One female singer who bucked this trend was the composer of 'The Long Black Veil', Marijohn Wilkin, who, in 1961, two years after Lefty Frizzell's recording, made her own, though it wasn't released for more than thirty years. Entitled 'My Long Black Veil', Wilkin's recording presents the song from the woman's point of view, but in most other respects the song is unchanged.

Another recording from 1961 was by Burl Ives, and this was significant. Ives's recording career had been devoted almost entirely to American folk songs, including a fair few murder ballads such as 'Frankie and Johnny'. Danny Dill's initial spur to write 'The Long Black Veil' had been Ives's singing, and while he was aware Ives specialised in traditional material, he believed he might be able to write something in the same idiom. Ives's recording of Dill and Wilkin's song was proof, then, of their success. It was, in Dill's own words, 'an instant folk song'.

23

Desolation Row

music and words by Bob Dylan

ALMOST FROM THE START OF Bob Dylan's career as a songwriter and performer, an industry of interpretation grew up around him. From the music critic Greil Marcus to Boston University's Professor of Humanities (and former Oxford Professor of Poetry) Christopher Ricks, commentators have been on hand to tell us what they thought Dylan's words and music – but especially the words – might mean. No song has received more attention than the eleven-minute epic 'Desolation Row', from Dylan's 1965 album *Highway 61 Revisited*.

'They're selling postcards of the hanging / They're painting the passports brown / The beauty parlour is filled with sailors / The circus is in town': from the opening lines, it is clear we are observing some sort of unsettling carnival. The circus has arrived and now bad things – or at least inexplicable things – are happening. The commissioner, the only authority figure, is blind and in a trance, while the riot squad – presumably under his command – is antsy and looking for action. It seems clear there will be trouble, though 'Lady and I', the spectators through whose eyes we will observe the parade of dysfunctionality, appear calmly detached as they 'look out tonight from Desolation Row'.

What we observe in this song at one level, is a phantasmagorical stream of consciousness. The characters that populate 'Desolation Row' are mostly familiar. They're from the Bible and Shakespeare, literature, mythology and history, ancient and modern, but few of them are behaving as we might expect them to. Cinderella has 'her hands in her back pockets / Bette Davis style'; Ophelia 'wears an iron vest'; the Good Samaritan is getting dressed for tonight's carnival; Einstein, who is 'disguised as Robin Hood' goes round 'sniffing drainpipes and reciting the alphabet'; the Phantom of the Opera looks like a priest; Casanova lacks confidence; the *Titanic* will sail at dawn but right now Ezra Pound and T.S. Eliot are 'fighting in the captain's tower / While calypso singers laugh at them'.

And those are just some of the names we recognise. Who is the jealous monk that's befriended Einstein? Who is Dr Filth and why is his world in a leather cup? Who are 'the superhuman crew' that are out rounding up 'everyone / That knows more than they do'? Why are 'insurance men' bringing kerosene 'down from the castles'? There is no shortage of answers in the literature.

For Christopher Ricks in *Dylan's Visions of Sin*, 'Desolation Row' is a key song representing not just one of the seven deadly sins, but 'a masque of all the sins'. Ricks compares it to the pageant of the sins 'that cavort in Marlowe's play *Doctor Faustus*', equating Dylan's Dr Filth with Faustus himself.

In an essay written for *Esquire* magazine in 1972, literary critic Frank Kermode and poet Stephen Spender call 'Desolation Row' 'a deliberate cultural jumble – history seen flat, without depth, culture heroes of all kinds known only by their names'. But they also note that in the song's final verse Dylan explains he 'had to rearrange their faces / And give them all another name'.

The Tennyson scholar Aidan Day, in his book *Jokerman: Reading the Lyrics of Bob Dylan*, points out links between the song's images. There are water/drowning references: Noah, Ophelia, the *Titanic*, the expectation of rain. There's entrapment: Ophelia in her iron vest, Einstein's memories locked in a trunk. By the end of the song, we are all trapped on Desolation Row, a broken door knob ensuring no one may leave.

And then, as many commentators have observed, there's T.S. Eliot's great poem 'The Waste Land', with which 'Desolation Row' shares so much of its imagery. We even find the poet himself, fighting with his friend Ezra Pound, the editor of 'The Waste Land' – 'il miglior fabbro' (the better craftsman), as Eliot dubbed him in the poem's dedication. In Dylan's song there's no love lost between these twin titans of modernist high art, and their fighting is mocked by mere calypso singers. Eliot's own imagery is unravelling, the 'lovely mermaids', as Ricks points out, seeming to have 'flowed over from "The Love Song of J. Alfred Prufrock"'.

But what of that first verse? Who is 'selling postcards of the hanging' and why? Kermode and Spender called it 'a surrealist town with a circus', but some of this verse's imagery appears to have been founded in reality. Once upon a time in America you could buy postcards of hangings – specifically lynchings of African Americans, which were photographed, turned into postcards and sold as souvenirs, or possibly as warnings. This continued well into the twentieth century. In the *Chicago Sun-Times* of 1 July 2001, journalist Dave Hoekstra recalled a particular instance from eighty-one years earlier.

On 15 June 1920 in Duluth, Minnesota, the circus was in town. A white girl was assaulted behind the circus tent and three young black circus workers, accused of the crime, were dragged from the Duluth Jail by a mob and lynched. Dylan's father, Abram Zimmerman, was eight years old at the time and lived with his family two blocks from where the lynching occurred. It seems unlikely the boy forgot it.

'Desolation Row' has one of Dylan's most fascinating and beguiling sets of lyrics, and it is hardly surprising that this is what the critics usually write about. But it is a song, not a 'poem' (as Kermode and Spender refer to it), so what of the music? What of Dylans's voice? The melody? The gorgeous, elaborate Spanish guitar of Charlie McCoy?

For all the dysfunction on offer in this made-over 'waste land' – for all the confusion, the hints of disaster, of end times, all the references to 'the cyanide hole' and 'the heart-attack machine' – 'Desolation Row' is a sweet-sounding song. Like many of Dylan's songs of the early 1960s, it belongs to the ballad tradition – the number of verses alone tells you this. But unlike other songs of the period, such as 'Masters of War' or 'A Hard Rain's A-Gonna Fall' or 'Girl of the North Country', it doesn't use a traditional template or a borrowed tune. The tune is original, and it is one of Dylan's loveliest. But the guitar gives it a Tex-Mex feel. In contrast to the Anglo-Celtic-Appalachian ballad traditions that lie behind those other tracks, 'Desolation Row' might be a cowboy song.

What Ricks and Day and Kermode and Spender (with their references to poems) nearly always fail to discuss is the music of Dylan's songs. That's particularly surprising given the sound of Dylan's voice – so familiar to our ears and yet perpetually strange. Dylan can stress a word – even a particular vowel – and colour our whole understanding of a lyric. Think of the way he delivers the opening line of 'Positively 4th Street', dripping with sarcasm: 'You got a lot of nerve to say you are my friend'. You wouldn't want to be in an argument with the singer of that song. But Dylan's singing on 'Desolation Row' is anything but dramatic. There's none of the spitting anger that characterises 'Masters of War' or the sneering delivery of 'Ballad of a Thin Man'. On the contrary, his diction is clear and his attitude deadpan.

In *Invisible Republic*, Greil Marcus writes about early performances of 'Desolation Row' that he experienced at concerts predating the song's release in 1965. Apparently, certain images – even whole verses – provoked laughter from the audience. And Dylan, Marcus reports, laughed too.

So the song is an enigma – bad news in the form of 'some kind of joke' – and the music, overriding the words, takes us out with one of Dylan's jauntiest harmonica solos, dancing in the face of desolation.

24

Mignon

music by Ludwig van Beethoven
words by Johann Wolfgang von Goethe

'ET IN ARCADIA EGO,' reads the Latin epigraph at the front of Goethe's *Italian Journey* – 'And I am in paradise.'

In the eighteenth century and before, northern Europeans longed for Italy. The sunlight, the warmth, the romance: Italy was the ultimate destination on the Grand Tour, and Goethe's book, first published in 1816, only added to the allure.

In September 1786, the playwright and poet 'slipped away' from his court duties in Weimar and headed south where he would spend the next eighteen months, principally in Rome, but also visiting Verona and Venice, Naples and Sicily. It was, according to W.H. Auden, a journey as much psychological as geographical, and Goethe himself felt he had undergone a personal renaissance.

Even before the belated publication of his travel journal, Goethe included a tantalising glimpse of his yearning for the place in *Wilhelm Meister's Apprenticeship* (1796). Here, he had the androgynous girl, Mignon, sing to the novel's hero of the homeland from which she had been kidnapped. The teenage Mignon is a mysterious figure made more mysterious by these words.

Kennst du das Land? Wo die Citronen blühn,
Im dunkeln Laub die Gold-Orangen glühn,
Ein sanfter Wind vom blauen Himmel weht,
Die Myrthe still und hoch der Lorbeer steht.
Kennst du es wohl?
Dahin! Dahin!
Mögt ich mit dir, o mein Geliebter, ziehn.

'Do you know the land where the lemon trees bloom, where golden oranges glow amid dark foliage, a gentle breeze blows from the blue sky, and the silent myrtle and tall bay grow? Do you know it well? It's there, there, that I would go with you, my beloved.'

'To have seen Italy without seeing Sicily, is not to have seen Italy at all', wrote Goethe in his journal, 'for Sicily is the clue to everything.' Sicilians believe it was their island, and specifically the clifftop town of Taormina, that Goethe was thinking of when he gave Mignon her song. The words would become so famous so quickly that in little over a century they had been set to music by nearly sixty different composers, Beethoven, Schubert, Schumann, Liszt, Wolf and Berg among them. Beethoven's setting, while not quite the first, is one of the best known.

We tend not to think of Beethoven as a songwriter. He composed so many famous sonatas and string quartets, and among his nine symphonies are the five that the world knows best. There is hardly room to consider his vocal music. And yet Beethoven's *An die ferne Geliebte* (To the Distant Beloved) constitutes the first real song cycle, at least by a composer you've heard of. Whether his setting of 'Kennst du das Land?' is a song exactly is a moot point. Goethe was certainly unimpressed, calling it a dramatic aria, but the poet's words encourage that approach and most musical settings make a virtue of the change of tone at the words 'Dahin! Dahin!', using them to introduce a different mood.

Beethoven's Mignon leans on her first word: '*Kennst* du das Land'? ('*Know* you the land?') There's yearning in her question. Beethoven composed his song in 1809, which was the year that Napoleon's invading troops laid siege to Vienna and began their heavy shelling of the city. Hiding in his brother's cellar, Beethoven was reduced to strapping pillows over his ears in order to protect what remained of his hearing from the din of the bombardment. Mignon's vision of a lemon-scented paradise to the south must have seemed more than usually attractive for this German.

Whether inspired by Beethoven's setting or whether Goethe's poem simply invites the approach, Schubert, Schumann, Wolf and Berg all follow suit and stress *Kennst*. Only Liszt does something different: 'Kennst *du* das Land?' But then German wasn't his first language.

But there are ample differences of tone between the various settings. Schubert's account of Goethe's words is innocent and unaffected, which is possibly how he saw Mignon herself. Schumann's setting is more chromatic, even ecstatic, the piano's right hand evoking a dappled light that strongly recalls the piano introduction to his earlier 'Mondnacht' from the second *Liederkreis*. Liszt's song has a suitably dreamy opening, becoming more rhetorical at the repetitions of 'Kennst *du* es wohl?' Wolf and Berg, as you might expect, offer still more chromatic settings, increasing the mystery, especially in Wolf's rather seductive account.

All these composers, except Berg, effect a change of musical tone involving an increase of tempo as Mignon invites Wilhelm to go with her at 'Dahin! Dahin!' But Beethoven's is a pure sharing of joy, his slow duple metre suddenly giving way to a sprightly 6/8.

Appropriately, it's the rhythm of a *siciliano* – a dance in 6/8 from Sicily – but it's too fast to actually be one. On the contrary, the music it most calls to mind is by Beethoven himself, though it would be more than a decade later that he composed it.

The 'Ode to Joy' in the ninth symphony is Beethoven's most famous 'song', and it's hard to believe he didn't have Mignon's invitation to the warm and fragrant south at the back of his mind when he created one of its most memorable moments, the turning of the famous theme into a skipping 6/8. It is generally held to be a 'Turkish march' – it is marked 'Alla marcia', and certainly the instrumentation suggests a janissary band – but perhaps it was Mignon's joy that prefigured this symphony's more public outpouring of the emotion.

25

Funiculì, Funiculà

music by Luigi Denza
words by Giuseppe Turco

IN 1886, AT THE SUGGESTION of Brahms, the 22-year-old Richard Strauss travelled through Italy. He had recently been appointed conductor of the Meiningen Court Orchestra on the recommendation of that great Wagnerian Hans von Bülow, but he had yet to make much of an impression on the world with his own music. This was about to change.

Abandoning the conservative style of his juvenilia, Strauss embarked on a series of symphonic tone poems that would include *Don Juan*, *Also sprach Zarathustra* and *Ein Heldenleben*. In less than a decade, he would be one of Europe's most famous composers.

The first of these tone poems, inspired by his grand tour, was *Aus Italien* – 'From Italy' – and he completed it a matter of weeks after his return to Germany. Its finale, 'Neapolitan Folk Life', was enlivened by the appearance of 'Funiculì, Funiculà', a traditional song the young composer had heard all around the Bay of Naples. *Aus Italien* had its premiere in Munich in March 1887, conducted by the composer, and while not a great success – the folksong finale was actually booed – it set him on the path to considerable fame.

Alas, 'Funiculì, Funiculà' was not a folk song at all. It wasn't even old, having been written a mere six years before Strauss encountered it. Few songs of the day can have entered the public's consciousness quite so swiftly. Within a year of its publication, 'Funiculì, Funiculà' had sold a million copies. No wonder the young Strauss heard it everywhere he went.

'Funiculì, Funiculà' is in the tradition of the Neapolitan song. 'Santa Lucia' is the best-known example of one that actually is traditional, and in the nineteenth century these songs enjoyed such popularity that an event, the Piedigrotta Festival, was established in 1830 with an annual competition to encourage new songs in the style. It ran until the middle of the twentieth century. This period – particularly the last two decades of the nineteenth century and the first two of the twentieth – was the heyday of the Neapolitan song, the age of Enrico Caruso, who took the songs to America and made the style internationally famous.

Perhaps the most famous composed Neapolitan song is 'O sole mio', written in 1898 by Eduardo di Capua and Giovanni Capurro, and sung not only by Caruso but Elvis Presley (as 'It's Now or Never'). Another well-known example is 'Torna a Surriento' ('Come Back to Sorrento') by Ernesto and Giambattisa de Curtis.

'Funiculì, Funiculà' was intended as something of a novelty song, a humorous celebration of the first funicular railway on Mount Vesuvius. It was the work of the composer and singing teacher Luigi Denza, and the journalist Giuseppe 'Peppino' Turco, whose lyrics are sung from the point of view of a man who heads up the volcano on the funicular in order to escape the taunts of his girlfriend, one Nanniné. But as the car turns around at the summit, so do his feelings. On the way down he realises he wants to marry her.

The song's chorus – 'Jamme, jamme 'ncoppa, jamme jà!' ('Let's go, let's go, let's go to the top!') – turns the word 'funicular' ('funicolare' in Italian) into the joyous nonsense refrain 'Funiculì, funiculà, funiculì, funiculàààààààà', and it does so (until the final attenuated syllable) on a single repeated note. The absence of melodic inflection here focuses our attention on the sound of the words, which emphasise the song's rhythm. 'Funiculì, Funiculà' is a tarantella, a dance, not only native to the south of Italy, but also associated with courtship.

There's nothing particularly bold about the tune (apart from those repeated notes) or the harmony. 'Funiculì, Funiculà' is a well-made song that punches out its diatonicism like most good popular music, and it is undeniably catchy. In the year of its composition it won first prize in the Piedigrotta competition, was published by Ricordi, and sold by the truck-load. It has remained a popular hit, taken up nearer our own time by the Three Tenors and Andrea Bocelli (Caruso had begun the association with tenors). It was also not long before it became something of a cliché. When

Noël Coward wrote 'A Bar on the Piccola Marina', he had the recently widowed and now bibulous Mrs Wentworth-Brewster knocking back the gin on the Isle of Capri, while loudly declaiming 'Funiculì, funiculà, funiculì, funick yourself!'

Luigi Denza moved to London not long after the success of his song and by the end of the nineteenth century was Professor of Voice at the Royal Academy of Music. By then, Strauss was a famous composer and it was only a matter of time before Denza heard *Aus Italien* and noticed the prominence of 'Funiculì, Funiculà' in the finale. When he did, he successfully sued Strauss, who was thereafter obliged to pay Denza a share of the royalties from each performance. Strauss, who readily acknowledged his error, was in no position to complain. More than any other composer before him he was an assiduous businessman, and in that capacity had been one of the leading figures behind the reform of German copyright law.

26

I Got Rhythm

music by George Gershwin
words by Ira Gershwin

Roly-poly

Eating solely

Ravioli

Better watch your diet or bust

IRA GERSHWIN NEVER INTENDED TO use these words for his brother's infectious new composition. According to Michael Feinstein it was a 'dummy' lyric, written to see how the rhyme scheme might fit the tune. Ira concluded that it didn't work, that it gave the tune a 'jingly, Mother Goose quality', so he wrote another dummy, this time without rhymes, that he found he liked better: 'Just go forward / Don't look backward / And you'll soon be / Winding up ahead of the game'.

The clue is in that first line, 'Just go forward'. When a song is too closely rhymed, as in the earlier example, it can feel a little like running on the spot. It's harder for the song to advance. Whereas the absence of rhymes makes the lyric more open ended – it moves forward and could go anywhere. And so 'I Got Rhythm' is a song that, except for the bridge, doesn't rhyme at all. 'I got rhythm / I got music / I got my man / Who could ask for anything more?'

Originally a slow song, written for the musical *Treasure Girl* in 1928, 'I Got Rhythm' found its proper place two years later in *Girl Crazy* as an up-tempo number sung by Ethel Merman, who was making her Broadway debut to great acclaim in the role of Frisco Kate Fothergill. The show also made a star of Ginger Rogers and introduced two more Gershwin classics, 'Embraceable You' and 'But Not for Me'.

Having come up with a lyric that pleased him, Ira Gershwin was initially going to call the song 'Who Could Ask for Anything More?' After all, that's the line that ends each stanza. 'I got rhythm', on the other hand, is merely the opening line. But not only is it a punchier title, it's more accurate. Rhythm is what the song is about.

The basic structure of the chorus is a straightforward AABA over thirty-two bars, but rhythmically it's an off-beat Charleston. If we assume the song to be in 4/4, then there's nothing on beat one, 'I' comes on beat two, and 'got' on the second half of beat three. The next bar puts 'rhy–' on the downbeat and '–thm' on the second half of beat two. The song trips across the metre and, at least for the first three lines, the rhythm is fixed. The melody is fixed, too. If we think of the song in its original key of D flat, the first line has four ascending notes of a pentatonic scale (A flat, B flat, D flat, E flat), the second has the same notes coming down, and the third line has them going up again. The fourth line is different, rhythmically and harmonically, hitting consecutive down beats on 'ask' and 'more', and introducing a diatonic F natural to put us squarely in D flat major.

'I Got Rhythm' quickly became one of the Gershwins' most popular songs, and one of George's most popular tunes. He often played a fast rag-time version of it as a piano showpiece, and his last orchestral work was a set of variations on the tune for piano and orchestra.

The timing of the song was also fortunate. The 1930s was the decade that cemented the relationship between Broadway and jazz, jazz singers and instrumentalists drawing on show tunes to provide what in time would get called 'standards' – a sort of canon of tunes that are common currency among jazz musicians. It was not only that the likes of Louis Armstrong, Benny Goodman, Art Tatum and Duke Ellington played and recorded 'I Got Rhythm', but that the chord changes themselves became ubiquitous as the 'rhythm changes' underpinning many new compositions. This practice developed in bebop, with Charlie Parker using the rhythm changes several times, while Thelonious Monk's 'Rhythm-A-Ning' advertises its source in its title. But in fact, the use of the 'rhythm changes' predated bebop – Lester Young's 'Lester Leaps In' was based on them as early as 1939, and so was Ellington's 'Cottontail'.

You can't help but wonder if George's tune would have gained the same ubiquity had Ira called it 'Who Could Ask for Anything More?' – or if it had been about eating too much ravioli.

27

America

music and words by Paul Simon

'AMERICA' IS A SONG ABOUT searching. The lyrics tell us we have 'walked off to look for America', then later 'They've all come to look for America'. But the song itself is also searching. For one thing, it's searching for a rhyme it never finds. And, in the end, it doesn't find America either, only the New Jersey Turnpike.

'America' appeared on Simon & Garfunkel's penultimate studio album *Bookends*, released on 3 April 1968, the day before the assassination of Martin Luther King Jr. This was followed two months later by the assassination of Robert Kennedy, and both the album and the song gained an added poignancy from those and other contemporary events: in August, there was rioting and violence at the Democratic National Convention in Chicago; in September, as the war in Vietnam dragged on, the Vietcong launched the Tet Offensive; in November, Richard Nixon won the presidential election with a large majority of the electoral college, but only forty-three per cent of the popular vote. 'Kathy, I'm lost,' Paul Simon sang. That year, a lot of Americans felt the same.

There really was a Kathy, and she'd already had a song to herself – 'Kathy's Song' on *Sounds of Silence*. She was Kathy Chitty, Simon's girlfriend, with whom he went on a brief road trip in 1964. In 'America', the trip takes Simon from Saginaw, Michigan, to Pittsburgh, Pennsylvania, where he and Kathy board a Greyhound that ends up on the New Jersey Turnpike, heading into New York.

As with 'Stardust' and 'I Got Rhythm', the absence of rhymes keeps 'America' moving, but it's not so much purposeful forward motion in this song as drifting. 'America' has an unconventional structure that increases this peripatetic effect and adds to the story in various ways.

It's worth exploring this in some detail. Take the opening:

> Let us be lovers, we'll marry our fortunes together
> I've got some real estate here in my bag
> So we bought a pack of cigarettes and Mrs Wagner pies,
> And walked off to look for America.

The first line has a perfectly ordinary melody, almost folk-like, an impression enhanced by its lilting 6/8 metre. The sinking bass line and attendant chords are straightforward too: D–D/C sharp–B minor–D/A–G. We heard them first in the hummed introduction, and now they underpin the beginning of the song, one for each stress of the opening line. But the second line comes up short – it only has four stresses – and the chords stop even before that, leaving us hanging in B minor. It's the first of several reverie moments in this rather cinematic song.

The third line is totally unexpected. Direct speech has given way to reportage, and as it does so, we find ourselves suddenly in F sharp minor. It's not that the chord is so remote (Schubert would have been happy with this modulation, though perhaps without the added seventh), but that we find ourselves here so quickly, the song barely underway. Then, as we walk off 'to look for America' in the fourth line, we're suddenly back in B minor.

At the start of the second verse, as the lovers get on the Greyhound, we find ourselves once more in the home key of D, while a distant organ decorates the melody. But the second line takes us back to B minor, to another moment of reverie. This time it's in the lyrics, too: Simon telling Kathy that Michigan now 'seems like a dream'.

And so to what passes for the song's chorus. (It's really only the fourth line of the verse, and we've already heard it once at the end of the first verse, but this time it is a little more insistent and we begin to notice it more.) We move via the dominant A to E major (the dominant of the dominant), then the home key of D, but with a dissonant C sharp in the melody on the elongated second syllable of 'A–ME–rica'.

The middle eight proper takes us to C major and to some light relief. A playful flute bubbles away as the lovers laugh and joke about their fellow passenger, 'the man in the gabardine suit'. But the mood dissipates. There's a sense of deflation and pointlessness on this return to the tonic D. A cigarette? No, we've smoked them. He just looks out of the window while she reads, and when that 'chorus' comes around the moment is subverted. This time there's nothing about America, just a moon rising 'over an open field'.

Back to the tonic D for the final verse and the drums kick in further. But while D major might be the song's harmonic home, the singer says he's 'lost'. He tells Kathy this, even though he knows she's sleeping. Has he perhaps waited until she was asleep?

'I'm empty and aching and I don't know why,' he adds, the last three words drawn out in frustration over the B minor chord. The reverie, then, is also subverted and he's reduced to 'counting the cars on the New Jersey Turnpike'.

But it's not all despair. The single-line chorus returns at the end of this final verse, and it's repeated. The D major chord, with the C sharp on 'A–ME–rica', is practically triumphant, Art Garfunkel's voice riding high above it all with its descant.

That's not quite the end of the song, though. The organ plays us out – it might be a fairground waltz – as 'America' fades away, Kathy still asleep and her boyfriend counting cars.

28

Baker Street

music and words by Gerry Rafferty

IT'S THE SAXOPHONE, OF COURSE – that's what everyone remembers about Gerry Rafferty's hit song. So much more than a riff, it's actually the song's wordless, voiceless chorus.

In 1978, Rafferty put out his first album in three years. Contractual restraints had prevented the release of anything earlier, and the songs on *City to City* in some ways reflected this frustrating period in the singer's life. The places of the album's title were Paisley in Scotland, Rafferty's home, and London. After the demise of his band Stealers Wheel, Rafferty had shuttled between the two cities, attempting to put his career back together. In London he would stay at a friend's flat in Baker Street. So the lyrics of 'Baker Street' are more than a little autobiographical. Written in the second person, Rafferty – or a version of Rafferty – seems to be the 'you' of the song, the one who winds 'your way down on Baker Street', where, 'light in your head and dead on your feet', you will 'drink the night away and forget about everything'.

But even knowing this background, interpretations remain open. In the second verse, the welcoming man behind the door with 'that look on his face' would appear to be more than just a friend. Is it actually a love song? And what are we to make of the information that 'he' dreams of 'buying some land', that he'll 'give up the booze and the one-night stands' and 'settle down'. This sounds more like Rafferty himself, known for heavy drinking and tired of the 'city to city' existence. But then, at the end of the song, in what we might think of as the second 'middle eight', we're told that 'you know he'll always keep moving ... because he's a rolling stone'. And, on the other hand, 'you're going home'.

Who is who now? It's confusing, but also tantalising. It's certainly far from the cut-and-dried slice of the singer's life that many fans of the song take it to be. Rather than presenting a narrative, 'Baker Street' is more a series of scenes – almost as in a dream – seen from different points of view and helped along by the use of only second and third person.

And this is where that famous saxophone comes in. Were it a more conventional first-person song, with a traditional chorus underlining a particular message and endlessly repeating the song's title ('Baker Street, ooh I'm livin' on Baker Street'), it might narrow the range of possible interpretations. It also wouldn't be a very good song. Instead we have Raphael Ravenscroft's triumphant sax, blazing away (albeit slightly flat) in D major, while the verses seem to float between the dominant A and its dominant E, and the middle eight, which is in D minor, guides us back to the sax.

There are various theories about this solo. One is that Ravenscroft made it up with no assistance from Rafferty – that the feature of the song that is so memorable is not the work of the copyright holder. This is not quite true. There is a demo recording on which the basic direction of the sax line is sketched in. It lacks the rhythmic flourishes, lacks the strong upbeat and lacks the energy of the final version, but the outline is there.

Another theory is that the solo resembles a sax line played by Steve Marcus on 'Half a Heart', composed by that great pioneer of the vibraphone, Gary Burton. There's no question that it does – it's even in the same key – and it's likely Ravenscroft would have known Marcus's 1968 album, *Tomorrow Never Knows*, featuring Marcus's version of the Beatles song of the same name as well as Burton's piece. What seems even more likely is that Rafferty knew it – hence the guitar sketch of the sax chorus on the 'Baker Street' demo in the same key as Marcus's recording.

But if 'Half a Heart' is in fact the origin of the sax chorus on 'Baker Street', it was never a simple theft. Like Rafferty's guitar sketch, the Marcus solo is a pale precursor of what Ravenscroft ultimately played. It's the added energy of that solo, and in large part it comes down to the instrument he used: Marcus played a soprano saxophone, while Ravenscroft, in the same key, opted for an alto. Much of the power of Ravenscroft's solo, then, results from the fact that instead of sitting safely in the middle of his instrument's range, as it would have on a soprano, it fairly burns in the upper register of the alto. It is this, the spirit of Ravenscroft's solo as much as the actual notes, that is the signature sound of 'Baker Street'.

29

Oh England My Lionheart

music and words by Kate Bush

In the opening scene of Michael Powell and Emeric Pressburger's film *A Canterbury Tale*, Chaucer's characters ride along the Pilgrims' Way, over the North Downs of Kent, as they journey to Canterbury to pay homage to the 'holy, blissful martyr' Thomas Becket. A narrator reads the opening lines of Chaucer's Prologue. Then we see a falconer looking up at his falcon wheeling in the sky above. As we watch, the bird turns into a fighter plane – a Spitfire, in fact – and the falconer becomes a soldier in a tin hat. 'Six hundred year have passed,' says the narrator, going on to wonder what Chaucer would have made of it all. The year is 1944.

Had Kate Bush seen the film? Did she think of this scene when she wrote 'Oh England My Lionheart'? The imagery in her song certainly recalls it: 'I'm in your garden, fading fast in your arms / The soldiers soften, the war is over.' So she's in Kent ('the garden of England'), thinking about soldiers at the end of World War II. It was in the skies over Kent that the Battle of Britain was fought. And later in the song there's this: 'Dropped from my black Spitfire to my funeral barge.' Whose funeral barge is this? Is it Churchill's, in 1965, making its way up the Thames as cranes bowed their heads? Or is it the torchlit barge that in 1603 took Elizabeth I by night from Richmond Palace down to Whitehall for her lying in state?

'I was, and am, entranced by this song's baroque-tinted concertina-ing of English history,' writes the novelist David Mitchell in his preface to *How to Be Invisible*, a selection of Bush's lyrics. He singles out that line about the Spitfire and the barge. 'Nine words condensing 500 years,' he writes, 'and an early example of how time can be compressed or ductile in Kate's lyrics.'

At first it was easy to miss Kate Bush's nostalgia. 'Wuthering Heights', the song that in 1978 made her instantly famous, had so much about it that was unusual, from the borrowing of Emily Brontë's characters (from a novel Bush later admitted she hadn't read) to the two videos featuring Bush dancing in red and white dresses, to the voice itself, unlike anything before it in pop music. All this from a nineteen-year-old with a debut album, *The Kick Inside*, that included darkly mystical songs about men and pregnancy and dreams, some of which she had written at thirteen and recorded at sixteen. Nostalgia hardly came into it. But it was always there – 'Wuthering Heights' itself a paean to a romanticised English rusticity.

'Oh England My Lionheart' is in a sense the title track of Bush's second album, called simply *Lionheart* and released the same year and only nine months after *The Kick Inside*. It was rushed, as Bush herself has said, and some of the songs sound it. 'Oh England My Lionheart' is one such, with Bush later admitting she was embarrassed by it. The lyrics, pace Mitchell, are not her finest. The half rhymes with 'Lionheart' – 'arms', 'Park' and 'barge' – are forced, and 'Park' is only there at all by dint of changing the name of London's Kensington Gardens. 'Flapping umbrellas', Shakespeare, Peter Pan, 'the rolling Thames', the legend of the ravens at the Tower, 'apple blossoms', 'wassailing', an orchard, a shepherd and an English rose: the lyrics are little more than an assemblage of clichés. But, as we have seen, lyrics alone do not make a song, and in this song it's the things unsaid that are most affecting.

Like 'Wuthering Heights' before it, 'Oh England My Lionheart' has a unique sound. There are no electric guitars here, no bass, no drums. The instrumentation consists of Bush's piano, Richard Harvey's multi-tracked recorders and Francis Monkman's harpsichord. Bush's voice is overdubbed to create a part-song effect in the choruses, a suggestion, perhaps, of the Elizabethan madrigal.

But it is the notes themselves that are most memorable. The song is in A minor, and the opening phrase takes us from an upbeat C ('Oh') on the submediant F major, to B to E ('Eng–land') on the dominant E minor, to C major (the relative major of A minor) with the melodic E rising, to B ('my Lion'), to the tonic note A ('–heart') but on the chord of D major, of which it is the dominant. It's a beautiful progression, moving us in a matter of seconds from poignancy to pride, and it has nothing to do with rock'n'roll. The chords in this song are triadic and tend to shift in blocks, often to chords that are a third or fourth away. In this they resemble Elizabethan music – the hymnody of Thomas Tallis or the viol consorts of William Byrd.

The song's chorus, most touchingly of all, begins in C major, the melody moving up from E to F to G and back again ('Oh England my'), only for it to land with the first syllable of 'Lionheart' on E, but against a chord of F major. The conclusion oscillates between E minor and F major, finally settling for G major. Bush sings 'I don't want to go', but G major is harmonically remote and the home key of A minor just a memory.

Whether or not Bush was inspired by Powell and Pressburger's film, she certainly sang this song for a time dressed in World War II airman's garb, performing in front of clips from wartime films that included the Spitfire scene from the same filmmakers' *A Matter of Life and Death* (1946). So the connection is there to be made. Bush's songs share with Powell and Pressburger's movies a devotion to bold storytelling, self-conscious quirkiness, unconventional structures, and powerful sentiment verging on sentimentality and occasionally succumbing to it. In their embrace of such elevated emotions, both the songs and the films effectively give the lie to that myth of England as a land of stiff upper lips.

Kate Bush's single-minded determination to realise her artistic vision influenced numerous later musicians with ambitions beyond the three-minute single. For Bush, as well as artists such as Björk, Rufus Wainwright and Kate Miller-Heidke, songwriting was like a modern-day version of Wagner's *Gesamtkunstwerk*, occupying a theatrical space where the intimate immediacy of the song blends with a dramatic spectacle rich in intertextual possibility.

30

Ja nus hons pris

music and words by Richard the Lionheart

KING RICHARD I OF ENGLAND (1157–1199) – Richard the Lionheart – is known to most of us as a character in the Robin Hood stories, a benevolent monarch as fictional as the outlaw himself. The historical Richard was rather different. For most of his 9½-year reign, the Plantagenet king was absent from his realm, invading foreign territories and fighting Crusades. Along the way, he also seems to have written one of the first prison songs, a genre that includes Leadbelly's 'Midnight Special', Johnny Cash's 'Folsom Prison Blues' and Paul Kelly's 'How to Make Gravy'.

Returning from the Third Crusade in 1192, Richard was captured by Leopold V, Duke of Austria, who believed the king to have ordered the murder of his cousin. Richard was imprisoned in a castle on the Danube, before being turned over to the Holy Roman Emperor, Henry VI, who locked him up in Trifels Castle in the Rhenish Palatinate. Both Leopold and Henry were subsequently excommunicated by the pope for imprisoning a crusader, but Richard would not be released until early 1194, after his mother, Eleanor of Aquitaine, had raised the required ransom money.

There are two stories about songs associated with Richard's imprisonment. One concerns Richard's faithful minstrel Blondel, who is supposed to have scoured the European continent in search of his missing boss. Richard and Blondel shared a love of the songs of the trouvères and troubadours, the itinerant singer-songwriters of northern and southern France. Finding himself beneath a high window at Trifels, Blondel sings the first verse of one of the Lionheart's favourite songs, whereupon the king responds with verse two from inside the tower. It's a good story with more than a whiff of the romantic quest about it, but for various reasons, it is unlikely. For a start, some people believe Blondel never even existed.

It's more probable that, while in prison, Richard did compose 'Ja nus hons pris', one of the most famous songs of the High Middle Ages.

> Ja nus hons pris ne dira sa reson
> Adroitement, s'ensi com dolans non;
> Mes par confort puet il fere chançon.
> Moult ai d'amis, mes povre sont li don;
> Honte en avront, se por ma reançon
> Sui ces deus yvers pris.

'No man in prison can speak his mind honestly, unless he speaks of his suffering, but he can take comfort in writing a song. I have many friends, but their generosity is lacking; it will be their shame if, for want of a ransom, I spend a second winter in prison.' That's the first verse of six in which the king, by turns, bemoans his lot and expresses his anger with those who have yet to fund his release. His friends knew exactly who'd banged him up and where he was being kept – another reason the story of Blondel's search is unlikely – but they seem to have been unable or unwilling to get the ransom money together.

The tune that Richard fitted to his poem is simple yet expressive, its opening consisting of four repeated notes, a minor third above the tonic, rising to the fifth on the negative 'ne'. The accompaniment (what would it have been – harp? cittern?) comprises just two chords, the tonic minor and a major chord, a tone lower (the dominant of its relative major). The song oscillates between these chords, as suits the structure of the lyric, which is as much a carefully constructed argument as a plaint: on the one hand this (chord I), but on the other that (chord VII).

The first five lines, which rhyme, are tetrameters – they have four stresses. But the sixth has only three stresses, its foreshortening depriving us of the rhyme. Instead, it ends on the word 'pris' ('prison') – all the verses do – driving home to the listener the king's plight. And, though the line is short, 'pris' is sung to two notes – the leading note and the tonic – the second of them held imploringly.

The typical trouvère or troubadour song was a poetic and musical manifestation of the art of courtly love, addressed to the object of that love, an entreaty to a lady whose cool indifference was, almost without exception, the cause of the singer's suffering. Richard directs 'Ja nus hons pris' to his older half-sister, Marie de Champagne, the first child of Eleanor of Aquitaine, by Louis VII of France. He makes a nice pun on 'pris' at the end of the song, where he addresses Marie directly, using the word to mean 'price' or 'fame' before returning to his original meaning in the final line.

> Contesse suer, vostre pris soverain
> Vos saut et gart cil a cui je m'en clain –
> Et por cui je sui pris.

'Countess sister, may your high fame be preserved and protected by the one who is keeping me in prison!' Passive aggressive or what?

What was Richard hoping for with this petition? Possibly he believed Marie might intercede on his behalf with another of her half-brothers, Philip II, King of France, and that Philip might buy Richard's freedom. If so, he was deluded. Philip – together with Richard's brother John – was already fundraising with a different aim. They hoped to bribe Henry to keep Richard in prison a while longer. Luckily for the Lionheart, his well-connected mother was able to raise twice as much.

31

Jerusalem

music by Hubert Parry
words by William Blake

'HE CEASED TO SPEAK, and put his finger on the note D in the second stanza where the words "O clouds unfold" break his rhythm. I do not think any word passed about it, yet he made it perfectly clear that this was the one note and one moment of the song which he treasured.'

These are the words of the conductor Walford Davies. He was recalling sitting with his old teacher Hubert Parry in the composer's room at London's Royal College of Music, looking over the score of 'And Did Those Feet in Ancient Time', the song we all now call 'Jerusalem'. Davies was preparing to conduct its first performance. The moment is recounted in Jeremy Dibble's biography of Parry. Today the words that Parry put to music are not only familiar but famous, yet their fame is down to composer rather than writer; prior to 1916, when the song was first sung, hardly anyone knew William Blake's words.

The poem was first published in 1808 as part of the preface to Blake's *Milton*, a long work in two sections, part literary criticism, part state-of-the-nation, part autobiography. And there the words remained until they were anthologised by Robert Bridges during World War I. Bridges, who was Britain's poet laureate, called his anthology *The Spirit of Man* and hoped it would lift national morale, which in 1916 was flagging as news continued to arrive of the carnage on the Western Front. It was Bridges, too, who saw the potential in Blake's words for a musical setting – a unison song in which everyone could join – and he asked Parry to tackle the job in time for a Fight for Right rally in London's Queen's Hall.

The song, for soprano soloist, chorus and organ, was a success, as you might expect, but even at the time Parry seems to have had doubts about the long-term ambitions of Fight for Right. Winning the war: yes, of course, but what did such violent patriotism presage for peacetime? Parry was considering refusing Fight for Right further performances, when the National Union of Women's Suffrage Societies approached him for permission to perform the song at a concert in 1918. The composer cheerfully agreed to the request. He orchestrated the organ part for the occasion, granted further permission for the song to become the Women Voters' hymn, and assigned them the copyright. After the vote was granted and the organisation disbanded, copyright was transferred to the Women's Institute, whose members still sing the song each year at their national conference.

'Jerusalem' has been sung at British Conservative Party conferences and alongside 'The Red Flag' at Labour Party conferences. It is the official song of the English Rugby League and, more recently, has been adopted by English cricket supporters. Each year on the final night of London's Promenade Concerts, it contributes to the traditional mixture of creepy jingoism and studied silliness in the Royal Albert Hall. It is, in other words, a song for all seasons.

But is it a hymn? It is certainly in the hymnbook, but the song's religious message is debatable.

> And did those feet in ancient time
> Walk upon England's mountains green:
> And was the holy Lamb of God,
> On England's pleasant pastures seen!
> And did the Countenance Divine,
> Shine forth upon our clouded hills?
> And was Jerusalem builded here,
> Among these dark Satanic Mills?

According to legend, Jesus visited England in his youth with his uncle, Joseph of Arimathea. Obviously, there is no evidence for this, so the only sensible answer to the questions posed in the first verse is a resounding no.

Its credentials as a Tory anthem are equally dubious. In Blake's poem, England, for all its 'mountains green' and 'pleasant pastures', doesn't seem to amount to much, what with those 'clouded hills' and 'dark Satanic Mills'. True, Bridges altered Blake's 'these' to 'those', putting the 'Satanic Mills' in the past, but still this is not a poem in praise of the status quo and conservative values, and evidently the words of the second verse are about improvement. Certainly that's how Clement Attlee saw them at the 1945 British general election when his Labour Party promised to build a 'new Jerusalem', and won in a landslide over the war hero, Churchill.

> Bring me my Bow of burning gold:
> Bring me my arrows of desire:
> Bring me my Spear: O clouds unfold!
> Bring me my Chariot of fire!
> I will not cease from Mental Fight,
> Nor shall my sword sleep in my hand:
> Till we have built Jerusalem,
> In England's green & pleasant Land.

So it could be about the second coming of Christ – that much chimes with the concept of building 'Jerusalem' we read about in the Book of Revelation. But the rest of Blake's imagery, though apocalyptic, is to do with self-help. A bow and arrows, a spear and a chariot, 'Mental Fight' and an unsleeping sword: this is the imagery not so much of revelation as revolution.

Parry wrote a superb tune for Blake's words, one so grateful and inspiring to sing it almost encourages the singer to believe the words mean whatever they want them to mean. The unison melody flows beautifully, the end of line one ('ancient time') becoming the opening of line two ('Walk upon Eng–'). Similarly, the third line resembles the first, except that now it leads us to minor chords and a sense of something like regret, perhaps that 'the holy Lamb of God' wasn't seen on 'England's pleasant pastures'. The tune winds its way back to the major at the end of the phrase 'shine forth upon', and the high point of the melody is on the second syllable of 'Jerusalem', as it should be.

In the second verse, the tune magically suits the meaning of the words as well as in the first, especially with the broken rhythm at 'O clouds unfold', of which Parry was so proud. This time the return from minor to major coincides with 'Nor shall my sword sleep in my hand', and the climax of the tune is no longer on the 'ru' of 'Jerusalem' but at the top of the phrase 'Till we have *built*'. The emphasis seems clear enough. If we want 'Jerusalem' we must make it ourselves.

32

Don't Dream It's Over

music and words by Neil Finn

There is freedom within, there is freedom without
Try to catch the deluge in a paper cup.

ACCORDING TO NEIL FINN, you can't put a 'paper cup' in a song without it being a reference to John Lennon. So why not go the whole hog? In the Beatles' 'Across the Universe', it's words that are flowing 'like endless rain into a paper cup'. Finn's cup is attempting to contain a veritable flood.

The Beatles were such a monumental force in pop music that for a decade after their disbanding, other musical acts seemed consciously to avoid their influence. In Split Enz, however, New Zealand's Finn brothers, Tim and Neil, embraced it wholeheartedly (this was long before 1990s Britpop, when everyone was at it), and the influence carried over to Neil's Australian band, Crowded House. In general, perhaps too much has been made of the Beatles–Crowded House connection, but it's there for all to hear in 'Don't Dream It's Over', where the narrow melody of the verse, all stepwise intervals, might easily have been written by Lennon. There is, however, nothing of Lennon in the famous chorus.

It was 1987 and 'Don't Dream It's Over', released in October the previous year, was a worldwide hit. It was the song you danced to at the end of the night, pressed close to the intriguing person you'd just met while wondering what might happen next. The palpable sincerity in Neil Finn's voice and the expansive melodic line of the song's chorus encouraged hope. The song was also fast becoming an anthem for Antipodeans overseas, the slightly maudlin counterpart to Men at Work's novelty song 'Down Under'. The latter was jovial and jokey, all plundering and chundering, fried-out Kombi vans and

Vegemite sandwiches: here was the larrikin abroad. But 'Don't Dream It's Over' was a serious song for the weary (and possibly homesick) traveller or expat. Before long, bands visiting Australia began to include it in their sets as a tribute.

Neil Finn's song is quite simple and symmetric. Melodic lines come in twos, the second half of the song repeats the first. Even a version of the organ solo that separates the two halves returns at the end. Above a relaxed, up-and-down strumming with a pronounced syncopated backbeat that, Finn says, New Zealanders refer to affectionately as the 'Maori strum', the four-line verse repeats those two lines of Lennonish melody over the same two chordal progressions: E flat–C minor–A flat–G.

Stepping back up a semitone to A flat, the melody of the chorus is more expansive – literally so, as it opens out from a falling perfect fourth on the first 'Hey now' to a falling major sixth on the second, to a rising octave (B flat to falsetto B flat) on 'Don't dream', coming down the scale to the tonic on 'it's over'. The harmony is simple stuff (IV–V–I), but it's effective, so, like the first two lines of the verse, Finn repeats it. In fact he repeats the expanding 'Hey now, hey now' line twice as the lyrics themselves expand ('They come, they come / To build a wall between us').

What is it about this melancholic but hopeful anthem of a song? The point of view of the lyrics is reassuring, even protective in a traditional sort of way. The other half of the relationship seems to be having doubts. We learn that the world is coming to 'build a wall' to separate them, and we're reassured that it won't succeed. There's an element of Weltschmerz – sentimental pessimism – in the lyrics: 'My possessions are causing me suspicion but there's no proof / In the paper today, tales of war and of waste / But you turn right over to the TV page …' There's an insular, even escapist side to the song, but it's all vague and it's precisely this vagueness that helps give the song its universal resonance.

The accompanying video has Finn walking through a house in which other members of Crowded House are sitting around, sometimes playing their instruments. It's a scene of nostalgic Australiana worthy of Men at Work. The house is a weatherboard; we even see a slice of toast spread with Vegemite. No wonder it became an anthem for Australians overseas. When the organ solo comes, the windows of this house are suddenly arched and have stained glass. It's fitting in this hymn to home.

33

Dancing Queen

music by Benny Andersson and Björn Ulvaeus
words by Benny Andersson, Björn Ulvaeus and Stig Anderson

WHO IS SHE, THIS DANCING QUEEN, this seventeen-year-old girl having the time of her life?

Who knows what the songwriters were thinking? Perhaps it wasn't far removed from Lennon and McCartney's thoughts in 'I Saw Her Standing There', the first track of the Beatles' first album, when they saw, standing there, another girl who was just seventeen. ('You know what I mean?'). After all, Benny, Björn and Stig give us 'You're a teaser, you turn 'em on / Leave 'em burning, and then you're gone'.

Stock-standard pop lyrics, then? Leering men and – at least in those men's imaginations – teasing girls? Perhaps, but that's not what we hear. The lyrics of ABBA songs were never really the point ('Can you hear the drums, Fernando?'); they were just something to sing, because songs – and singers – need words. And the singers were Agnetha and Frida, that strong, confident, triumphant blend of voices. The song might have begun in the minds of three men, but in the singing of two women it becomes a fantasy of independence.

It's a dream of a song. On this dance floor there is no unwanted attention, no sexual predation; there isn't even a whiff of cigarette smoke – and this was the 1970s when you came home from a night at the disco red-eyed and reeking. 'Dancing Queen' is a song of empowerment, a vividly imagined teen dream, without acne, bullies or peer pressure; where the stage, the glitter of the disco ball and the attention of the world are yours and yours alone.

It's the transformational song of a generation (or two, or three), and the transformation is achieved with melody and harmony more than words. The song is in A major, though heading quickly for F sharp minor, and the mood of the verse is sultry: 'Friday night and the lights are low. / Looking out for a place to go / Where they play the right music / Getting in the swing / You come to look for a king.' Not only are the lights low, but so is the singing, and it drops even lower as the verse continues, down to the E below middle C (on 'look' and, later, 'mood'), which isn't wholly comfortable territory for the singer. But then we begin swinging back up again, at the line 'And when you get the chance'. The harmonies brighten as they descend via the chain of fifths from F sharp minor to B minor 7 to E7, and finally to the tonic A and subdominant D, the voice rising confidently all the time. Suddenly 'You are the dancing queen / Young and sweet, only seventeen'. It's like a spotlight scanning the dance floor, finally picking out the girl.

The chorus proper, which we've already heard at the beginning of the song, starts in the dominant E: 'You can dance, you can jive, / Having the time of your life.' Opening a song with its chorus is hardly unusual, beginning on the dominant (chord V) is more so, but although that's where the vocals come in, the song's introduction is in the tonic A. However, the *very* first thing we hear is a flourish, the pianist's downward sweep of the keyboard. It's one of those instantly recognisable starts – you're out of your seat before the glissando has reached its bottom note – very similar in nature and function to the synthesiser sweep at the start of Cyndi Lauper's 'Girls Just Want to Have Fun', another feel-good manifesto of female independence and empowerment written by a man – in that case, Robert Hazard.

The key to the fantasy of 'Dancing Queen' lies inside the listener's head. The glittering piano, the relaxed disco beat (George McCrae's 1974 hit 'Rock Your Baby' is known to have been an influence), the seductive vocals are calling us to the dance floor, and the dance floor is the song itself.

Over the years, 'Dancing Queen' has had pride of place in films such as *Muriel's Wedding* (about an awkward young woman escaping banal everyday life into a fantasy world of ABBA and wedding dreams) and, of course, *Mamma Mia!*. But there *was* an actual queen. At the time of the song's release and ABBA's album *Arrival*, Sweden was about to become the adopted home of Silvia Sommerlath, a young woman of German and Brazilian descent. Her wedding to King Carl Gustaf XVI in June 1976 was widely televised, and the nation's longest serving queen went on to become something of a role model for many Swedish women. On the eve of the wedding, ABBA's 'Dancing Queen' had its Swedish premiere at a televised gala concert – and in 1993, an a cappella version of the song was performed in honour of Queen Silvia's fiftieth birthday.

But 'Dancing Queen' belongs to everyone. It's an anthem for the queer community; it's a DJ's foolproof last resort (according to a 2014 survey, it's Britain's favourite floor-filler just before Michael Jackson's 'Billie Jean' and 'Twist and Shout' by the Beatles); it brings toddlers and parents to the dance floor at a preschool disco; it's a staple of hens' nights and wedding receptions. The reason? While you may think you can't dance, the song insists and then demonstrates that – in your private fantasy, at least – you can.

34

I'm into Something Good

music by Carole King
words by Gerry Goffin

THE FIRST THE WORLD SAW AND HEARD of the Manchester group Herman's Hermits was Peter Noone singing 'I'm into Something Good' through a shy, toothy grin. The band itself may now be little more than a stalwart of the club circuit, a footnote to 1960s British pop, a novelty act among more serious bands such as the Beatles and the Rolling Stones, the Animals and the Kinks. But in September 1964, 'I'm into Something Good' dislodged the Kinks' 'You Really Got Me' from the top of the UK singles chart and Herman's Hermits were big. In Britain, at least, it was their first and last number one.

In fact, there was nothing British about the song. Composer Carole King and her lyricist husband Gerry Goffin had begun writing together at college in New York. When King, still only seventeen, became pregnant, college was abandoned in favour of full-time writing, and the hits followed swiftly. There was 'Will You Love Me Tomorrow' for the Shirelles; 'Chains' for the Cookies (and later the Beatles); 'The Loco-motion' for Little Eva; 'Go Away Little Girl' for Steve Lawrence; and 'It Might as Well Rain until September', which was sung by King herself. By the time they wrote 'I'm into Something Good' they were two of the most successful songwriters in America.

Carole King always said the song, with its high, floaty backing vocals, was an early homage to the Beach Boys (more than forty years later, Brian Wilson would record his own version), but the main part has the structure of a twelve-bar blues, complete with a so-called 'blues turnaround'. In place of Western music's standard cadential chord progression of IV–V–I, the blues commonly reverses chords IV and V, producing a softer, less final cadence. 'I'm into Something Good' makes a feature of this, because the climax of the tune – 'Some–thing tells me' – not only occurs on chord V but marches steadily up the arpeggio itself – G–B–D–G – landing on the song's highest note, before happily resolving with the song's title on chords IV and I.

If you know only Herman's Hermits' hit, you could be forgiven for missing the blues connection, but the grinning, clapping Peter Noone was not the first to record 'I'm into Something Good'. In late 1963, the Cookies were on tour with their latest Goffin–King hit, 'Chains', when singer Earl-Jean McRae became pregnant. The father turned out to be Gerry Goffin himself. Rather than boot her philandering husband out of the marital home, King agreed that they should take care of the singer financially. They also gave her 'I'm into Something Good', which she recorded under the name Earl-Jean, with King writing the arrangement and playing piano. The record was a minor hit in the United States, but it was soon eclipsed by Herman's Hermits' cover.

The two recordings were made just a few months apart and have much in common, Mickie Most's production for Herman's Hermits making broad use of Carole King's arrangement. But the differences in detail, though minor, give each a distinctive feel, the bright and breezy innocence of Herman's Hermits' hit at odds with the earthier tones of Earl-Jean's original.

The Cookies that Earl-Jean had joined in 1961 was the second group with that name. The earlier manifestation of the group had been transformed into Ray Charles's backing singers, the Raelettes, and the new Cookies retained a strong element of R & B in their sound. Earl-Jean's recording of 'I'm into Something Good', then, makes the blues template a little easier to hear, especially because she's inclined to embellish the vocal line with little melodic inflections redolent of soul – like the way she scoops up to the note on 'boy'.

There are subtle differences to the lyric as well. It's not only that Noone's 'new girl in the neighbourhood' was originally a 'new boy', it's also a matter of attitude. Noone sings that 'she danced close to me', though 'only … for a minute or two', after which she 'stuck close' to him 'the whole night through'. But though Earl-Jean and her boy 'only *talked* for a minute or two', it felt like she'd known him her 'whole life through'. He then 'danced *every slow dance* with me as I hoped he would'. The clean-cut Noone, a grinning boy with a hint of a lisp, is pleased to have met a new girl, but the relationship, you feel, is unlikely to progress much beyond hand-holding, and the reference to a 'one-night stand' always did seem odd. Earl-Jean was singing about physical desire, and she didn't have to ask this boy if he'd still love her tomorrow; she '*knew* it wouldn't be just a one-night stand'.

These differing lyric emphases are borne out in the sound of the music. The tempo of the original record is also slower than the more familiar version, roughly 120 beats to the minute, as opposed to 132. It's not a big difference, but the heavier use of tom-toms and King's more pronounced rolling piano seem to situate the song in a different world. In contrast, Herman's Hermits' cleaner vocals and quicker tempo are underpinned by the nonstop hand claps and a skipping triplet rhythm tapped out on a cymbal and later a tambourine. The instrumental break on Earl-Jean's record features a saxophone solo, brimming with passion albeit somewhat distantly recorded, while the Herman's Hermits cover has an anodyne electric guitar lick.

Herman's Hermits recorded the song in C, Earl-Jean in the higher key of E flat; yet Earl-Jean's husky and more intimate voice seems lower than Noone's. The song ends with a descent to its lowest note on the tagline 'Something good, oh yeah, something good'. The boyish Noone can barely produce a sound on his bottom note – and it's only the C below middle C, a pitch on the range of even a high-tenor voice. Earl-Jean's bottom note is E flat, which is low for any female voice, yet when the moment comes she leans in close to the microphone to croon a rounded, almost triumphant 'Something *good*'.

35

Thule, the Period of Cosmography

music by Thomas Weelkes
words: Anon

WE DON'T KNOW VERY MUCH ABOUT the Elizabethan composer Thomas Weelkes (1576–1623), but his reputation as a drunk appears to be solid enough. As organist of Chichester Cathedral from 1601 until his death, he was dismissed more than once for inebriation, as well as for loudly cursing and blaspheming during a service. On one occasion, he urinated on the dean from the organ loft. The fact that he was always reinstated is doubtless testimony to his talent, and perhaps we may also deduce that he was a passionate man. His music certainly seems to bear this out.

'Thule, the Period of Cosmography', his madrigal of 1600, is a song about fire and ice. It's also about desire, about having a heart frozen with fear yet burning – *frying* – with love. Its analogies come from the voyages of discovery undertaken by European explorers in the fifteenth and sixteenth centuries and refer to such wonders as the volcano 'Hecla, whose sulphureous fire / Doth melt the frozen clime'; of merchants bearing 'cochineal'; and oceans 'full of flying fishes'.

The poem Weelkes chose for his madrigal was chock-full of unusual words, two of them in the title. 'Thule' dates back to the Ancient Romans and Greeks, who used it to name a place six days' sail north from Britain. At the time this was the Shetland Islands, but later the term came to refer to Iceland, and it is at least partly in this sense the poet intends it here, since Hecla (or Hekla), mentioned in line two, is an Icelandic volcano. The Elizabethans, however, used Thule in a more general sense to refer to the remotest north – *ultima Thule*, beyond the known world – and in a poem that draws its imagery from the marvels of Renaissance cosmography, that meaning is certainly implied. Here's the whole text:

Thule, the period of cosmography,
Doth vaunt of Hecla, whose sulphureous fire
Doth melt the frozen clime and thaw the sky;
Trinacrian Etna's flames ascend not higher:
These things seem wondrous, yet more wondrous I,
Whose heart with fear doth freeze, with love doth fry.

The Andalusian merchant, that returns
Laden with cochineal and china dishes,
Reports in Spain how strangely Fogo burns
Amidst an ocean full of flying fishes:
These things seem wondrous, yet more wondrous I,
Whose heart with fear doth freeze, with love doth fry.

Even now, part of the magic of this madrigal is the unusual sound of its words, but in 1600 some of these words would have seemed very strange indeed. The Oxford English Dictionary tells us that the adjective 'sulphureous' first appeared in the language less than fifty years before Weelkes's madrigal, while 'cochineal' was an even newer concept, first coined in 1586. More remarkable is that while the names Trinacria (the Greek word for Sicily) and Andalusia, were, if exotic, nevertheless long established, their adjectival forms, 'Trinacrian' and 'Andalusian', appear to have been later coinages – later than 1600, according to the dictionary – as was 'china' (in the sense of porcelain). These words were not merely strange, then, but to all intents and purposes unknown. The poem isn't just describing things that 'seem wondrous', the words themselves seem wondrous.

And then there's Weelkes's music.

This six-voice madrigal sets out from the word 'Thule', sung by a soprano voice on an isolated B flat. The possibilities of this voyage of discovery seem infinite; the music might go anywhere. Soon enough, however, it settles on the key of E flat as the other five voices join it in elaborate, imitative counterpoint. The music is full of pictorial effects, most memorably flying fishes, which leap melodically and flutter alliteratively. This is standard Renaissance word painting, but wonderfully well done. There's symbolism too: at the word 'Trinacrian', which means three-pointed, the music moves momentarily into a triple metre. And there are musical portraits of the volcanoes too: Hecla's sulphureous vapours swirling in contrary motion, Etna's flames ascending in the sopranos, and Fogo drooping with mysterious chromatic harmonies.

But the strangest harmonies are reserved for the poet's marvelling at his own emotional state, and these arrive without warning each time, taking the listener by surprise in much the same way as the freezing/frying feelings seem to surprise the poet. 'These things seem wondrous,' the voices sing, suddenly in slow motion and stepping on to a chord of D flat, before ratcheting up the dissonance for 'Yet more wondrous, *I* ...' The chord on 'I' is F major. We are by now quite remote from the home key of E flat, in the harmonic equivalent of Thule.

The notion of peppering a love song with long words may not strike us as odd, particularly if we have some knowledge of the so-called Great American Songbook of the mid-twentieth century. In the heyday of Tin Pan Alley, lyricists would inject mystery, sophistication and humour into their love songs by using big words, words the listener would have to think twice about. 'Yesterdays, yesterdays / Days I knew as happy, sweet / sequestered days,' wrote Otto Harbach for Jerome Kern. Then, in 'Mountain Greenery', Lorenz Hart upped the ante: 'How we love sequestering / Where no pests are pestering.'

In the musical *A Connecticut Yankee*, Hart has the twentieth-century Martin woo Alice in King Arthur's court with a mixture of cod Shakespearean English and American slang: 'Thou swell, thou witty, thou sweet, thou grand / Wouldst kiss me pretty? Wouldst hold my hand?' But it's the slang that wins – 'Hear me holler, / I choose a / sweet lolla– / palooza / in thee' – notwithstanding the fact that 'lollapalooza' is a kind of grand slang, and in 1927 still relatively new.

Ten years later, for the film *Ready, Willing and Able*, Johnny Mercer wrote a lyric about this practice for Ross Alexander to sing to Ruby Keeler – actually, not sing, but speak, à la Rex Harrison – during a scene in a library. In 'Too Marvellous for Words' (music by Richard Whiting), having first tried and abandoned 'glorious, glamorous / And that old standby amorous' as descriptions of Keeler, Alexander insists that she is 'Much too much / And oh so very, very / To ever be in Webster's Dictionary'. But he doesn't give up, his attempts growing ever more recherché as he rejects 'magical' and 'mystical' as 'just too apathistical' (unemotional) and complains that 'the sweetest words / In Keats or Shelley's lyric' are still not 'sweet enough / To be your panegyric'.

36

You Can't Hurry Love

music by Lamont Dozier and Brian Holland
words by Eddie Holland

ACCORDING TO ABDUL 'DUKE' FAKIR of the Four Tops, having a song written for you by Lamont Dozier and the Holland brothers, Brian and Eddie, was like visiting a bespoke tailor to be measured for a suit. They were the Motown label's principal writing and production team Holland–Dozier–Holland, one of the great hyphenated songwriting legends of the post–World War II era, along with the likes of Leiber–Stoller and Lennon–McCartney. Duke Fakir was right: there was nothing off-the-peg about their work.

'I need love, love, to ease my mind...' Though they were still called the Supremes in 1966, becoming Diana Ross and the Supremes only in 1967, Ross's gentle, slightly nasal delivery dominates this song, the voices of Florence Ballard and Mary Wilson pushed well into the background. 'You Can't Hurry Love' was a summer hit for the trio, offered in their typically sophisticated manner. Elegant and serious, the Supremes' routine was minimal, the three singers swinging from the hips while standing on the spot. It was in contrast to the comparatively freeform stage presence of the Four Tops and the choreographed dance routines of the Temptations, though 'You Can't Hurry Love' did come with a finger wag from Ross as she repeats Mama's advice: 'No, you've just got to wait'.

Most of the Supremes' biggest hits, and they had a few, were penned by Holland–Dozier–Holland. These included the trio's first hit single, 'Where Did Our Love Go' (1964), as well as 'Baby Love' (1964), 'Stop! In the Name of Love' (1965) and 'Reflections' (1967). Structurally, these songs were simple, but 'You Can't Hurry Love' is a slightly unusual case.

The song's first verse is just four bars long: 'I need love, love to ease my mind. / I need to find, find someone to call mine. / But mama said...'

And with that, we're straight into the first chorus. It's as though Mama has interrupted the song right at the beginning in order to make the point that 'You can't hurry love', Ballard and Wilson's voices like distant, nagging reminders.

Following the chorus in B flat, there's a striking bridge starting in D minor (the relative minor of chord V), with the singer's protest, 'But how many heartaches must I stand / Before I find a love / To let me live again'. And then later – because the song has a second bridge – 'I grow impatient for a love to call my own'. Each time the bridge ends with the singer recalling Mama's advice – 'I remember Mama said' – and each time it crashes into the chorus, 'Mama said' colliding with 'You can't', as though the song itself is now impatient, trying to hurry love along in spite of the warning.

After the initial four-line, four-bar verse, three choruses and two eight-bar bridges, comes another verse, this time twelve bars long. It restates and elaborates the music and sentiments of the original verse, but in the last four bars Ballard and Wilson begin singing their backing vocals from the chorus. It's the song's last collision – verse and chorus superimposed – and it brings us to the final chorus proper, and the reiteration of Mama's life lesson: 'You can't hurry love, / No you just have to wait. / She said, "Trust, give it time, / No matter how long it takes"'.

The last two lines of the chorus don't quite fit the tune and have to be pulled around by Ross in order to get the sense across: 'She said, "Tru-u-ust, *give* it time, / No matter … how *long* it takes"'.

Perhaps the reason for this is that the words are borrowed from another song. Mama's lesson about life and love was first heard in the 1950 song '(You Can't Hurry God) He's Right on Time', written by Dorothy Love Coates and recorded by her with the Original Gospel Harmonettes. Here's the chorus: 'You can't hurry God, / No, you just have to wait. / You have to trust him and give him time, child, / No matter how long it takes.' Borrowing from Gospel to furnish pop (and vice versa) was at least as old as Ray Charles and Aretha Franklin, and here the imagery and diction are almost identical to the second half of the Supremes' chorus. Even the use of 'child' in the original song matches Mama's words in 'You Can't Hurry Love'. And the fact that the tunes of the two songs are unrelated easily explains why the words no longer fit. None of which, for a moment, detracts from the effectiveness of one of Motown's greatest hits.

Above all, the Supremes – and Motown in general – offered a sound. Pounding drums and agile bass, lots of tambourine, a prominent horn section, and singing so syncopated it's almost never on the beat. It's a style that defines black American music of the 1960s, and the most successful remake of 'You Can't Hurry Love', by Phil Collins in 1982, sensibly left these things untouched. He even included two backing singers who, in the video, turn out to be replicas of Collins. A drummer himself, Collins heard in the Supremes' record, and the Motown sound in general, a kind of rhythmic perfection, something to be dazzled by, learnt from and emulated, but not messed with.

37

It Might as Well Be Spring

music by Richard Rodgers
words by Oscar Hammerstein II

BETWEEN THE EARLY 1940S and mid-1960s, Rodgers and Hammerstein's musicals enjoyed unprecedented success, on stage and then on film. *Oklahoma!* and *Carousel*, *South Pacific*, *The King and I* and *The Sound of Music* remain such staples of holiday television, their stage shows regularly revived around the world, that it's hard to hear their songs without imagining the dramatic scenes that gave rise to them. 'Surry with a Fringe on Top', 'This Nearly Was Mine' and 'Shall We Dance?' are all linked to specific stories and images. It requires a few degrees of separation – say, John Coltrane's version of 'My Favourite Things' – before we can put from our minds a nun comforting a bedroom full of children frightened by a storm.

'It Might as Well Be Spring' is different. *State Fair* (1945) was the only time Rodgers and Hammerstein wrote a musical for Hollywood. While the film was a success in its day, earning the composer and lyricist team their only Academy Award, it is now sufficiently obscure that it's possible to listen to 'It Might as Well Be Spring', the song that won that Oscar, without imagining its narrative context. And yet, as always with these songwriters, the song – even its title – is intrinsically tied to a dramatic rationale.

Rodgers and Hammerstein created a new style of musical. Where Rodgers and Hart had produced romantic musical comedies, now musical theatre was a genre that could deal with domestic violence (*Carousel*), racism (*South Pacific*; *The King and I*) and Nazis (*The Sound of Music*). It was a process Hammerstein had begun fifteen years before *Oklahoma!*, with Jerome Kern on *Show Boat*, but it reached a new level of sophistication in his partnership with Rodgers, and it was partly down to the way they worked.

Most songwriting teams of the mid-twentieth century began with the music. Rodgers would come up with a tune and Hart would fit words to it. But Hammerstein liked to write the words first, so, suddenly working in the manner of a classical composer, Rodgers became a setter of words to music. This meant that the sense of the song could lead, and consequently a song might advance a story.

In *State Fair*, as the Frake family looks forward to the Iowa fair ('Don't miss it, don't even be late'), adolescent Margy Frake is down in the dumps. Her mother can't understand it. 'I don't know what's got into you lately,' she says. 'All you do is sit around and mope.' Margy disagrees, but she's as puzzled as her mother: 'What *has* got into me anyway?'

Hammerstein wanted Margy's hormonal stirrings to be 'spring fever', except that he was aware that American state fairs are always held in autumn, and he was a stickler for the facts. He told Rodgers his dilemma: how could Margy have spring fever when it isn't even spring? Rodgers pointed out that Hammerstein had both his song and its title.

Hammerstein gave the verse a simple, childlike diction: 'The things I used to like, I don't like anymore; / I want a lot of other things I've never had before.' Rodgers, the word-setter, finds childlike music for them. Five-finger exercises from D up to A ('things I used to like) and again ('don't like anymore'), and then – because this is piano practice and the student is growing in confidence – up and down and up again ('I want a lot of other things / I never had before'). Margy's mother calls from downstairs, delaying the first chorus, but when it finally begins, the melodic word-painting intensifies. Take only the first two lines: 'I'm as restless as a willow in a windstorm / I'm as jumpy as a puppet on a string.'

The branches of the willow may be restless, but the tree is rooted to the spot, and so, to begin with, is the tune. It starts on the dominant A, leaving that note only to move to B, a tone higher, on the first syllables of 'restless' and 'willow', dropping back to A each time, then up to the tonic D and B again on 'a wind–', returning to A once more on '–storm'. Restless, then, but safely grounded – as the critic Gerald Mast pointed out, in soft, alliterative syllables ('willow'/'windstorm') – and, like Margy herself, going nowhere.

But then in line two she's 'as jumpy as a puppet on a string' and so is the melody, with its dotted rhythm and wide intervals. Up it jumps to F sharp (a major sixth), then the A above it; down it falls, A to D (a perfect fifth), F sharp to A (the major sixth again), D to A (a perfect fourth), collapsing on to a dissonant C (in D major) on 'string'.

As the song goes on, the melodically grounded first line of each chorus contains images that suggest the furrowed brow of concentration ('vaguely discontented' and 'busy like a spider spinning'), while the jumpy second is more active ('giddy ... on a swing'). Only the line about 'a nightingale without a song to sing' doesn't fit the pattern, though notice how that line is a precursor for Hammerstein's more famous (and oddly meaningless) 'like a lark who is learning to pray' in the title song of *The Sound of Music*.

State Fair, the film, may now be largely forgotten (there were no other hit songs in it), but the close association of words and music in 'It Might as Well Be Spring', and the near universality of the experience they describe, have ensured it remains one of the songwriters' best-known works, sung and recorded by hundreds of artists. One of those recordings offers further insight to the workings of the song and the way the music and lyrics constantly play off each other. Blossom Dearie included it on her first American recording in 1957, singing it languorously in French. As Gerald Mast observed, her version 'proves how lifeless [the song] is without Hammerstein's sensitivity to the sounds of English vowels and consonants' – and, he might have added, without their clear justification for Rodgers' tune.

38

Im wunderschönen Monat Mai

music by Robert Schumann
words by Heinrich Heine

IT STARTS WITH A DISSONANCE. C sharp with D natural, neighbouring notes on the piano keyboard. Except that here the right hand plays and holds the C sharp, while the left hand plays the D two octaves lower. So it's not only dissonant but disjunct. Then the music unfolds, gently chromatic, seeking a key, seeking its home.

It's the mysterious opening of a mysterious song. A song without a real ending. A song so rich in possibility that, even once it stops, possibility continues. This is the beginning of Schumann's great cycle *Dichterliebe* – 'A Poet's Love'.

> Im wunderschönen Monat Mai,
> Als alle Knospen sprangen,
> Da ist in meinem Herzen
> Die Liebe aufgegangen.
>
> Im wunderschönen Monat Mai,
> Als alle Vögel sangen,
> Da hab ich ihr gestanden
> Mein Sehnen und Verlangen.

'In the magically beautiful month of May, when all the buds opened, love sprang up in my heart. In the magically beautiful month of May, when all the birds were singing, I told her about my love and my longing'. May, of course, is the time for new love ('a long, long while' from December, as Maxwell Anderson and Kurt Weill remind us in 'September Song'), but this new love seems troubled from the start, and it's the music that lets us know.

Robert Schumann composed *Dichterliebe* in 1840, his year of song. This was the year Schumann married Clara Wieck following a drawn-out and difficult courtship, of which Clara's father, Friedrich, strongly disapproved. Robert and Clara finally applied to a court for permission to marry, their wedding taking place one day before Clara's twenty-first birthday, whereupon she would have been free to marry even without the old man's blessing. Robert celebrated by writing songs – more than 130 of them in one year – most of them love songs, many among the greatest of the nineteenth century. In addition to *Dichterliebe*, they include two *Liederkreis* cycles, *Frauenliebe und -leben*, the *Myrthen* songs (a wedding present to Clara) and settings of poetry by Justinus Kerner and Robert Reinick.

So why isn't *Dichterliebe* a more cheerful piece? Why, in this magically beautiful month of May, is our lovelorn 'poet' so wistful? Some of that, of course, is down to the actual poet, Heinrich Heine, whose words seem to have inspired most of the nineteenth century's composers – not only Robert and Clara, who also set his poetry to music, but Schubert, Fanny and Felix Mendelssohn, Brahms and Tchaikovsky.

Heine's great-grandnephew was the American lyricist Lorenz Hart, who together with Richard Rodgers wrote such songs as 'Isn't it Romantic', 'My Funny Valentine' and 'Bewitched, Bothered and Bewildered': romantic songs laced with doubt and humour, but romantic nonetheless. 'This can't be love, because I feel so well', went another of his lyrics. It is as though he inherited the talent from Heine, whose poetry often has a similar bittersweet quality (Hart was funnier).

But the words of *Dichterliebe*'s opening song are not, on the face of it, wistful or bittersweet. It's May – springtime for Heine! – buds open and so does love; birds sing and love is declared. It's all quite straightforward, though admittedly it's happening in the past tense. It's Schumann, in the throes of nuptial bliss, who brings to these ostensibly simple lyrics a set of notes that force us to wonder what is really going on.

Perhaps Schumann took his cue from the poem's tense. Yes, it was spring, the buds opened, the birds sang and love was in the air. But now it's not. The song is sung by one who knows how this story will play out, and at every turn it unsettles as it beguiles.

The poet's happy words about the awakening of love are sung to notes that belong to the key of A major, but the song is really in the relative minor of F sharp. Certainly the piano is playing in F sharp minor. So it's a little like a scene in a film where the main character's cheerful demeanour is under-cut by the composer's knowing score, which tells the viewer that all is not well. But there's more to the song than that, too, for, as Eric Sams points out in his indispensable book, *The Songs of Robert Schumann*, while F sharp minor might be the key of the song, not only is the singer in A major, but nowhere in the piano part is there an F sharp minor triad, not even at the end. *Especially* not at the end, one might say, for here the piano settles onto a dominant seventh chord that is only resolved by the start of the next song.

Things go from bad to worse in *Dichterliebe*. She leaves him, she marries someone else, he pretends he doesn't care, but he cares deeply. At the end, he asks for a coffin – it must be huge, he says, because he intends to put his love and his grief in it. The imagery is slightly deranged, there's no doubt about it, but the music of the final song suggests acceptance or at least resignation.

Almost a century after *Dichterliebe*, in the verse of 'Spring Is Here', Heine's illustrious descendant, Lorenz Hart, wrote:

Once there was a thing called spring
When the world was writing verses like yours and mine
All the lads and girls would sing
When we sat at little tables and drank May wine.
Now April, May and June are sadly out of tune,
Life has stuck a pin in the balloon.

39

আমার সোনার বাংলা
(Amar Sonar Bangla)

music by Rabindranath Tagore, after a melody by Gagan Harkara
words by Rabindranath Tagore

WHEN BOB DYLAN WAS NAMED Nobel Prize–winner for Literature in 2016, objections were raised about his suitability for the award. Song lyrics, the argument went, however astonishing they might be, were not literary because they depended upon performance. In Dylan's defence, his critics were reminded that Homer had performed his lyrics with musical accompaniment and so had the author of *Beowulf*. Another argument might have been mounted based on precedent, for Dylan was not the first songwriter to win the prize. That was the Bengali polymath Rabindranath Tagore in 1913.

Born in Calcutta in 1861, Tagore wrote more than two thousand songs as well as novels, plays and essays, and was also a painter. A greatly loved figure in India during the British Raj, he used his prominence to call for independence, but he also championed Bengali identity and in 1905 wrote the poem 'Amar Sonar Bangla', 'My Golden Bengal', fitting it to a melody he adapted from a well-known song by the Baul poet and composer Gagan Harkara. In 1971, thirty years after Tagore's death and during Bangladesh's war of liberation, his song was taken up as the new country's national anthem.

Most of the world's national anthems have a sabre-rattling quality. Some of those from countries in the Middle East and South-East Asia are, in effect, military marches, while the more elaborate marching anthems heard in South America often seem to have escaped from Verdi operas – the anthem of Uruguay, for example, contains passages that are almost interchangeable with the 'Anvil Chorus' from *Il trovatore*.

Even those national anthems you can't march to – 'God Save the Queen' and 'The Star-Spangled Banner', for example, are both in triple time – tend to have bellicose lyrics. The US anthem describes resilience in battle and ultimately victory, while the British anthem follows its 'happy and glorious' first verse with this little-sung second:

O Lord, our God, arise,
Scatter her enemies,
And make them fall;
Confound their politics,
Frustrate their knavish tricks;
On thee our hopes we fix:
God save us all.

But there is nothing warlike about the Bangladeshi anthem. In spite of its adoption at a time of genocidal conflict, with refugees fleeing across the Indian border in their hundreds of thousands, the new government of Bangladesh chose as its national hymn Tagore's celebration of nature.

My golden Bengal, I love you.
Your skies, your air always tune my heart as if it were a flute
Oh my mother! The springtime scent of your mango orchards drives
    me crazy,
Ah, what a thrill!
Oh my mother! In late autumn what sweet smiles fill the blossoming
    paddy fields!
What beauty, what shades, what affection, what tenderness!
What a quilt have you spread at the feet of the banyan trees and along
    all the river banks!
Oh my mother! The words from your lips are like nectar to my ears.
Ah, what a thrill!
Oh my mother! If sadness casts a shadow on your face, my eyes are
    filled with tears!

Tagore's hymn to Bengal is not unique in its concentration on nature and its refusal of jingoistic nationalism. The Swedes, who in any case lack an official anthem, sing as their de facto national song 'Du gamla, du fria', which celebrates the Nordic landscape and is so devoid of nationalist sentiment it fails to mention Sweden at all. What makes 'Amar Sonar Bangla' unique is its music.

Harkara's song was about longing and love – themes found also in Tagore's hymn – and perhaps that's why Tagore chose it as the basis for his own song. As adapted by Tagore, the tune is sung or played to *Dadra* – a *tala*, or rhythmic pattern, of two groups of three, like a Western 6/8 metre. The melody itself is remarkably flexible. As heard at sporting events and the like, it is fitted out with simple chords so that it can be played by a band with a cymbal crash on the first and fourth beats of the six-beat *tala*. It never convinces, because the arrangement, which tends to sound like a quick waltz, robs the song of the yearning quality that gives it its distinction.

There are wistful vocal performances of the song, also with chords, that have considerable charm. But sung above a drone, as Tagore presumably intended, the melody reveals all its twists and turns. With its soulful, plangent descent on the words 'Amar Sonar Bangla', and its tugging quarter-tone embellishments as the melody rises again, it is one of the most beautiful, hopeful and friendly national anthems on earth.

40

The Battle Hymn of the Republic

music: Anon.
words by Julia Ward Howe

Glory, glory, hallelujah!

THIS TUNE IS SO WELL-KNOWN and has been used for such a variety of words and occasions, it's surprising we don't know who composed it or when it was written.

The American Civil War marching song 'John Brown's Body' provides the first famous set of words for the tune, but other versions predate it. Its composition was claimed by one William Steffe, who, years after the fact, insisted that he had written it in the 1850s. But we know it was in circulation at Christian revivalist meetings long before that. Provenance theories abound: that the tune was originally a Swedish drinking song, an African American wedding song and that it was a sea shanty in the British merchant navy.

Wherever it came from, it is certainly well made, its catchiness a function of simple diatonicism allied to an agile, yet eminently singable, melodic line that spans exactly an octave. This agility is reminiscent of both New England shape-note hymnody and the so-called West Gallery singing of Low-Church Anglicanism, both characterised by spirited and joyful melodic lines. Perhaps this accounts for the popularity of the tune at camp meetings from the late 1700s, where it came to be used for a hymn entitled 'Canaan's Happy Shore', with its opening, thrice-repeated line, 'Oh, Brothers will you meet me' or 'Say, brothers will you meet us' (' … on Canaan's happy shore'). It was at these meetings that the tune first acquired the chorus 'Glory, glory, hallelujah!' that would remain with it in both its most famous versions.

By 1861, at the start of the American Civil War, the tune was ubiquitous enough for it to have jokey words put to it by soldiers in the Second Massachusetts Regiment. Two years earlier, the abolitionist John Brown had led an attack on the US arsenal at Harpers Ferry, Virginia, hoping to initiate a slave rebellion. The raid failed, Brown was tried for treason and hanged. The Massachusetts Regiment had a soldier named John Brown, the butt of many jokes, and the song 'John Brown's Body' became one of them.

'John Brown's body lies a-mouldering in the grave / His soul is marching on' went the song, and it caught on fast. So much so that, before the year was out, the poet Julia Ward Howe had been persuaded by her friend, the preacher and theologian James Freeman Clarke, to write a more lofty and elaborate set of words:

> Mine eyes have seen the glory of the coming of the Lord
>
> He is trampling out the vintage where the grapes of wrath are stored,
>
> He has loosed the fateful lightning of His terrible swift sword,
>
> His truth is marching on.

'The Battle Hymn of the Republic', as it was called, was sung alongside the 'John Brown's Body' words, though it never replaced them. They simply coexisted. But the 'Battle Hymn' went on to acquire an unofficial place at the heart of American life, sung on solemn occasions, its words quoted (and misquoted) in other songs and in literature. The first line gave Martin Luther King Jr the closing line of his final sermon. The title of John Steinbeck's *The Grapes of Wrath* refers to the song's second line.

Gaining in popularity, the anonymous tune continued to accrue new lyrics, and a curious thing happened to it: the lines became longer, and they acquired more syllables. Consider the following, which are all sung to the same eight pitches:

> 'Oh, brothers, will you meet me?'
>
> 'John Brown's body lies a mouldering in the grave'
>
> 'Mine eyes have seen the glory of the coming of the Lord'

As the melody became busier, subdividing its beats to accommodate the extra syllables, it also gained in urgency and dynamism, a function of the newly dotted rhythm. And then, just over half a century after Howe's version of the song was penned, it got longer still.

> When the union's inspiration through the workers' blood shall run.
> There can be no power greater anywhere beneath the sun;
> Yet what force on earth is weaker than the feeble strength of one,
> But the union makes us strong.

This version is now so closely associated with Pete Seeger, we are liable to forget that it was written four years before his birth – and two years before the Russian Revolution – for the International Workers of the World. The author was Ralph Chaplin and the words are even more overwrought than Howe's. At last, however, there is a new chorus, 'Glory, glory, hallelujah!' replaced by the song's title: 'Solidarity forever.'

And so this tune, which might have been Swedish or African American in origin, a wedding song or a sea shanty, goes marching on, transformed at political meetings and in playgrounds, at sporting fixtures and in nursery schools: 'Glory, glory, hallelujah! / Teacher hit me with a ruler'; 'Glory, glory Leeds United!'; 'Father Christmas do not touch me!': 'Little Peter Rabbit had a fly upon his nose'.

41

O God of Earth and Altar

music: Anon. (arr. Ralph Vaughan Williams)
words by G.K. Chesterton

O God of earth and altar,
bow down and hear our cry,
our earthly rulers falter,
our people drift and die;
the walls of gold entomb us,
the swords of scorn divide,
take not thy thunder from us,
but take away our pride.

THE WORDS HAVE A STARTLINGLY MODERN ring to them, and you might find it surprising to stumble across them in *The English Hymnal*. But for the hymnal, first published in 1906, modernity was the point. This was the Anglican Church renewing itself at the start of the twentieth century – today they'd probably call it being relevant – and in their attempt to offer an alternative to the stolid Victoriana of *Hymns Ancient and Modern*, the publishers of the new book engaged a young composer to edit it.

According to his second wife, Ursula, Ralph Vaughan Williams was an atheist, but he believed in musical communities and viewed Anglican congregations as a good example of them. He took his task seriously, commissioning new tunes, composing some himself, and sifting through history for forgotten gems. One of his finds was a hymn tune by the Tudor composer Thomas Tallis that Vaughan Williams later made the basis of his famous *Fantasia on a Theme by Thomas Tallis*. He also appropriated traditional melodies, but in this he had an ulterior motive: Vaughan

Williams was on a mission to save the folk song, which was threatened with extinction.

Writing the introduction to his book *Traditional Tunes: A Collection of Ballad Airs*, published in 1891, Frank Kidson reported:

> This class of song is fast disappearing before the modern productions, and any young ploughboy who should sing the songs his father or grandfather sung would be laughed to scorn ... The old traditional songs are fast dying out, never to be recalled. They are now seldom or never sung, but rather remembered, by old people.

Vaughan Williams wasn't alone in his attempts to rescue these songs. Inspired partly by nationalism and partly by the belief that traditional music might be a way to discover new sounds to inspire their own compositions, Béla Bartók and Zoltán Kodály, Gustav Holst and Percy Grainger went on excursions into the countryside and to small towns across Europe to 'collect' songs from those who still remembered them. On one such collecting trip to Norfolk in January 1905, Vaughan Williams struck gold in the harbour town of King's Lynn. The seas were rough that week, too dangerous for sailing, and the pubs were full of fishermen. In seven days, the composer noted down sixty-seven songs encountered in beer-fuelled performances. One of them was 'Van Diemen's Land'. It's a ubiquitous song with a dozen different tunes, but the one Vaughan Williams heard (also sung to the words 'Young Henry the Poacher') made a deep impression on him. It's in the hymnal under the title 'King's Lynn', the tune attached to 'O God of Earth and Altar'. The words are by the writer and Catholic convert G.K. Chesterton, best known today as the creator of the priest detective Father Brown.

Chesterton's poem was first published in a magazine, *The Commonwealth*, in 1905, the same year Vaughan Williams learnt the tune, and its sentiments have scarcely dated. Here's the second verse:

> From all that terror teaches,
> from lies of tongue and pen,
> from all the easy speeches

that comfort cruel men,
from sale and profanation
of honour, and the sword,
from sleep and from damnation,
deliver us, good Lord!

It is, alas, a lyric for the ages, and perhaps that's what Vaughan Williams recognised when he fitted it to the stout modal melody he'd collected in that King's Lynn pub. The mode in question is the aeolian, which you can think of as a minor scale with a flattened seventh. If you play up the white notes from A to A, there it is. A minor would have a G sharp accidental, but the aeolian mode – sometimes called the natural minor scale – has a G natural. 'King's Lynn' makes much use of that note. (In *The English Hymnal*, 'King's Lynn' is actually in D minor, but let's keep this discussion focused on the white notes.)

The first line ('O God of earth and altar') climbs up to the G natural, landing on it with the second syllable of 'al–tar', before the second line resolves to the tonic A, an octave lower. The next couplet ('our earthly rulers falter …') climbs further, reaching the high A and staying there (on 'fal–ter'), resolving to the dominant E ('our people drift and die'). The third couplet, ('the walls of gold entomb us …') again reaches the A, but immediately drops back to the G ('–tomb us'), resolving once more onto the dominant. Finally, the fourth couplet repeats the melody of the first.

Melodically, it's the third couplet that's significant. Thomas Anderson, the singer from whom Vaughan Williams recorded the original song, varied the tune here – doubtless for expressive purposes – rather than repeat the melodic line of the second couplet. You might have expected Vaughan Williams to iron out that difference in the hymnbook, because having the same line twice would have made it easier on the congregation, and anyway the rationale for the variant was gone. But Vaughan Williams kept it, and in doing so, as the musicologist Julian Onderdonk has pointed out, was thinking both as a composer (the variant still works, because it calls our attention to Chesterton's words) and as a musical nationalist, faithful to the music of his people.

It's hard not to wonder if any of those modern-minded ploughboys later sang the hymn in church, and if they recognised the tune as one that their grandfathers had sung. You might also wonder what fans of heavy metal made of the tune. With metal's apocalyptic mindset and fondness for grand imagery, it's perhaps not surprising that words from 'O God of Earth and Altar' should have found their way into an Iron Maiden song. But 'Revelations', from the band's 1983 album *Piece of Mind*, used Chesterton's complete first verse, together with the 'King's Lynn' tune, and – at the end of the song – adapted Chesterton's third and final verse.

Chesterton had written this:

Tie in a living tether
the prince and priest and thrall,
bind all our lives together,
smite us and save us all;
in ire and exultation
aflame with faith, and free,
lift up a living nation,
a single sword to thee.

On 'Revelations', which is fundamentally a humanist anthem, Iron Maiden's singer Bruce Dickinson gives us a verse that begins: 'Bind all of us together, / Ablaze with hope and free ...' It is pugnacious, certainly, but not as pugnacious as Chesterton, who wanted the whole lot of us smitten, in readiness for a fresh start.

And was that sentiment also at the back of Vaughan Williams' mind when he fitted the poet's words to a traditional melody? Did it occur to him that he was giving an endangered tune a fresh start?

42

We Will Rock You

music and words by Brian May

QUEEN'S 'WE WILL ROCK YOU' is one of the simplest songs of the 1970s. Lasting only two minutes, it consists of three verses and three choruses accompanied by nothing but stamping and clapping, followed by thirty seconds of an apparently unrelated solo for electric guitar. That's it. But then, after you've had a major international hit with a grandiloquent slab of operatic prog rock, where on earth do you go?

At nearly six minutes and supported by a video as memorable as the song itself, 'Bohemian Rhapsody' was unique, its intricate, multilayered vocals and ever-changing moods and tempos tending to stop you in your tracks. You certainly couldn't dance to it. That song appeared in late 1975. 'Somebody to Love', the following year, retained the close vocal harmonies, multiplied many times until the sound resembled a large choir, but this time in the more conventional context of a gospel number – Freddie Mercury's call answered by the choir's response.

Call and response is also a feature of 'We Will Rock You'. Released in 1977 as the B side of 'We Are the Champions', the song could hardly have been more different from its chart-topping predecessors. And yet, like 'Bohemian Rhapsody', it was sui generis, the odd simplicity of its design and the urgency of its delivery almost guaranteeing the song's success. Guitarist Brian May, who wrote it, said in a radio interview at the time that its anthemic nature was inspired, in part, by an audience spontaneously singing 'You'll Never Walk Alone' following a Queen performance at Bingley Hall in the English Midlands. Since the 1960s, that song, from Rodgers and Hammerstein's musical *Carousel*, had become a favourite of sporting crowds, particularly supporters of Liverpool FC; and sporting crowds were quick to claim both 'We Are the Champions' and 'We Will Rock You'.

The template that underpins 'We Will Rock You' is the US army tradition of 'cadence calls' sung by military personnel on training runs ('I don't know, but I've been told ...'). They are, in effect, work songs, and are derived from both the field hollers of the antebellum South and also chain-gang songs. All those traditions use blues scales and so does 'We Will Rock You', its opening lines oscillating between just two notes, a bluesy flattened seventh and the tonic, a tone above it: 'Buddy you're a boy, make a big noise / Playing in the street, gonna be a big man some day ...'

It is only on the word 'man' that a new note appears – the fourth note of the scale, falling back to a flattened third on 'some day' and cementing the blues feel. The flattened seventh/tonic oscillation continues in the next line ('You got mud on your face, you big disgrace'), until the last line ('Kicking your can all over the place') outlines the entire scale as it drops down the octave.

The connection to the cadence calls and other American work songs is made all the more clear by the complete absence of instruments. The steady sound of the GIs' feet, running or marching, or the constant dig of a chain gang's hoes is replaced here with a heavy beat – stomp-stomp / clap (rest) – that marks out the song's duple time. The stomps and claps were provided by the band members themselves, overdubbed multiple times like the 'choir' in 'Somebody to Love'.

After the verses and refrains comes May's guitar solo. The singing has been in the key of E minor, but the guitar is in the slightly surprising key of A major, where it remains, quickly going through a display of distorted pyrotechnics as the song fades. If the singing in 'We Will Rock You' was inspired by the sound of a big crowd at an outdoor concert, the guitar solo is the band's grateful reply from the stage, another instance of call and response.

But there's also a small joke behind this song. Anyone of Brian May's vintage who, like May, had attended an English grammar school, would have heard and possibly sung 'The Rocking Carol'. Translated from the Czech by Percy Dearmer, it was first published in England in the *Oxford Book of Carols* in 1928 and by the mid 1960s, when May was at school, had become a familiar item at Christmas services, thanks in part to a recording by Julie Andrews. 'The Rocking Carol' is a saccharine thing, a close relative of 'Away in a Manger', addressed to the Christ Child from the point of view of a group of children ('Little Jesus, sweetly sleep, do not stir'), and its chorus – as far from the stadium anthem as you could wish – is 'We will rock you, rock you, rock you.'

43

Wiegenlied

music by Johannes Brahms
words: Anon. (from Des Knaben Wunderhorn),
second verse by Georg Scherer

LULLABIES ARE AS OLD AS singing itself and they create a special link between a parent and a child. The child cannot understand the words – which in any case are often rather unsuitable ('When the bough breaks, the cradle will fall') – but understands very well the parental voice at its kindest. As Mark W. Booth has written, in lullabies, 'whatever version of mother-hood the words express, the mother's voice is especially motherly'.

The most famous European lullaby is actually an art song, the 'Brahms Lullaby.' How many other art songs are known by their composer's name and a nickname? Symphonies and concertos, yes: Schubert's *Unfinished*; Tchaikovsky's *Pathétique*. Beethoven's *Emperor*; 'Rach 3'. But the 'Brahms Lullaby' – or, to give it its proper title, 'Wiegenlied' Op. 49, no 4 – is unique in this regard.

'Wiegenlied' ('Cradle Song') is the most famous art song ever written, but it long ago escaped the confines of that categorisation in recordings by Bing Crosby, Frank Sinatra, Rosemary Clooney, and many more. Perhaps its popularity stems from the fact that it doesn't seem like art – melodically it's more like a folk song. And perhaps that, in turn, comes from the words – the first verse of which are indeed folkloric: 'Guten Abend, gut' Nacht ...' ('Good evening, good night ...'). *Des Knaben Wunderhorn* – 'The Youth's Magic Horn' – is a collection of folk poetry assembled at the start of the nineteenth century, the century that, in Northern Europe alone, gave us *Danmarks gamle Folkeviser*, Walter Scott's *Minstrelsy of the Scottish Border* and the Finnish *Kanteletar* (not to mention the *Kalevala* epic and the fairy stories of the Brothers Grimm). The poems in *Des Knaben Wunderhorn* are not only for children, but a lot of them are. Many nineteenth- and early twentieth-century composers set these words, and Mahler was especially drawn to them, particularly early in his career.

> Good evening, good night,
> Covered with roses,
> Festooned with cloves,
> Slip under the bedsheets,
> In the morning, God willing,
> You will wake again.

To this, the poet Georg Scherer added a second verse, more overtly Christian and more sentimental:

> Good evening, good night
> Watched over by angels
> Who will show you in your dreams,
> the Christ-child's tree:
> Sleep happily and sweetly,
> See heaven as you dream.

The melody is a model of lucidity, making much use of the rising and falling minor third, the interval employed universally for calling. Here it calls the child to sleep in that famous opening phrase. Brahms must have been fond of this phrase as it crops up elsewhere in his music in slightly different forms. A version of it is in the waltz in A from his Op. 39 set for piano duet (there's also a solo version in A flat), and the second subject of the second symphony has a related theme. Perhaps a clue to this, as suggested by Brahms's biographer, Jan Swafford, is that the cradle song was written for the second child of Artur and Bertha Faber. Brahms had known and loved Bertha Porubzsky when she was just a girl, and the tune of the lullaby forms a counterpoint to a song she had once sung to him.

Lullabies are work songs for parents. Like sea shanties or cotton-picking songs, they exist to get the work done, the cradle rocked and the baby to sleep. Like other work songs, lullabies adopt the rhythm of the work and so are usually in 6/8. A cradle goes gently back and forth: a slow push and a little hold (1,2,3), a slow return and another little hold (4,5,6).

Brahms's lullaby is nominally in 3/4 – the piano's left hand plays three crotchets to the bar throughout – but the composite rhythm, taking the right hand also into account, mostly fills that out to six quaver beats. Interestingly, though, the figuration isn't smooth. There are ties across bar lines, the right hand is often ahead of the beat. This, you sense, is a slightly rickety cradle – one that has rocked generations of babies to sleep.

The cradle motion is enhanced by the song's harmonic structure. 'Wiegenlied' is in E flat major and the chord changes are simplicity itself – just I, IV and V. But even such basic harmonic changes imply movement, and while the cradle may be rocking back and forth it is not actually going anywhere. Underpinning the whole song is the sense of a drone, for the first bass note of every single bar is the tonic E flat, and this is irrespective of the chord above it.

The music of lullabies is intended to inspire feelings of safety – that while the child sleeps, all will be well. The E flat, reliable in its repetition, offers the reassurance that nothing will change. Tomorrow, the child will awake, as usual, and everything will still be the same.

44

С куклой (S kukloy)

music and words by Modest Musorgsky

WHEN THE COMPOSER OLIVER KNUSSEN wrote to the author and illustrator Maurice Sendak, hoping to turn his children's classic *Where the Wild Things Are* into an opera, the author rang him up.

'What is the best children's opera?' Sendak asked down the phone. The obvious options included Humperdinck's *Hänsel und Gretel*, Ravel's *L'Enfant et les sortilèges* and Britten's *Noye's Fludde*.

'The second act of *Boris Godunov*,' Knussen replied.

'Right answer!' said Sendak, their collaboration off to a good start.

Musorgsky's grand opera about the troubled reign of the Russian tsar at the turn of the seventeenth century veers from the clanging pomp and ceremony of Boris's coronation (quoted, in fact, by Knussen in *Wild Things*) to the oppressive darkness of his growing paranoia. But Act II is set in Boris's children's nursery. It's a dramatic masterstroke, offering light relief while simultaneously throwing the main events into a new perspective. We come to worry about the children, exposed to their father's mental deterioration and its potentially violent outcome, but equally we witness their childishness through Boris's eyes and ears, and it begins to seem like a symptom of his decline.

Modest Musorgsky (1839–1881) gained a reputation, even in his lifetime, for being a bit of an amateur. Good ideas, yes, but if only he had enough technique to realise them fully; if only his music were more polished. The drunken and dissolute lifestyle of the composer's later years probably added to this impression. After his death, his fellow composers, doubtless well-intentioned, set about correcting his errors of judgement and making his music more suited to the world of professional performance. Accordingly, there are many versions of Musorgsky's best-known works, edited by Rimsky-Korsakov, Anatoly Lyadov and others.

These days, we tend to feel differently about the composer. What struck Rimsky-Korsakov and his colleagues as clumsy and oafish now seems vital and compelling. Debussy always knew this. He was greatly influenced by *Boris Godunov* in writing his only completed opera, *Pelléas et Mélisande*, and once observed to a friend who was attending a performance of the former, 'You will find all of *Pelléas* there'.

Musorgsky's influence on Debussy is most clearly detectable in the Frenchman's word-setting, where lyricism is sacrificed to the rhythms and contours of normal speech. In the case of Yniold, the boy in Debussy's opera, Boris's children are role models, but so are the children of Musorgsky's group of songs called *Detskaya* – literally, 'The Children's Room', though in English the songs are usually called *The Nursery*.

Musorgsky wrote five songs between 1868 and 1870, then two years later, as the first set was being published, began composing five more. Just two of these later songs survive and perhaps only two were ever completed.

With a single exception, the songs in *The Nursery* are sung from the point of view of the child, with a child's diction and tone. As often as not, the melodic contour is rather narrow, the line rising and falling as the child's actual speech might. In the first song, 'S nyaney' ('With Nanny'), we encounter childish prattle. The child wants a story, the scary story about the horrible bogeyman who took children into the forest and ate their white bones … Or maybe not – maybe the story about the Tsar and Tsaritsa might be better, about how the Tsar had a limp and when he fell down a mushroom grew, and the Tsaritsa had a cold and when she sneezed she cracked the windows. Yes, that would be better.

It is rare in song to find such accurate representation of a child's characteristic speech patterns, now obsessed, now distracted. Oscar Brown Jr's lyrics for Bobby Timmins' 'Dat Dere' certainly achieves it – 'Hey what dey doing dere? / And where dey goin' dere? And, Daddy, can I have dat big elephant over dere?' – but he doesn't keep it going, interrupting the persistent questioning to comment, paternally, on the child's inquisitiveness. Musorgsky, however, sustains the tone to the end of each song. More importantly, in 'Dat Dere' we are meant to laugh, but Musorgsky takes his children as seriously as they take themselves.

In 'S kukloy' ('With the doll'), the child sings her doll a lullaby.

Tyapa, bay, bay.
Tyapa, spi, usni,
Ugomon tedya vozmi!
Tyapa! Spat' nado!

'Dolly, bye, bye. Dolly go to sleep, so lie down quietly! Dolly, it's time to sleep!'

This is an action song. As the child sings her made-up song – and it *sounds* as if she's making it up – she falls asleep herself. The words of the song don't tell us this: we hear it happening; we hear the child occasionally lose focus, then continue; we hear pauses (for yawns?), before she ploughs on with her song, repeating the same phrase, willing herself to stay awake even as the doll goes to sleep. And in the end, the child is asleep, too.

Anyone who has ever overheard a child singing herself to sleep will recognise how accurately Musorgsky has captured this. Debussy certainly did, writing in *La Revue blanche* in 1901: "The Doll's Lullaby" seems to have been taken down word for word, thanks to enormous powers of assimilation and an ability to inhabit those magic landscapes so special to a child's mind. The end of this lullaby is so beautifully restful that even the little girl who is telling the story falls gently to sleep at the sound of her own voice.'

In his article, Debussy recognises and praises the extreme simplicity of the music. But he comments that while, for Musorgsky, one chord was often enough, 'Monsieur So-and-so' would doubtless object to such parsimony; and when Musorgsky surprises us with an unlikely modulation, 'Monsieur What's-his-name' will complain that he can't find it in any textbook. Debussy adds that these two grumpy gentlemen are, of course, 'the same person'. He doesn't mention Rimsky-Korsakov by name.

45

Twisted

music by Wardell Gray
words by Annie Ross

'TWISTED' IS AN EARLY EXAMPLE of what jazz musicians call 'vocalese' (pronounced voca–*lees*), and it is the opposite of classical vocalise (pronounced the same way). For while the classical version involves wordless singing – think of the famous song without words by Rachmaninov – to jazz musicians the term indicates words applied to an existing instrumental solo, thus turning it into a song. You could argue, indeed, that vocalese is the antithesis of jazz, since what had begun as an improvised line ends up fixed forever.

For some reason, it is nearly always saxophone solos that are thus transformed, and in the case of 'Twisted' the solo was the work of tenor player Wardell Gray, who recorded his instrumental in 1949. Three years later, this became the starting point for the 22-year-old bebop singer Annie Ross, who took Gray's record – and, significantly, its title – as the basis of her song.

The legend is that Ross wrote her lyrics overnight, which, if true, is quite an achievement, for Gray's sax line is twisted indeed. Vocalese is not simply a matter of putting words to a tune, which lyricists do all the time, but of fitting a syllable to each note of the solo, and 'Twisted' has a lot of notes. It's also linear, because it is an improvised solo, not a strophic song, and so invites a narrative structure. Most examples of vocalese are, in fact, short stories and Ross's is no exception. Vocalese also tends to be humorous, and 'Twisted' is certainly that – a shaggy-dog joke with a punchline. (It may be relevant that Ross was born to two Scottish vaudevillians – her father was a comedian – and by the age of four was herself a child actor.)

Ross's genius starts with her inspired decision to situate her 'Twisted' in a psychiatrist's office with the blunt statement, 'My analyst told me that I was right out of my head.' This will be a song about a 'twisted' mind, but also one that never strays far from a self-reflexive enjoyment of its own idiom. It abounds in words for madness – 'out of my head', 'crazy' 'out of my mind', 'nuts', 'wild', 'insane' – but also jazz terms such as 'jive' and 'swingin''. And there are some jazz conceits, too.

In Gray's original, he had quoted another song as jazz improvisers of his vintage were wont to do. In the 1944 film *Going My Way*, Bing Crosby, as Father 'Chuck' O'Malley, sings Johnny Burke and Jimmy Van Heusen's 'Swinging on a Star' to the wayward boys of his parish. It's a song for children – a novelty song – and it became a number one hit. Gray quotes just a line from the tune, and Ross can hardly ignore it, so at that point she brings in a line about children – indeed wayward children: 'I heard little children were supposed to sleep tight / That's why I drank a fifth of vodka one night'. She even finishes the verse with the line 'I was swingin'' ('on a star').

Then immediately she goes one better, introducing her own reference to a different song, the Gershwins' 'They All Laughed'. In the original 'They' laughed at such explorers and inventors as Christopher Columbus, Edison, Wilbur Wright (and his brother), and Marconi and Henry Ford, among others. In 'Twisted', it's 'A. Graham Bell', Edison (again) and Einstein.

Throughout it all, Ross sticks tenaciously to Gray's original recording, repeating the music of the head – the first verse – but leaving nothing out except Gray's short second solo that comes just before the reprise of the head. Others have sung it since – Joni Mitchell (on her album *Court and Spark*) and Bette Midler – but neither kept to Gray's original line. No reason that they should, of course. By the time they recorded it the song was already, thanks to Ross, a standard, and other singers were at liberty to make it their own, Mitchell changing some of the words and music, Midler situating the song among a group of ladies who lunch (and dish the dirt).

But the sheer exhilaration of Ross's recording is in the breathlessly accurate way the singer cum lyricist reproduces Gray's convoluted saxophone line down to its intonation – what an ear she had! – in the process giving every note a specific meaning.

46

I'm in the Mood for Love

music by Jimmy McHugh
words by Dorothy Fields

THE KEY TO THIS SONG'S SUCCESS is the word 'funny' and its placing in the harmony.

'I'm in the Mood for Love' was first sung by Frances Langford in 1935 in Raoul Walsh's film *Every Night at Eight*, a musical comedy starring George Raft and Alice Faye. In its review of the movie, *The New York Times* failed even to mention the music, but the song quickly became Langford's calling card (she sang it in two more films) and, before the end of 1935, it was a hit for Louis Armstrong. That was just the start, though.

Over the years, the song only became more popular, spawning a famous vocalese, 'Moody's Mood for Love', a minor ska hit and a hip-hop version. It's not impossible that it also gave rise to another great standard, Vernon Duke's 'Taking a Chance on Love', which can be sung quite convincingly over Jimmy McHugh's chord changes. On a live recording in Carnegie Hall, Ella Fitzgerald sings 'Taking a Chance on Love' then slips into a chorus of 'I'm in the Mood', before returning to 'Taking a Chance' for her big finish. It's seamless.

One reason for the success of 'I'm in the Mood for Love' is the tight knit between McHugh's music and Dorothy Fields' words. Fields was a superbly natural writer of song lyrics. Stephen Sondheim singled her out for her seemingly effortless mix of simplicity and brilliance, which, he wrote, was matched among her contemporaries only by Frank Loesser. She had a long career during which she worked with composers as various as Sigmund Romberg, Jerome Kern and Cy Coleman, yielding songs that included 'The Way You Look Tonight' and 'Big Spender'. But her first hits were with McHugh in the 1920s and 1930s.

Fields' lyrics seldom draw attention to themselves (another thing Sondheim admired) and on the page the first stanza of 'I'm in the Mood for Love' looks humdrum enough with its almost symmetrical ABBA structure:

I'm in the mood for love,
Simply because you're near me.
Funny, but when you're near me,
I'm in the mood for love.

Harmonically, it is routine I–IV–V–I stuff, with the exception of the start of the third line: here we slip through chords III (first with an added seventh, then diminished) and II (also with a seventh), the melody following suit with a chromatic twist and turn. And this is where 'Funny' comes in, Fields' placing of the word at the beginning of that line not only disrupting the symmetry of the lyric, but also making sense of the harmony.

In a recording of the song from 1949, James Moody's tenor saxophone solo seems to take its cue from this moment. It is gloriously chromatic throughout, always unpredictable and full of wild bravura, rhetorical flourishes and phrases that seem to start on the wrong note. Eddie Jefferson heard it and, via vocalese, turned it into a whole new song.

'Moody's Mood for Love' acquired its title in 1954 when King Pleasure made his famous recording, and it has since been sung by Aretha Franklin, George Benson, Van Morrison and Amy Winehouse, to name only a few. Even James Moody, though not much of a singer, took to performing the song that had been based on his improvisation.

What Moody had done in 1949 was to perform a standard bebop trope. Charlie Parker, a big influence on Moody, would often create brand-new pieces improvised over the chord progressions of jazz standards. Most famously, Parker's 'Ornithology' derives from changes to Morgan Lewis's 'How High the Moon'. The original tune has gone, and no one would be likely to spot it from chords buried beneath the new tune.

But in calling his vocalese 'Moody's Mood for Love', Jefferson had drawn attention to its origins, audible or not, and Jimmy McHugh, as the composer of 'I'm in the Mood for Love', believed he was entitled to some compensation. His legal action was only partially successful, but Moody, evidently a magnanimous fellow, agreed to share his royalties with McHugh.

But there's one last twist: in putting his new words to Moody's solo, Eddie Jefferson also drew attention to the resemblance between 'I'm in the Mood for Love' and 'Taking a Chance on Love'.

John La Touche and Ted Fetter's lyrics for the latter begin: 'Here I go again. / I hear those trumpets blow again.'

'Moody's Mood for Love' begins: 'There I go, there I go, there I go, / *There* I go!'

47

I Touch Myself

music and words by Christina Amphlett,
Tom Kelly, Mark McEntee and Billy Steinberg

'I TOUCH MYSELF' WAS the work of four songwriters, the hit-making team of Tom Kelly and Billy Steinberg (whose previous work included 'Like a Virgin' for Madonna and 'True Colours' for Cyndi Lauper), and Christina Amphlett and Mark McEntee of Divinyls. But whoever had the idea of putting the second syllable of 'about' on the note C deserves the lion's share of royalties.

This is not the only song about masturbation – far from it. There's Cyndi Lauper's 'She Bop', Lady Gaga's 'Dancing in Circles' and the Who's 'Pictures of Lily'. And there are many other songs that refer to masturbation, most famously – because it led to a confrontation in the United States Senate between Frank Zappa and Tipper Gore of the Parents' Music Resource Centre – Prince's 'Darling Nikki'. Still, given masturbation is presumably the most common form of sexual activity, it's surprising there aren't more songs on the subject. What makes Divinyls' song special is that it's an action song: the music seems to act out the words, and the key to it all is that C.

Divinyls was a quintessentially 1980s, post-punk, new-wave rock band, and Chrissie Amphlett, in a school uniform, was not only its voice but its image (beside McEntee, the rest of the personnel kept changing). The band's appearance grew more glamorous with the passing years, but Amphlett remained the focus. Their biggest album, *diVINYLS*, was released in 1991, and ahead of it, at the end of the previous year, came its lead single, 'I Touch Myself'.

You could argue that, by definition and of its very nature, rock'n'roll is a musical representation of sex. The term itself is an early euphemism for the act. 'My Man Rocks Me (with One Steady Roll),' sang Trixie Smith as far back as 1922; 'Rock that Thing,' sang Lil Johnson seven years later. Pure 1950s rock'n'roll, with its simplified rhythm and heavy backbeat, was a sonic metaphor for sex, and boy-girl relationships were rock's principal subject matter. In fairness, they had also been the subject of most jazz standards, quite a lot of lieder and nearly all troubadour songs, but rock was increasingly explicit and sometimes it was not just lyrically, but musically explicit. Marvin Gaye may have sung about 'Sexual Healing', but other songs embodied it. Joan Armatrading's 'Love and Affection', for example, starts slowly, almost nonchalantly – 'I am not in love, but I'm open to persuasion' – and then the musical persuasion begins. 'But with a lover I can really move, really move,' she sings, as the song settles into a slow, driving, rhythmic groove. 'I Touch Myself' does something similar. The verse is all foreplay, but the chorus provides the action.

Even before Amphlett sings, the steady introduction (heavy guitar chords and chromatic organ embellishments) creates a sense of anticipation. When the words come, they present a wish list: 'I love myself, I want you to love me / When I feel down, I want you above me / I search myself, I want you to find me / I forget myself, I want you to remind me.'

The singer may love herself, but she needs 'you' to fulfil her desires. The words are suggestive, full of double meanings. 'When I feel down, I want you above me': is that 'feeling down' mentally or physically? When, in the next line, she searches herself, is she indulging in self-reflection or what we used to call self-abuse? The verse is a come-on. Chrissie Amphlett's voice is sleepily seductive, circling around itself in the narrowest of ranges. It's in C major, the melody rising from E to F ('I love myself'), then dropping to D, C, D and back to C ('I want you to love me'). This flattish melodic shape is repeated for each line until the fourth, where on the second syllable of 'remind' Amphlett jumps up a sixth to A. It's not much, but it's the only melodic action we've had, and it's a harbinger of the chorus.

'I don't want anybody else / When I think about you, I touch myself.' She says she doesn't want anybody else. But is that anybody but 'you', or anybody at all? Does the chorus represent a change of heart or a change of plan? She seems to be doing all right on her own.

The chorus is in B flat, the melody oscillating between two notes a semitone apart, F and E. The notes are next to each other on a piano keyboard and to play them you'd use two fingers, back and forth: 'I don't want anybody else' (F–E–E–E–F–F–F–F), 'When I think a-*bout* you, I touch myself' (F–F–F–F–C–E–E–E–F–F). And there it is: that jump up to C, that sudden little 'ow' of pleasure.

Of course there's more to it than that. There's McEntee's guitar solo, which is every bit as minimally obsessive as Amphlett's vocal line, and there's the long coda with its multiple repetitions of 'I touch myself' – more than a dozen of them, punctuated only by the occasional, breathless, 'I honestly do'. But take away that C in the chorus, and the song would not have been the hit it was.

After Amphlett's death in 2013 from breast cancer and complications with multiple sclerosis, the Cancer Council of Australia adopted her most famous song in an attempt to encourage women to conduct regular breast inspections. Ten female Australian singers, including Amphett's cousin Little Pattie, Olivia Newton-John, Deborah Conway, Megan Washington, Sarah Blasko and Katie Noonan, sang a largely a cappella version of 'I Touch Myself' in a video that ended in silence with the words 'Touch yourself' appearing on the screen.

48

There Must Be an Angel
(Playing with My Heart)

music and words by Annie Lennox and David A. Stewart

LOVE AT FIRST SIGHT. It's Ezio Pinza singing about the stranger across a crowded room in *South Pacific*, it's the Monkees' Micky Dolenz undergoing instant conversion as he sees 'her face' and becomes 'a believer', it's Charles Trenet's heart going '*Boum!*' But sometimes, the room can be empty and the heart can still go boom.

When the British duo Eurythmics released their only chart-topping single in 1985, the lyrics informed us that the room where 'the heart goes boom' was empty, but in fact Annie Lennox and David Stewart had installed in it a 'multitude of angels' in the form of a gospel choir, a string section, a harpsichord, an opera singer, Stevie Wonder playing a fabulous harmonica solo and a whole lot of synthesiser.

Eurythmics was a duo born in a hotel room in Wagga Wagga, when two members of the Tourists, playing around with a portable mini-synthesiser, decided to go their own way. Portable synthesisers made many things possible, and over the years the clever songwriting team of Annie Lennox and Dave Stewart grew very professional. While a lot of the pop music of that era sounds its age, 'There Must Be an Angel' is a record that hasn't dated in sync with the synths.

It's not a deep song. On the contrary, it is, as Gabriel Roth pointed out, a 'silly slab of plastic soul', and the 'room/boom' rhyme is only a small part of that. The melody, disguised by Lennox's ornate vocals and all the other fireworks, might not sound simple, but structurally it is. Harmonically it is the common progression I–V–IV–ii–I; melodically, it is built around the first six notes of the C major scale. Ignoring the ornamentation (we'll come to that), the first phrase of the first verse ('No one on earth could feel like this') climbs the four notes from E to A, while the second line ('I'm thrown and overblown with bliss') takes us down the C major triad, and back up to E. The first part of the verse ends with the lowest three notes of the scale, reinforced by the leading note. (We can't resist pointing out that 'Some Enchanted Evening' in *South Pacific* uses the same notes.)

But this simple material is only the skeleton that will be fleshed out with ornamentation, and before we hear a word of verse one, before we hear a single instrument, we are awash in that. It is the song's signature gesture, Annie Lennox's high unaccompanied vocalisation that starts the song: 'Da da do da da da do daa ...' This is the song's real essence, and it is from this that its most memorable features seem to derive, including the harmonica solo. Unless, of course, it was the other way around. The typically ebullient ornamentation that Stevie Wonder brings to his playing is so similar to Lennox's decoration of the melody – particularly at the lines about walking 'into an empty room' – that one is forced to speculate that she may have rerecorded her vocals in light of his contribution. Ornamentation is everywhere in this song, not least in the overdubbed vocals of the opera singer, over the little chorus-like chant of 'Must be talking to an angel' in the subdominant F major/minor, but Roth is not wrong to label the song 'soul' (albeit 'plastic soul').

The path to Wonder's solo, about three minutes in, is a bridge passage in B flat, which introduces the gospel choir and lets Lennox's powerful soul voice off its leash. The song appeared on the album *Be Yourself Tonight*, which also featured Lennox's duo with Aretha Franklin, 'Sisters Are Doing It for Themselves'. The music chimes well with the words here, since both step aside from the main song, the latter to comment on all that's happened to date: 'I must be hallucinating / Watching angels celebrating.' But with Wonder's harmonica, the hallucinations only get more lurid. It's a magnificently elaborate thing, full of disjunct rhythms, leaping intervals, staccato squeaks and ornamental roulades and it elevates the song to new heights. It's like the gilt curlicues in high-baroque architecture.

The high-baroque reference is apposite not merely because of the ornamentation in 'There Must Be an Angel', but also because of Eddie Arno and

Mark Innocente's accompanying video. Annie Lennox is a diva performing on stage at the Versailles palace of Sun King Dave Stewart. Louis XIV was a great patron of the arts, the playwrights Racine and Molière and the composers Lully and François Couperin all benefitting from his patronage. The big-budget in-house productions over which Louis presided, and in which he liked to participate as a dancer, especially early in his reign, doubtless came to the directors' minds after hearing the lavish production involved in the song. The harpsichord probably helped, too.

Two winged cherubs pull the curtain, Lennox sings, and behind her are figures that might be angels, though they would seem equally at home in Ancient Rome. Richard Cross, who supplied the backing vocals, is on hand to camp it up in a pair of wings, and a little boy stands in for Stevie Wonder, miming his harmonica solo (well, everyone else is miming).

Nothing was real in the entertainment dished up for the Sun King, and nothing is real in this song or this video. It's rococo pop.

49

A Case of You

music and words by Joni Mitchell

THIS IS A SONG RICH in meaning. Even the title is rich.

In the context of a love song, the usual sense of 'case' would be illness, 'a case of you' the amorous equivalent of a case of measles. The imagery is centuries old. From the troubadours of the Middle Ages to the Romantics of the nineteenth century to the blues to Peggy Lee ('You give me fever'), love has been portrayed as a malady – 'a bad case of loving you', to quote Moon Martin's song.

But Joni Mitchell was never one for clichés, so having set up the expectation of this well-worn trope, she presents us, instead, with a different image, the more powerful for having first misled us: 'I could drink a case of you,' she sings at the end of the chorus, 'and I would still be on my feet.' So it's a case of wine – 'holy wine', what's more.

But what does she mean by this metaphor? That she can't get enough of him? We know from the song's first line that the affair is over. Perhaps she means the opposite, that in contrast to the singer of 'You Go to My Head', who tells us that 'like a sip of sparkling Burgundy brew ... you intoxicate my soul', Joni can drink twelve whole bottles of this fellow, and be as sober as a judge. He might have intoxicated her in the past, but since their 'love got lost' he has no effect on her at all. Is that what she means?

'A Case of You' is a song from Mitchell's fourth album, *Blue*, which, on its release in 1971, brought her the greatest success of her career to date. The songs were among her finest, the singing perhaps the best she ever achieved, and her instrumental accompaniments, moving from guitar to piano to dulcimer and making a feature of each, were bold and varied.

'Just before our love got lost, you said: / "I am as constant as a northern star." / And I said: "Constantly in the darkness – where's that at? / If you want me, I'll be in the bar."' You can read those opening lines as prose. There is no sense of metre and the only hint that it might be the start of a song lyric is the rhyming of 'star' with 'bar'. It is, then, a perfectly typical Mitchell lyric, the words tumbling over themselves to fit her expandable melodic lines. No one else wrote songs that do quite this. Mitchell's great contemporaries, Bob Dylan and Leonard Cohen, though wordsmiths first, were not above faking a rhyme and truncating or obscuring sense to make their words fit their tunes. Mitchell, a far more sophisticated and inventive musician than either man, wrote melodies and chord structures that seemed infinitely elastic, allowing her to say exactly what she wanted.

There's a theory that Cohen is the 'you' of this song; there's another theory that it's Graham Nash. Cohen is perhaps more likely on the basis of the quotation from Shakespeare. In *Julius Caesar*, the doomed emperor tells his circling assassins, 'I am constant as the northern star, / Of whose true-fix'd and resting quality / There is no fellow in the firmament'. Moments later, he is dead.

Are we meant to conclude that Joni's ex-lover is pretentious? Possibly, and in this opening exchange she certainly gives herself the last word ('If you want me, I'll be in the bar.'). But in the second verse, by which point the insufferable fellow is paraphrasing Rilke ('Love is touching souls'), she is more acquiescent ('Surely you touched mine.') So what are we to think? Is her sobriety real or does he still go to her head, pretensions and all? She wouldn't be the first drunk to insist she was stone cold sober. Is she over him or not? To discover the song's meaning, we must hear not only the words, but also the music.

The Appalachian dulcimer is the principal instrument here, strummed in a staccato manner that underlines the distinctive rhythm of a song that seems to want to be a tango, especially at the line: '*I* – could *drink* – a *case* of you'. The other instruments are James Taylor's guitar and Russell Kunkel's congas, absent from the song until the final line of the first verse and the words 'O Canada'. This is a significant moment in the song. Mitchell, a Canadian, was, by the time of *Blue*, a resident of California – there's a song on the album entitled 'California' – and so when she finds herself in the darkened bar drawing 'a map of Canada … with your face sketched on it twice' it is doubly nostalgic. 'O Canada' is the title of the Canadian national anthem, its significance highlighted by the arrival of the other instruments, and the song's first high note as the last syllable of 'Canada' takes her sailing up the octave. (Of course Cohen, too, was Canadian.)

This is both a nostalgic song and a song *about* nostalgia. Mitchell is a character in the song, but also a detached observer. The action of the verses is in the past tense, the chorus in the present. The bar with 'the blue TV screen light', the 'cartoon coaster' with the sketched map, 'that time' he told her about 'touching souls', the woman she met with the mouth like his: these things have all passed, like their lost love, and yet, in the chorus he is there in her blood 'like holy wine'.

The song is in the key of D flat (the octave leap on 'Canada' is from D flat to D flat), and the verses of the song are contained within that octave with just the odd dip down to the dominant A flat or the leading note C, to reinforce the D flat-ness of it all. But the chorus floats up out of the octave to E flat: 'You are in my blood like holy wine.' (And it's worth remembering that holy wine – communion wine – is meant to be 'the blood of Christ'.)

The song's three choruses aren't exactly the same musically or verbally (for example, in the second and third choruses, the word order changes to 'Still I'd be on my feet'), but 'blood' is always on that high E flat, and in a song where the word-setting is preponderantly syllabic, the 'you' in 'I could drink a case of you' always comes with a melisma. The first time it is relatively restrained, but as the song continues the melisma soars up to an F, the song's highest note. This is in contrast to the clipped – one might say *sober* – manner in which she sings 'I could drink a case'.

There can't be much doubt about Mitchell's true feelings. The mostly syllabic singing in the past-tense verses may be from her head, but the present-tense choruses, with their ever-expanding melismas, are from her heart.

50

Ne me quitte pas

music by Jacques Brel and Gérard Jouannest (uncredited)
words by Jacques Brel

ACCORDING TO JACQUES BREL, this famous love song wasn't a love song at all, though if women wanted to think of it that way it was fine. In an interview in 1966, Brel said 'Ne me quitte pas' ('Don't leave me') was about the pathetic dependency of men – a hymn, in truth, to their cowardice. 'This is the story of a jerk and a loser,' he said, 'nothing to do with a woman.' ('C'est l'histoire d'un con et d'un raté, ça n'a rien à voir avec une femme.')

The singer of the song certainly appears needy, repeating over and over the phrase 'Ne me quitte pas' or, in Brel's Dutch version, 'Laat me niet alleen' ('Don't leave me *alone*'). Rod McKuen's polite English translation – 'If you go away' – doesn't approach this level of desperation.

It's seldom a good idea to assume that songs are autobiographical, and in the case of 'Ne me quitte pas' it is probably unhelpful. For one thing, there were several women who believed the song to have been addressed to them. Brel was married with three children, the third born around the time 'Ne me quitte pas' was composed, but the family had moved to Belgium. In Paris, Brel was having an affair with the singer Suzanne Gabriello, who later declared the song had been written with their break-up in mind. In another theory the song was addressed to his estranged wife. In any case, it seems quite likely that when Brel spoke of the man as a 'jerk' and a 'loser', he was talking about himself.

Brel recorded 'Ne me quitte pas' three times, but he was not the first. The first singer was in fact a woman, Simone Langlois, in January 1959, and so the song's point of view became female. The arrangement of that first recording by François Rauber is lush and reassuring, but the vocals are anguished – not quite in Brel's league of loserdom, but close – Langlois and Brel phrase the song similarly. Perhaps she had heard Brel sing it.

Brel made his first recording, in French, in September that same year. In contrast to the arrangement on Langlois's recording, Brel's – also by Rauber – is, from its opening moments, a work of angst-ridden expressionism. A high, quavering line of near atonal melody is played by an ondes Martenot, an eerie-sounding electronic instrument beloved of the composer Olivier Messiaen (who spotlit it in his *Turangalîla-Symphonie*), but more commonly heard in horror movies of the period. Next enters the piano, playing the 'Ne me quitte pas' figure, then repeating it an octave higher, a gesture amplified at the beginning of Brel's second French recording from 1972. By that time the ondes Martenot was gone.

The pianist in both recordings is Gérard Jouannest. We can safely assume from the romantic, rhapsodic manner of his playing that the opening figuration was down to him, but he seems to have had a more pivotal role. The second part of the melody, first heard with the words 'Moi, je t'offrirai des perles de pluie venues de pays où il ne pleut pas' ('I offer you pearls of rain from a country where it doesn't rain'), quotes – or at least toys with – the central slow section of Liszt's Hungarian Rhapsody No 6, which was a popular enough classic, and one the Paris Conservatoire–trained pianist would have known and possibly played.

Brel and Jouannest often collaborated, even trying things out side by side at the same piano keyboard. It has been speculated that at the time they wrote 'Ne me quitte pas', Jouannest was not a member of SACEM, the French performing-rights society, and therefore could not receive royalties; but if this were true, why was the attribution not remedied, especially given his other collaborations with Brel? It's a mystery.

But back to Brel's own performance. That he considered it a song about male dependency and viewed such men with scorn obviously colours our listening. His Dutch version, recorded in 1961 for the album *Marieke*, is ripe for consideration in this regard. Though French-speaking, Brel's Belgian family was of Flemish ancestry and he recorded a number of his songs in Dutch – *Marieke* contains several. But his Dutch wasn't fluent and so, with the assistance of the poet Ernst van Altena, 'Ne me quitte pas' became

'Laat me niet alleen'. Perhaps it was the more guttural tones of the Dutch language, but Brel's performance here, though it uses the same arrangement as his original 1959 recording (ondes Martenot and all), takes a radically different approach. Much of it is adopts a spoken tone, some of it is actual speech, and the overall mood is obsessive and unsettling. This is far removed from the Seekers singing 'If You Go Away'.

Mind you, the obsession is already embedded within the song. It is not only the repetition of the first line that creates this effect (though it is hard to think of many other songs that repeat their title over and over so many times), but more subliminally, the melodic line that goes with the words, which is heard everywhere. In fact its rhythm never really goes away – even in the 'Hungarian Rhapsody' section, the insistent 'Ne me quitte pas' rhythm, a beat less here, a beat more there, underpins the melodic invention.

Throughout it all, however, we must remember that Brel was not only a singer and songwriter, but a cabaret performer and film actor. The stage was his world and to watch one of his French TV performances of 'Ne me quitte pas' is instructive. The earliest is from 1959 and already he is shot in close up, sweating under the studio lights. But there's a later version. By now the song is a hit – the audience applauds at the first words – and Brel is in extreme close-up, the sweat running off him as he pleads desperately before the camera. To sing a song for others is to perform; and to perform, as Edith Piaf knew, is to be an actor – at least a little. Is Brel acting here? A lot!

51

Good Morning Heartache

music by Irene Higginbotham
words by Ervin Drake

BILLIE HOLIDAY FIRST RECORDED THIS, one of her most famous songs, in 1946, and she sang it ever after, right to the end of her life. It became as much her signature tune as 'God Bless the Child' and 'Strange Fruit'. In addition to Irene Higginbotham and Ervin Drake, the producer Dan Fisher usually gets a credit, as in those days producers often did. However, it's hard to say what his contribution was, beyond bringing the song to Billie Holiday's attention.

Irene Higginbotham (1918–1988) is an interesting figure. She was a niece of jazz trombonist J.C. Higginbotham, who played with the likes of Louis Armstrong and Red Allen, but her own musical education seems to have been largely classical, and she worked as a concert pianist as well as a composer and songwriter. While 'Good Morning Heartache' is far and away her most famous song, Higginbotham was evidently prolific. Her songs were sung by Bing Crosby, Nat King Cole, Dinah Washington and Fats Waller, and played by Duke Ellington's and Benny Goodman's orchestras. But it's a messy history, partly because some of her early output might be by her uncle – 'Harlem Stomp', recorded in 1940 by Louis Armstrong, is now generally considered to be J.C.'s work – and partly because much of the time she used a pseudonym. In the 1930s and 1940s it was rare to encounter a female composer on Tin Pan Alley, rarer still an African American woman, so Higginbotham often published under the name Glenn Gibson. It's possible she used other pseudonyms, too, and that consequently we'll never know the extent of her songwriting.

'Good morning, heartache, you old gloomy sight / Good morning, heartache, thought we'd said goodbye last night': Drake's personification of heartache in response to Higginbotham's slow blues is a masterstroke. Turning on its head the notion of 'sleeping it off', the song posits the unwelcome reappearance of the singer's heartache the following morning, 'with the dawn'. She'd like to 'shake' him, but can't. And it's not only a 24-hour problem, but seven days a week. As the song's best lines put it, 'I've got those Monday blues / Straight through Sunday blues'. The clincher is the singer's acceptance of the situation. Nothing's going to change, heartache is going to keep turning up, and all the singer can do is extend a polite welcome: 'Good morning, heartache, sit down.'

Doubtless much of the song's success – and Billie Holiday's immediate identification with the material – was down to the sad nexus it formed with her own life and its string of abusive relationships with men, booze and hard drugs. In this context, it's particularly touching to hear the resignation in the line 'Good morning, heartache, what's new?'

Holiday, it hardly needs saying, was one of the greatest vocal stylists of the twentieth century. She and Frank Sinatra, both born in 1915, shared similar gifts. They had immaculate timing, an inherent sense of swing and perfect diction. This last quality, allied to a tone of voice that in both cases we might call 'dry', gave their singing a spoken quality, and this was particularly true when a song involved direct speech. Sinatra's famous recording of Arlen and Mercer's 'One for My Baby (and One More for the Road)' is an example, the whole song addressed to Joe the bartender at 'quarter to three' in the morning; 'Good Morning, Heartache' is another.

Holiday took her one-sided dialogue with the mute 'heartache' into the recording studio twice, first in 1946, and again ten years later for the album *Lady Sings the Blues*. The change in her voice is marked – by 1956, much of the tone has drained from it – but the performance has grown and the song seems still more powerful. There's now a wry amusement in her voice as she sings the line, 'Might as well get used to you hanging around'.

Two years later, there was hardly any voice left, though some days were better than others. On a live recording from October 1958, at an outdoor stage at the first Monterey Jazz Festival, the elderly sounding 43-year-old is in variable form. She starts her set confidently but, perhaps spooked by a passing plane, soon deteriorates. Her band is losing it, too. But it's compelling stuff, and we can't turn it off. By the time she reaches 'Good Morning, Heartache', most of the actual notes aren't there, and some that are sound out of tune. And yet, the words and the timing and the humour are there, and there's a wonderful lightness of touch. Then along comes another plane, and this one isn't distant at all. It comes and keeps on coming, like a B-52 bomber, gradually, but inexorably obliterating this rare, late recording. Holiday and her sensitive piano player, Mal Waldron, disappear, and so does Gerry Mulligan's burbling baritone sax. All we can hear is the plane. It's an awful moment, but more awful still is that, as the plane passes, we realise Holiday has never stopped singing. She is finishing the song that nobody heard. Ten months later, she was dead.

52

Lush Life

music and words by Billy Strayhorn

'AH YES, I WAS WRONG!' That's the hinge on which this structurally surprising song turns. It consists, you might say, of a verse and a chorus, but these might as well be a recitative and an aria.

'Lush Life' isn't unique in having this form. Rodgers and Hart's 'My Funny Valentine' is similarly brief and to the point. But that song had a dramatic rationale: in the 1937 musical comedy *Babes in Arms*, a woman named Billie sings it to a man named Valentine, telling this 'slightly dopey gent' with the 'laughable' looks that, in spite of his IQ and appearance, she likes him the way he is. In contrast, 'Lush Life' has no dramatic rationale but its own, and that is every bit as remarkable as the song's structure.

'My Funny Valentine' is often sung without its verse (and changes its meaning in the process), but 'Lush Life' depends on the set-up in its verse to justify the high-flown language of its more musically conventional chorus. Given the convoluted melodic line and unusually chromatic harmonies of both parts of the song, it might be wiser to think of 'Lush Life' as a continuum. On the famous 1963 recording of the song by Johnny Hartman and John Coltrane, there really is nothing useful Coltrane can contribute until Hartman has sung the entire song. You sense Coltrane's impatience in the first few notes of his solo, which arrives more than three minutes into the track.

Billy Strayhorn (1915–1967) was Duke Ellington's arranger and in-house composer, and the bandleader liked to give him his due. The Duke Ellington Orchestra would seldom play its signature tune without Duke himself introducing it as 'Billy Strayhorn's "Take the A Train"'. But 'Lush Life' was written before Strayhorn and Ellington met, for the song is the work of a teenager. And here's the first surprise.

'I used to visit all the very gay places / Those come-what-may places / Where one relaxes on the axis / Of the wheel of life'. The lyrics are wonderfully, wittily rhymed. The internal rhyme of 'relaxes on the axis' is brilliant enough, but the axis belongs to the 'wheel of life' where one gets 'the feel of life / From jazz and cocktails'. And we're not done, because the next stanza describes girls with 'sad and sullen grey faces / With distingué traces', all that remains after a life of daytime drinking: 'Twelve o'clock tales' (to rhyme with cocktails).

This is virtuoso rhyming from the teenage Strayhorn. It's worthy of Cole Porter or Noël Coward, and so is the fulsome sophistication. Distingué, indeed! It would be another twenty years before Billie Holiday released *Songs for Distingué Lovers*, and most English speakers, then as now, would struggle to explain the meaning of the word (it means a distinguished manner). But if this sophistication – self-conscious or not – is hard to credit in a high-school boy, it's worth remembering that 1933, the year Strayhorn started work on the song he initially called 'Life Is Lonely', was also the year he first heard Ellington's orchestra. Perhaps some of the Duke's own sophistication wore off.

The song was written and first published in the key of D flat and in spite of chromatic excursions and lots of added sixths, sevenths and ninths, remains anchored by that chord for the first two stanzas as the singer remembers his dissolute past. Suddenly we modulate.

'Then you came along, / With your siren song, / To tempt me to madness.' This 'siren song', in F major, actually tempts us to further chromaticism – all the way to a C flat ninth chord, a tritone away, before the singer realises his mistake: 'Ah yes, I was wrong / Again, I was wrong.'

And now we're back in D flat and the chorus, if we want to call it that. At any rate, we're finally in the present tense: 'Life is lonely again', the song tells us, and nothing can help; 'A trough full of hearts could only be a bore'. And while 'A week in Paris will ease the bite of it' (this is a Pittsburgh schoolboy, remember!), he's resigned to living 'a lush life / In some small dive', and to rot there with 'those whose lives are lonely too'.

The music of the chorus is authentically chromatic, the chords that underpin the melody often descend stepwise. For example, at the words

'A trough full of hearts', which melodically pits the B flat of the key signature against B natural and the tritone E natural, the harmony oscillates between the tonic D flat and D7. The song ends with the melody creeping up the chromatic scale from C flat to F natural, sounding all the notes in between.

This is a hard song to pull off. As Blossom Dearie, introducing a live performance on her album *Needlepoint Magic*, says, 'Lush Life' is 'very difficult to play and even harder to sing; and on top of that it's sad'. She admits it took her eleven years to learn. The hardest thing about singing it is the chromaticism. Even Strayhorn himself, who, it must be said, wasn't much of a singer, has trouble keeping it in tune, especially the final chromatic ascent. It's remarkable how many singers come unstuck with the lyrics.

The most common mistake is to sing 'distant gay traces' instead of 'distingué traces', though in some cases it might be mispronunciation. Strayhorn himself got it right, as you would expect, and so did Kay Davis at an Ellington concert at Carnegie Hall in 1948, introducing the song to an audience for the first time with Strayhorn at the piano (fifteen years after he began work on it). But Hartman sang 'distant gay', so did Nat King Cole, so did Blossom Dearie (who often sang in French, so had no excuse), and so did Rickie Lee Jones in an extraordinary live performance on *Girl at Her Volcano* where she seems to be method-acting her way through the song. Hartman also turned 'trough full of hearts' into 'thoughtful of hearts' (what did he think this meant?), while Cole, apparently unaware what a 'siren song' was, sang 'you came along with your siren *of* song'. He also sang 'strifling' for 'stifling' and 'those *who* lives are lonely' instead of 'whose lives'. These last two might have been slips of the tongue, but no one seems to have thought they were worth fixing.

'Lush Life' is a bear trap of a song, but is it, as Dearie suggested, sad? It's worth listening to Strayhorn's own live recording from 1964. He might have difficulty holding the tune, but his diction is clear and bright, and the performance doesn't linger. By turns breezy and amused – perhaps by the thought of his teenage self – he despatches the song in record time. Let's not take ourselves too seriously, seems to be his attitude.

53

Come on in My Kitchen

music and words by Robert Johnson

AS THE WRITER AND BROADCASTER Garrison Keillor once pointed out, the kitchen is a place for confidences. Things that are hard to say elsewhere in the home may be spoken in the kitchen. Perhaps this is because, traditionally, it is a mother's domain, the room in which she is especially motherly. But 'Come on in My Kitchen' is not Robert Johnson being motherly.

It's a stretch to say that Johnson (1911–1938) actually wrote this song, either the words or the music. It seems to have been more a matter of choosing phrases from a library of blues stock, a standard oral-tradition technique. It's even possible that Johnson made his selection on the fly, for on 23 November 1936 at the Gunter Hotel in San Antonio, Texas, he recorded the song twice and the second time it was different.

The first performance of this eight-bar blues was slow and brimming with despair, the second faster with a hint of ragtime. Johnny Shines, who for a time travelled and worked with Johnson, reported that the singer could make grown men and women weep with his performance of 'Come on in My Kitchen'. Is that why the record producer Don Law asked for a more cheerful version? This was Johnson's first time in a studio and he seems to have been happy to oblige, not only singing and playing it faster, but leaving out beats at the ends of lines to move things along. The vocal delivery is changed on the second recording, and so is the guitar playing. It's much more of a display case for Johnson's virtuoso technique than the austere earlier version. This was the technique that had the young Keith Richards wondering who the second guitarist was when his fellow Rolling Stone Brian Jones played him a recording.

But perhaps most significant about these two versions of the same song, recorded on the same day, is that they have substantially different lyrics.

We are listening as Johnson mixes and matches familiar blues phrases. The second, up-tempo account contained more verses than the first, but it's that slower first version that is the more powerful of the two. Both sets of vocals begin with the singer's moaning. This is how the first version continues:

> You better come on in my kitchen,
> Well, it's goin' to be rainin' outdoors.

> Ah, the woman I love, took from my best friend,
> Some joker got lucky, stole her back again.
> You better come on in my kitchen,
> It's goin' to be rainin' outdoors.

> Oh, she's gone! I know she won't come back.
> I've taken the last nickel out of her nation sack.
> You better come on in my kitchen,
> It's goin' to be rainin' outdoors.

> Hey, can't you hear that wind howl?
> Oh, can't you hear that wind would howl?
> You better come on in my kitchen.
> It's goin' to be rainin' outdoors.

> When a woman gets in trouble, everybody throws her down.
> Lookin' for her good friend, none can be found.
> You better come on in my kitchen,
> Baby, it's goin' to be rainin' outdoors.

> Wintertime's comin', it's goin' be slow
> You can't make the winter, babe, that's dry, long, so.
> You better come on in my kitchen,
> 'Cause it's goin' to be rainin' outdoors.

On the second recording, Johnson starts with the verse 'When a woman gets in trouble' and leaves out the one about the 'nation sack', but adds three more verses that aren't part of the first recording. The first of these is about his woman being 'up the country' and not writing to him, the second has him going to a mountain, and the final verse explains that he is an orphan and has no one 'to love or care' for him. If anyone is to be motherly here it will be the figure he is inviting into his kitchen.

Food is prepared in kitchens and, in the blues, food is often a euphemism for sex, albeit sometimes hard to pin down precisely. 'Jelly roll', for instance, represents either male or female genitalia, depending on whose account you accept. (Since 'jelly roll' is a long, cylindrical cake, like a Swiss roll, and since it was the sobriquet of the notoriously macho Jelly Roll Morton, it's difficult to believe that it could be anything other than a phallic symbol.) There are later examples of food representing sex in popular music, generally from a male point of view. The Rolling Stones' 'Brown Sugar' is one that seems more unsettling with every passing year, and another is the Strangeloves' 'I Want Candy' (though Annabella Lwin turned this on its head when she sang it with Bow Wow Wow).

In the 1930s, women were mostly the purveyors of kitchen imagery when it came to 'dirty blues' in recordings that were never played on radio but have, nonetheless, survived. Blues singer Lil Johnson (no relation to Robert) seems to have specialised in culinary euphemisms for sex. She boasted in one song that her 'stove' was in 'good condition', and variously sang of her love of 'hot nuts' ('Get 'Em from the Peanut Man') and 'Meat Balls'. Bessie Smith sang 'I need a little sugar in my bowl / I need a little hot dog in my roll.' And in the vaudevillian blues, 'Kitchen Man', by Andy Razaf and Edna Alexander, also recorded by Smith, a smorgasbord of double meanings is served up:

His frankfurters are oh so sweet;
How I like his sausage meat!
I can't do without my kitchen man.

Oh, how that boy can open clam!

No one else can touch my ham.

I can't do without my kitchen man

There is nothing vaudevillian in Robert Johnson's kitchen; there's only pain – too much pain, one imagines, for producer Don Law. After all, these recordings were being made in the hope that they would be released as 'race records', appealing to white record buyers. They would be more successful if they were cheerful or, if cheerful couldn't be managed, at least energetic. The second recording achieved the latter and was duly released the following year on the Vocalion Records label.

But that first recording of 'Come on in My Kitchen' is a study in despair. The singer moans, the wind howls and the guitar gently weeps. The key to the despair is the verse that Johnson left out of the second recording: 'Oh, she's gone! I know she won't come back. / I've taken the last nickel out of her nation sack.' There's some dispute about how the 'nation sack' got its name, but we know what it was. It was a small purse, tied around a woman's waist and worn beneath her undergarments. In it she kept charms – a lock of hair from her lover, for instance – and money. The money wasn't necessarily for spending, it could also be a charm for good luck in love. Sometimes there was a dollar bill that had been soaked in the urine of the woman's lover. The nation sack kept the relationship together. So when Johnson sings he has 'taken the last nickel' from his woman's nation sack, he's done more than rob her of money, he's removed the last piece of luck from their relationship. This is why he *knows* she's not returning.

But then who is he addressing, if the woman herself has gone away? Who is he inviting into his kitchen? Perhaps it's us, his listeners. Perhaps, after all, he simply wants to unburden himself in that room that the blues associates with sex, but that the whole world uses for sharing confidences. In this song, Robert Johnson asks his listeners not only into his kitchen, but also into his confidence. And perhaps that's why some of us still weep.

54

Ich bin der Welt abhanden gekommen

music by Gustav Mahler
words by Friedrich Rückert

MAHLER'S SETTING OF RÜCKERT'S POEM is perhaps this book's most beautiful song. But then beauty – sublimity, rapt stillness – is the point of it.

When we think of Gustav Mahler (1860–1911) we think of symphonies – dramatic, discursive works for the concert hall lasting anywhere up to an hour and a half. But songs were central to this composer's art, and they feature in his first four symphonies.

The first symphony begins with an awakening of nature, before a purposeful tune strides out in the cellos. It's straight from one of Mahler's *Songs of a Wayfarer*, our hero walking across dewy fields on a beautiful morning as birds and flowers call out to him, 'Isn't it a wonderful world?'

The second symphony – the *Resurrection* – introduces actual voices, rather a lot of them in the final choral movement, but before that there are two songs to words from *Des Knaben Wunderhorn*, the collection of folk poetry that had provided Brahms with the words of his famous lullaby. In the central third movement of his symphony Mahler presents a version of his own setting of one of these songs, again for orchestra alone, and in the following movement a solo alto voice sings another *Wunderhorn* song. More singers and more *Wunderhorn* songs appear in the third and fourth symphonies. But the fifth symphony has no singer and, apparently, no song. Mahler began it in the summer of 1901.

Mahler was better known in his lifetime as a conductor than as a composer. He was one of the first superstars of the art, with an international career that took him from Prague to Budapest, Leipzig to Hamburg. He was conductor of the Vienna Court Opera, then (simultaneously) of the Vienna Philharmonic's subscription series. In the last years of his life, he conducted the New York Philharmonic and the Metropolitan Opera. The work kept him away from composing, so summer holidays were sacrosanct. Each summer, Mahler took himself off first to Steinbach on the Attersee, then Maiernigg in Carinthia, where he composed in a hut on the Wörthersee. This is where he began the fifth symphony, and where he set to music a number of Rückert's poems. That summer of 1901, he completed seven songs to words by the poet (including three that would later belong to the *Kinder-totenlieder* – 'Songs on the Deaths of Children') and probably the first three movements of the symphony. In one of the Rückert songs it is impossible not to feel Mahler is composing his own experience, cut off from the hurly-burly of daily life.

> Ich bin der Welt abhanden gekommen,
> Mit der ich sonst viele Zeit verdorben,
> Sie hat so lange von mir nichts vernommen,
> Sie mag wohl glauben, ich sei gestorben.

'I am lost to the world, where I once wasted so much time; it has heard nothing of me for so long that it probably thinks I am dead.'

The music comes tentatively to life. Two notes, then three notes, then four. The solo instrument that plays them is the cor anglais or English horn, offering us a premonition of the composer's great farewell to life, 'Der Abschied' (The Farewell) from *Das Lied von der Erde* (The Song of the Earth). This Rückert song, however, is only a temporary farewell. Mahler may, for the moment, have abandoned the world, but he's sending it a postcard.

We associate the symphonic Mahler with big orchestras, with lots of extra woodwind and brass, batteries of percussion and the occasional off-stage band. This group of five *Rückert Lieder* is for a small orchestra, and this particular song has especially reduced forces by Mahler's standards: an oboe; the aforementioned cor anglais; pairs of clarinets, bassoons and French horns; a harp and a small body of strings. There's nowhere in the song where these instruments all play simultaneously. The orchestration is delicate and detailed. Take the opening, where the cor anglais doles out its meagre notes against a fragmented tapestry of sound created by a single low note from the harp (repeated once), a soft, two-note chord played by muted violas, and then short phrases from a bassoon and a horn. The music is hardly there, an impression reinforced by the absence, at first, of the tonic note, E flat. The harmony is rootless, the music levitates.

The structure of the piece is unconventional. Rückert's poem has three stanzas, and Mahler's song three verses. Yet before the first verse is over, before we hear Rückert's words about the world imagining his death, the orchestra has gently interrupted the singer and started up the introduction once more – that rapt, still, weightless, rootless music. It is as though the composer, like the poet, is so cut off from the world, surrendering himself so utterly to his art, that he is no longer in control. The music comes and goes as it pleases.

The words of Rückert's final stanza underline this impression:

Ich bin gestorben dem Weltgetümmel,
Und ruh' in einem stillen Gebiet.
Ich leb' allein in mir und meinem Himmel,
In meinem Lieben, in meinem Lied.

'I am dead to the world's pandemonium, residing in a tranquil realm. I live alone in my heaven, in my love, in my song.'

The cor anglais is as much a feature of this song as the singer. Rather than providing a musical commentary in the form of a Bachian obbligato, it is the singer's alter ego; it has the first word and the last. It takes over from the voice, and when Rückert's poem gives out and the singer, absorbed by the song, gives up, the cor anglais just goes on singing, the song now disembodied.

When Mahler composed this song, he had yet to write the final two movements of his fifth symphony. The following summer he returned to Maiernigg to complete the work and it was there, on the shores of the Wörthersee once more, that he wrote perhaps his single most famous stretch of music: the fifth symphony's *Adagietto*. Was he reminded of the previous summer? Was he seeking to recapture – or possibly unable to resist – the rapt mood of 'Ich bin der Welt'?

The great Mahlerian, Donald Mitchell, suggested that the *Adagietto* resembled the second song of the *Kindertotenlieder*, 'Nun seh' ich wohl' ('Now I see well'), written two years after the symphony. And so it does. They both feature strings and harp – though 'Nun seh' ich wohl' employs other instruments, too – and they even share some melodic material. The song, it seems clear, was inspired by the *Adagietto*.

But the principal point of reference for the *Adagietto* seems to be this earlier Rückert song. From its tentative opening, with its delay of the tonic, the *Adagietto* floats free in just the same way as the song, leaving the cruel world behind. When Visconti included it, over and over, in his film *Death in Venice*, he used it to create precisely this effect.

55

Gracias a la vida

music and words by Violeta Parra

'IN THE MIDST OF LIFE we are in death', reads one of the funeral sentences from the Book of Common Prayer. Or, to put it another way: death comes and life goes on. The charango accompaniment in Violeta Parra's most famous recording is the sound of life going on, even as she sings what many believe to have been her suicide note.

A charango is a sort of lute played throughout the Andes. It resembles a ukulele, with a not dissimilar tone, and like the ukulele comes in a variety of sizes. The back of the standard charango was traditionally made of an armadillo shell, but these days it's more likely to be some sort of wood. In 'Gracias a la vida', the charanguista strums a gentle and unchanging 12/8 pattern as Parra sings, quite freely, her 'Thanks to life'.

Violeta Parra (1917–1967), singer, songwriter, poet and visual artist, was a vital figure in Chilean and South American song, specifically as a founder of the Nueva canción ('new song') movement. The movement was moored in the rediscovery of traditional Chilean music during the 1950s and 1960s, and Parra was a leader of the revival.

Although traditional songs were already sung in Chile's cities, these tended to be 'official' arrangements, their words edited and even censored. Parra, along with singers such as Victor Jara, went to the countryside to find original songs – and not just songs, but also stories, sayings and recipes. They performed the songs they learnt, often accompanied by traditional instruments such as the charango, and began to write new songs using folk idioms. The exercise was as much political as cultural. Its aims were to counter the commercialisation of Chilean culture coming from the United States and give voice to the lives and experiences of rural Chileans. In 1970, the movement, formalised the previous year as Nueva canción Chilena, played an important role in the election of Marxist president Salvador Allende, but by then Parra was dead.

'Gracias a la vida que me ha dado tanto' ('Thanks to life, which has given me so much'): the words of her best-known song are subject to some debate. She seems to have written it in 1965 or 1966, during or after the breakdown of her relationship with the Swiss flautist Gilbert Favre. But can we take the words at face value? There are those who believe we can't. Parra's life might have been full and frequently passionate, but it was hardly easy. The Chilean-born composer Daniel Rojas hears the song as Parra's equivalent of the 'Heiligenstadt Testament', the long letter of existential angst that Beethoven, in his encroaching deafness, wrote to his brothers but failed to send. But there's no obvious angst in 'Gracias a la vida'.

Parra thanks life for her eyes (she calls them stars), which enable her to distinguish between black and white, and to see her lover; for her hearing, which brings her crickets and canaries, the sound of working machinery and her lover's voice; for words, with which she can write 'mother', 'friend', 'brother', and through which she can address her lover; for the steps of her weary feet that have taken her from cities, deserts and mountains to 'your' house and garden (now, presumably, addressing her lover); for the heart that enables her to distinguish good from evil, and to look into the depths of 'your' eyes; and for the laughter and tears, with which she may tell joy from pain, and so may create songs – her own songs, 'your' songs, everyone's songs. It's not Pollyanna's view of life, but neither is it a list of complaints.

There is, however, the music. The charango's rhythm, Rojas says, is a sirillo (a descendant of the Spanish triple-time dance, the seguidilla), found on the Southern Chilean island of Chiloé. Above its chugging continuum, Parra's voice, gentle, reassuring, perhaps a little tired, sings her short phrases, most of which descend in pitch. The chords seem to descend, too, often dropping by a tone or a semitone (A minor on 'tanto' at the end of the first line to G7 in the next line, F major on 'blanco' to E7 in the next line. Overall, the effect of this lovely, lilting song of thanks is of its music forever falling gently down. Even when the harmony resets itself at the start of each verse it seems still to be descending, a bit like an Escher staircase. The other strange effect in this song is that the longer Parra sings, the more reverb is added to her voice, so that she seems to be fading away.

Parra and Favre returned to Chile from Europe in 1964, and the following year she and her son Ángel set up 'La Carpa de la Reina', a circus tent in the neighbourhood of La Reina on the outskirts of Santiago. If you came to the tent, Parra would sing for you, but this was more than a stage, it was also a cultural centre.

Favre moved to Bolivia; Parra followed but couldn't persuade him to return. Chile's Christian Democrat government offered reforms in housing and education, but they weren't enough for her. Radio stations wouldn't play her music. The tent in La Reina was failing to attract interest. On 5 February 1967, Parra took a gun to the tent and shot herself.

Four years later, 'Gracias a la vida' was recorded by the Argentine singer Mercedes Sosa, becoming a bestseller right across South America and beyond. In 1974, Joan Baez included the song on her album *Gracias a la vida* as 'a message of hope' to Chileans now living under a military dictatorship. In 1976, the Brazilian singer of jazz and samba Elis Regina included it on *Falso Brilhante*; in 1977, the Greek singer and activist Maria Farantouri recorded the song. All the recordings were in the original Spanish. In 1978, Arja Saijonmaa recorded a whole album of Parra's songs in Finnish, including 'Gracias a la vida'. Saijonmaa also recorded the song in Swedish and went on to sing it at the funeral of the assassinated Swedish prime minister, Olof Palme. Within a decade of Parra's death, 'Gracias a la vida' had become international.

In Chile itself, the song also took on a greater significance. Following the CIA-assisted coup of 1973 and the installation of military dictator Augusto Pinochet, many of the leaders of Nuevo canciones were rounded up and taken to the notorious general stadium in Santiago. Among them were Victor Jara and Ángel Parra. Jara was tortured there and subsequently murdered. 'Gracias a la vida' was among the songs banned by the Pinochet junta. But when you ban a song you give it life, and Violeta Parra's song became an anthem of the Chilean resistance.

Pinochet's regime ended in 1990. In 1998, the former dictator was indicted for violating human rights. Corruption charges followed, including embezzlement. At Pinochet's death in 2006, approximately three hundred criminal charges against him were pending.

'Gracias a la vida' lives on.

56

O Breath

music by Elliott Carter
words by Elizabeth Bishop

'O BREATH' IS A SONG of great complexity but also great intimacy – the singer counts the hairs on the breast of her sleeping lover (nine in total, 'four round one // five the other nipple').

In 1975, after almost thirty years of writing purely instrumental music, the American composer Elliott Carter (1908–2012) returned to word-setting with six poems by Elizabeth Bishop. *A Mirror on Which to Dwell*, the resulting cycle of songs, is particularly interesting in hindsight. Carter followed it up with a big piece to a poem by John Ashbery and another to six poems of Robert Lowell. Bishop, Ashbery and Lowell were all themselves American and Carter's contemporaries, and by the time the composer had finished his Lowell cycle in 1981, these three vocal works were regarded by his admirers as harbingers of a lyrical late style. Carter was seventy-three.

But the songs weren't that late, it turned out. Carter still had another thirty years of composing ahead of him (he died just before his 104th birthday), including musical settings of words by Ashbery (again), E.E. Cummings, T.S. Eliot, John Hollander, Marianne Moore, Ezra Pound, Wallace Stevens (twice), William Carlos Williams and Louis Zukofsky – a who's who of American modernist poetry.

What had kept the composer from writing vocal music for three decades was the complexity of his music. The rhythmic, textural and harmonic richness of works such as the Concerto for Orchestra (1969), the third string quartet (1971), and the Duo for violin and piano (1973) made them fiendishly difficult to pull off. In early performances of the quartet, for example, the four players had required earpieces carrying individual click tracks – electronic pulses – just to keep the show on the road. The composer doubted that singers existed who could do justice to his way of writing, but *A Mirror on Which to Dwell* proved him wrong.

It's interesting that Carter should have returned to songwriting with Bishop. There's a certain domesticity about her poetry. Comparing her to Chekhov, the English poet and critic Craig Raine pointed out that Bishop examined life 'even in extremity, with the calm and precision of a gifted family doctor'. This chimes with the way in which Carter sometimes spoke of his chamber music in terms of domestic scenes, the players participants in a conversation. He certainly saw his string quartets in this way, comparing them to the ensembles in Mozart's operas, where a number of characters will sing simultaneously, while expressing different points of view and exposing their individual personalities. There's something of this instrumental role-play in *A Mirror on Which to Dwell*, which, in addition to a soprano voice, is scored for a little chamber orchestra of nine instruments, and it is hard not to feel that Carter is using Bishop's poetry to make sense of his typical musical concerns, verbal explanations for the way his music behaves.

In 'O Breath', the last of the six Bishop poems in the cycle, the poet is in bed with her sleeping lover. The ensemble uses mellow instruments in low lying ranges – the flautist plays an alto flute, the oboist a cor anglais, the clarinettist a bass clarinet; the violin barely gets out of its first octave and the other strings play in a similar range. Texturally, they form a bed of sound beneath the singer.

The rhythmic structure of the ensemble music is detailed and complex. The players execute a three-part polyrhythm the component parts of which begin every forty-third semiquaver, every thirty-seventh quintuplet semiquaver and every sixty-fifth triplet semiquaver. You are not meant to discern this – no one could discern it with their ears, because it is too complex and also too slow – but you *are* aware of a semi-regular rising and falling of gentle chords. So a technique that is pure Carter, and which might form part of any of his musical structures, here gains a rationale from the text, which describes someone sleeping. The words have explained the music.

The first words we hear are not from the body of Bishop's poem, but are her title, 'O Breath', sung melismatically, over and over. It's a gentle outpouring of notes akin to the call of a songbird, which the composer instructs the singer to perform 'as if out of breath'. In the context of the whole cycle, the melismas are a noteworthy moment. In these songs, as in all his late vocal music, Carter's vocal writing tended to be syllabic – one note per syllable – but here there are as many as ten. Following this opening, the syllabic style returns, the words sung dispassionately, almost as though the singer herself is falling asleep.

Bishop's text is regretful. As she watches the rising and falling of the 'celebrated breast' of her sleeping lover, the poet realises her own separateness.

> Equivocal, but what we have in common's   bound to be there,
> whatever we must own   equivalents for,
> something that maybe I   could bargain with
> and make a separate peace   beneath
> within   if never with.

The poems that Carter chose are more or less autobiographical – all Bishop's poems were – and in 'O Breath' the poet seems to be especially aware of being a poet. Those caesuras – those midline breaks – belong to Bishop's great poet-predecessor Emily Dickinson, and this poem was the only time Bishop used them.

Carter's cycle is itself also self-referential. He makes use of a solo oboe (the composer's own instrument) in the earlier song 'Sandpiper' – the bird in question is a metaphor for Bishop – and, like the poet, he doffs his cap to an illustrious composer of the recent past: surely that's Charles Ives's marching band in the fifth song, 'View of the Capitol from the Library of Congress'! But in all these songs, Carter seems to be saying, via Bishop: these are some of the things my music is *about*.

In 'O Breath' the relationship between the poet/singer and her sleeping lover is characterised by pitch. Or, to put it perhaps more correctly, one of Carter's typical pitch devices is explained by the poem. In the instrumental role-play of his chamber music – and even in big works such as the Concerto for Orchestra – Carter frequently allocated different intervals to different players or sections of an orchestra. It was a way of emphasising their individuality within the complex whole. In 'O Breath', the chamber orchestra is restricted to perfect fourths and minor sevenths, while the soprano voice never sings those intervals, but takes up all the others – so while the two might strike a musical 'bargain', 'a separate peace', they remain 'never with' each other. And by the time the last word of the song – of the whole cycle – comes around, the orchestra has already finished, the singer left as alone as the poet feels in that bed.

Elizabeth Bishop disliked what Carter did to her words, writing to a friend that she hoped, at least, there might be some good publicity in it. But she was hardly the first writer to object to a composer's music. A.E. Housman had loathed *On Wenlock Edge*, Vaughan Williams's song cycle to poems from *A Shropshire Lad* (he seems to have disliked all musical settings of his words); and Henrik Ibsen was unhappy with Grieg's music for *Peer Gynt*. When, on the strength of his famous score, Grieg's name was proposed to the playwright for another project, Ibsen is said to have scoffed: 'You thought that was good, did you?'

A composer asks a poet's permission to use her words. After that, the matter is out of the poet's hands. Of course, like the poet in 'O Breath', the poem itself continues to have a separate existence on the page, and even within the song, the words 'beneath // within / if never' *quite* 'with' the music.

57

O viridissima virga

music and words by Hildegard of Bingen

WHAT MUST IT HAVE SOUNDED LIKE? Were they good singers, those nuns? How many of them were there? Was there a sounding drone, above and around which Hildegard's melodious chant rose and curled? Did the nuns' song fill the echoey chapel?

Hildegard of Bingen (1098–1179) was a Benedictine abbess, born in the Rhineland. She lived a long life, during which she founded monasteries at Rupertsberg in 1150 and Eibingen fifteen years later. She was a mystic and a visionary, a theologian, a natural scientist with a particular interest in medicine, and a composer. It is not always possible to disentangle these activities. Her visions, for example, contained ideas about nature that are reflected in her pioneering work in natural science, her theological writings and her compositions. *O viridissima virga* is a good example of this.

Veneration of the Virgin Mary began early in the history of Christianity and received recognition at the Council of Ephesus in the fifth century, where the Virgin was for the first time officially named the Mother of God. During the early Middle Ages her popularity grew exponentially throughout Western Europe, sometimes to the point of cultishness. The Blessed Virgin – 'Our Lady' – was represented in paintings and statuary, poetry and music – Marian hymns, such as *Ave maris stella*, *Salve Regina* and *Alma Redemptoris Mater*, date from this time. In 1160, construction began on the great cathedral of Notre-Dame de Paris – 'Our Lady of Paris'.

The Benedictines had been early adopters of Marian devotion, so it isn't surprising that Hildegard's nuns at Rupertsberg and Eibingen should have venerated the Blessed Virgin, especially since they were themselves led by such a strong and brilliant woman. Many of Hildegard's hymns and songs are dedicated to Mary, often employing imagery that might startle us today.

In *Ave, generosa*, for example, the nuns sang of God's pleasure as he impregnated the Virgin, holding her in his grip (*amplexione*) and implanting in her the heat (*calor*) of his love. Hardly less remarkable is *O viridissima virga*, which progresses from the association of the words *virgo* (virgin) and *virga* (branch or twig), and is an example of what Hildegard called *viriditas*. In English the word means greenness, and Hildegard used it in a sense that has a distinctly modern ring to it.

Hildegard believed that the natural world, created by God, was also a depiction of his grace, and that the quality of *viriditas* was therefore sacred: 'O viridissima virga ave,' her hymn begins: 'O hail to the greenest branch.' But there was another aspect to the imagery in her hymn, both ancient and specific. In the Book of Isaiah in the Old Testament, we read the prophecy of Christ's birth: 'And there shall come forth a rod out of the stem of Jesse, and a Branch shall grow out of his roots.'

The Tree of Jesse was a common image in medieval art, purportedly showing, in the manner of a family tree, Christ's ancestors going back to King David and his father, Jesse. So Hildegard's 'greenest branch' – Mary, 'Our Lady', the mother of Jesus, the Mother of God – grows not only from nature, but also from this mythological tree, and from this branch comes Jesus.

> Nam in te floruit
>
> pulcher flos qui odorem dedit
>
> omnibus aromatibus que arida erant.
>
> Et illa apparuerunt omnia in viriditate plena.

'For the beautiful flower [Jesus] grew out of you, giving all dried up perfumes back their scent. And these things have reappeared in full greenness.'

And this is how Hildegard's music sounds. It is an unstoppable outpouring of song that belies its narrow range of a single octave (a fifth above and a fourth below the tonic/drone) with constant movement. The melodic line proliferates like the spreading greenness of *viriditas* itself, and the last word of the stanza, *plena* (full), has the longest and widest melisma (the fullest of notes) in the whole song. Now nature's womb brings forth corn; the birds of the air build their nests on her.

Deinde facta est esca hominibus
et gaudium magnum epulantium.
Unde, o suavis Virgo, in te non deficit ullum gaudium.

'Then the harvest was gathered for humankind, and a great joy was among those who feasted, such as the sweet virgin herself never lacked.' So it's a song of joy, a hymn of praise to Mary in all her virginal fecundity, in all her greenness. But there's a twist. There's one last tree to be recalled – the tree of knowledge of good and evil – and in the poem's penultimate line, we are reminded that, in the Garden of Eden, Eve rejected greenness: 'Hec omnia Eva contempsit'.

Nothing, however, can derail the purpose of this song. While Hildegard's melodic line grew more elaborate for nature's bounty and Mary's greenness and joy, there is no equivalent word painting, no narrowing of the range or shortening of the phrase for Eve's contempt. The melody simply flows through this moment into the final line of the song: 'Nunc autem laus sit Altissimo' – 'Now let there be praise to the Highest!'

58

The Holly and the Ivy

music and words: Anon.

WHATEVER THE BUMPER STICKERS may say, Jesus is not 'the reason for the season'.

Jesus was an interloper, a gatecrasher at a party that had been in full swing for centuries. Each December, when days were at their shortest and the sun farthest away, the Ancient Romans celebrated Saturnalia in honour of their sun god, Saturn. Early Christians very sensibly co-opted these festivities. When 25 December was adopted as the birthday of Jesus, it was already the solstice in the Roman calendar.

In northern Europe, the midwinter celebration was called Yule, and it still is – 'jul' in Swedish, Danish and Norwegian, 'joulu' in Finnish. The twelve days of Yule were a festival of light around the solstice. Songs were sung, food and drink consumed and presents exchanged, as the Nordic people cheered themselves up in the cold and the dark. Today, the northern European Christmas has retained much of the attendant pagan symbolism of Yule, including the use of evergreens for decoration. In the British Isles, holly and ivy are especially common. The prickly holly and soft ivy are representations of the male and female, and in the earliest versions of the famous carol – which fail even to mention Mary or 'sweet Jesus Christ' – the two plants vie for dominance, with holly winning the day.

Holly hath birds a fair full flock,
The nightingale, the popinjay, the gentle laverock.
Nay, ivy, nay, it shall not be I wis;
Let holly have the mastery, as the manner is.

Good ivy, what birds hast thou?
None but the owlet that cries how, how.
Nay, ivy, nay, it shall not be I wis;
Let holly have the mastery, as the manner is.

In the more familiar version of the carol, the power struggle is over before it's begun:

The holly and the ivy,
When they are both full grown,
Of all the trees that are in the wood,
The holly bears the crown.

In fact this is the only mention of ivy in the entire song, the remainder of the lyric concerning itself with the dominant holly and its grafted-on Christian imagery.

The grafting is certainly successful, the holly bush yielding one Christian symbol after another. Its blossom is 'as white as the lily flower', its berry 'as red as any blood', its prickle 'as sharp as any thorn' and its bark 'as bitter as any gall'. Here is the life of Christ in four images: the pure child of the Nativity, the Crucifixion, the crown of thorns, and the drink of vinegar and gall proffered and refused at Golgotha. And if this seems a dark set of images for Christmas, it's not out of place in a story where wise men deliver myrrh to the manger, an aromatic blend of resin and oil used to anoint the dead. Baby Jesus, we are being reminded, is born so he may die for our sins.

As sung, of course, 'The Holly and the Ivy' is anything but dark. It has a bright, diatonic tune in a dancing triple metre, and if that seems at odds with the imagery of the words, there is a reason. Both the words and tune of 'The Holly and the Ivy' are traditional, but they fit each other so poorly they can only have had independent origins: 'The holly and THE ivy' places the phrase's highest note on a word of no importance; 'And Mary bore sweet Jesus Christ to be our sweet sa–VIOUR' and 'for TO redeem us all'. The marriage of poem and melody is forced.

But it's a good tune – and a memorable one, or it wouldn't have retained its popularity. The opening phrase rises to a piquant major sixth from the tonic, falling back to the fifth and then the third, so completing the major triad. Simplicity itself. The next line repeats the phrase, except this time there's no third, the triad incomplete. The third line makes up for this, descending stepwise ('Of all the trees') from the fifth to the tonic, rising to the third once more, then dropping down below the tonic, to the sixth and then the fifth below ('that are in the wood'). The fourth line completes the tune with a run from the tonic up to the fourth and back again. It's a lovely, generous melody, yet it employs just six notes, from the tonic up to the sixth – eight notes, if you count twice the sixth and fifth notes sounding in two different octaves. This simple tune is used for both the verses and the chorus, variety coming from the changing rhythm brought about by trying to cram all those words into a foreign metre: 'The playing of the merry organ / Sweet singing in the choir'.

In this carol, indeed, the only lines that seem to fit the tune are the two that start the chorus, and you wonder whether they have survived from whatever song was originally sung to the tune, because they have nothing very obvious to do with Christmas or Christianity. On the contrary, they wear their paganism proudly.

> Oh the rising of the sun,
> And the running of the deer.

59

Take My Hand, Precious Lord

music: Anon. (adapted by Thomas A. Dorsey)
words by Thomas A. Dorsey

THOMAS A. DORSEY (1899–1993) WAS the W.C. Handy of gospel music. He didn't invent it any more than Handy invented the blues, but he helped to codify, package and sell it. And he created some of its lasting standards. 'Take My Hand, Precious Lord' is Dorsey's 'St Louis Blues'.

'Precious Lord, take my hand, / Lead me on, let me stand. / I am tired, I am weak, I am worn.' This consoling song is so central to gospel music – sung at various times by Sister Rosetta Tharp and the Blind Boys of Alabama, Mahalia Jackson and Aretha Franklin, B.B. King, Elvis Presley and Lawrence Welk – that it can seem as though it's a spiritual, part of an oral tradition. But Dorsey was nothing if not professional.

Here's another sample of his work: 'I wear my britches up above my knees, / Strut my jelly with who I please.' The lines come from 'It's Tight Like That', which Dorsey recorded with blues guitarist Tampa Red in 1928 under the pseudonym Georgia Tom (he seems to have had a dozen such alter egos). It's a catchy ragtime number and it sold a million.

A darker side of Georgia Tom emerges in 'If You Want Me to Love You', where the singer makes a list of demands to his woman, of which this is the last: 'Take a butcher knife, cut off your head, / Send me a telegram that your heart is dead.'

It was a telegram that inspired 'Take My Hand, Precious Lord'. In 1932 in Chicago, Dorsey's wife Nettie Harper died in childbirth while he was on stage in St Louis, their baby son dying the following day. Dorsey buried them in the same coffin and went home to write 'Precious Lord'. It is an agonising story and one the songwriter himself often told in old age, speaking of the words to the song coming to him 'like drops of water from a crevice of a rock above'.

The story would be even better had Dorsey, at this very moment, seen the light and abandoned the blues, but this was no road to Damascus. Alongside the blues, Dorsey had been writing and singing gospel songs since the mid-1920s, and by the time of 'Precious Lord' he was already director of music in a couple of Baptist churches. His St Louis gig had been a revivalist meeting. Moreover, the success of this song now led him to establish his own publishing company, the Dorsey House of Music. He knew the business: earlier in his career, he had been an arranger for the Chicago Music Publishing company and a talent scout for Vocalion Records.

What Dorsey achieved in 'Precious Lord', however, and in other songs such as 'Peace in the Valley', is a personalisation of musical worship, in the Pentecostal tradition. It's why he's sometimes called the father of gospel music. His inspiration, no doubt, was the old spirituals, but where those songs had tended to speak on behalf of a whole people – even when employing the first-person singular – Dorsey's songs are about a one-to-one relationship between the singer and his or her 'precious Lord'.

While the words of 'Take My Hand, Precious Lord' might have dropped on Dorsey from above, the tune already existed, though it's hard to say where it came from. It seems like an old hymn tune – indeed, it resembles more than one. So, in terms of originality, it is hardly inspired, yet in its very ordinariness it gets the job done, a musical conveyor of Dorsey's words. Moreover, the simplicity of the tune has provided a springboard for any number of musical elaborations, some of them elaborate indeed. To hear Aretha Franklin sing it at the memorial service for Martin Luther King Jr – 'sing' is such a poor word for what she does; she is *possessed* by the song – is to leave the tune a long way behind, lost in a cloud of vocal roulades and ululations, cries of anguish and shouts of hope.

'Precious Lord' had been King's favourite. It was sung at Mason Temple in Memphis, Tennessee, on the eve of his assassination, the night of one of his most famous speeches. 'I've been to the mountain top,' King told his congregation, as though the promise of the song had been fulfilled. 'Mine eyes have seen the glory of the coming of the Lord.' According to Jesse Jackson, who was on the motel balcony the following evening when King was shot, the civil rights leader's last words were about the song. They were addressed

to band leader, Ben Branch, who was due to perform at an event that night –
an event King was meant to attend. 'Ben,' he said, 'make sure you play "Take
My Hand, Precious Lord" in the meeting tonight. Play it real pretty.'

60

Hallelujah

music and words by Leonard Cohen

LEONARD COHEN'S 'HALLELUJAH' is a song about a powerful sexual obsession, ennobled by Old Testament references to King David and Bath-sheba, and Samson and Delilah. But it's also more than that. It must be, or why would it have been sung – complete with its references to being tied to a kitchen chair – by a large chorus at the memorial service for the victims of the 2009 Black Saturday bushfires in Victoria?

Though the song is now ubiquitous, it was what they call a 'sleeper'. Its first appearance, on Leonard Cohen's album *Various Positions*, came at the end of 1984 and went practically unnoticed except by Bob Dylan, who performed it at concerts four years later. John Cale recorded the song for his tribute to Cohen, *I'm Your Fan*, in 1991. Then Jeff Buckley included it on *Grace* in 1994. Still, it was only after Buckley's death in 1997 and then the use of Cale's version in the film *Shrek* (2001) that 'Hallelujah' became ubiquitous. The *Shrek* soundtrack album, with Rufus Wainwright now singing the song, sold millions, k.d. lang included 'Hallelujah' on her all-Canadian album *Hymns of the 49th Parallel* (2004) and there was no looking back. The song kept turning up in movies and TV series (generally to underline moments of sadness), TV talent-show contestants sang the song (to demonstrate sincerity) and it was used to sell everything from the Church of Jesus Christ of Latter-day Saints (minus its words) to neo-Nazism (with completely new words). By the time of Cohen's death in 2016, 'Hallelujah' was his most famous song, a song that, like Parry's 'Jerusalem', could mean virtually anything to virtually anyone (though nearly always something important).

Part of the song's ubiquity is to do with the variety of its lyrics. Long before political extremists began bending it to their needs, there were hardly two recordings of 'Hallelujah' that included the same verses. Cohen is said to have written as many as eighty verses for the song over a period of five years, though on *Various Positions* he only sang four of them. These are the ones beginning 'I've heard there was a secret chord', 'Your faith was strong but you needed proof', 'You say I took the Name in vain', and 'I did my best; it wasn't much'. We might call this the 'official' version of the song, and in Cohen's published selection of poems and song lyrics, *Stranger Music*, these are the four verses that appear. But they are followed in the book by three 'additional verses', beginning 'Baby I've been here before', 'There was a time you let me know' and 'Now maybe there's a God above'.

For his studio recording, Cale sang the first two verses from Cohen's official version (in fact everyone seems to sing these), then the three 'additional' verses, and since it was *Shrek* and Cale's recording that really made 'Hallelujah' famous, these additional verses have become rather better known than the last two official ones. Buckley and Wainwright both recorded the same verses as Cale, and so did lang, although she omitted the middle additional verse. In his later performances of 'Hallelujah', sung on tour in the years before his death, Cohen always sang the four official verses, but often supplemented them with 'Maybe I've been here before' and 'There was a time'. The lyrical fluidity of the song tends to militate against saying precisely what it is about, except that it is clearly about sexual desire and some of its consequences.

The 'secret chord that David played' is presumably a reference to the young shepherd psalmist in the first Book of Samuel, soothing King Saul of Israel with his harp playing. But who is the 'baffled king composing Hallelujah'? Not Saul – he isn't the composer. Is he merely composing the word, or have we jumped ahead in the story to the point where David has become king?

It is certainly King David, in verse two, ogling the naked Bathsheba, but already the song's point of view has shifted. We're in the second person ('You saw her bathing on the roof', 'She tied you to a kitchen chair'). This can't be the same 'you' mentioned in the first verse, because we know that David does 'care for music'.

There's more confusion to come. In the second Book of Samuel, it was King David who had all the power, forcing himself on Bathsheba, but in

Cohen's song she's the one in charge. She's cutting the king's hair ('your hair') and emasculating him in the process (breaking 'your throne'), rather as Delilah did to Samson in the Book of Judges. She also draws 'from your lips … the Hallelujah'. So what is this? A BDSM safeword? An exclamation of sexual ecstasy? Is he – are you, are we – taking pleasure in this moment? In the additional verse that begins 'There was a time', a verse that is explicitly sexual, the word 'Hallelujah' is orgasmic: 'I remember when I moved in you / And the holy dove was moving too / And every breath we drew was Hallelujah!'

Those who decided to have it performed at the Victorian bushfire memorial service must have known what they thought it meant, and it was surely little of the above. So does 'Hallelujah' have a broader meaning?

The words offer a mixture of ancient and modern, formal and informal – sometimes combining them humorously, which is surely part of the attraction. This is best demonstrated by the rhymes Cohen finds for his title and one-word chorus. The word 'Hallelujah' is derived from two Hebrew words which, taken together, mean 'Praise God' ('Yah'). The song rhymes 'Hallelujah' with 'do ya', 'overthrew ya', 'to ya' and, less satisfactorily, 'fool ya'. So it's a kind of joke – the high-flown Hebrew contrasted with colloquial English – though for some reason Rufus Wainwright insists on singing 'you', in the process destroying both the rhymes and the joke.

But surely it's the music that explains the song's exponential appeal. After all, the lyrics of the first verse are about the power of music. They even describe it from a technical point of view.

'It goes like this', the song explains, offering a real-time analysis of the chord structure: 'the fourth, the fifth / The minor fall, the major lift'. The song is in C major and as Cohen names the chords we hear them: 'the fourth' (F major – chord IV), 'the fifth' (G major – chord V), the minor fall ('A minor'), 'the major lift' (F major). Whether we really hear a lift with F major is a moot point. The word 'lift' is there not so much for musicological reasons, but because it (almost) rhymes with 'fifth'. We're meant to think of minor keys as dark and major keys as bright, whatever the evidence of our ears. (In another song that describes its own harmonic structure – Cole Porter's 'Every Time We Say Goodbye' – the 'strange … change from major to minor' is more a 'lift' than a 'fall'.)

But what of 'Hallelujah' – the word and the chorus? Cohen's words in the little-sung third official verse tell us there is 'a blaze of light' in the word, whether it's 'the holy or the broken Hallelujah'. The music of the chorus reflects this, repeating the word as the harmony rocks back and forth consolingly between F major (IV) and A minor (the relative of the tonic C major). More lifting and falling? It's impossible to say.

Inscrutability seemed written across the faces of the religious and political leaders ('baffled' kings?) sitting in the front row of the large audience at Rod Laver Arena at the bushfire memorial, as the Melbourne Symphony Orchestra and a choir of 500 voices performed their secular 'Hallelujah'. Was this 'a holy or a broken Hallelujah'? Surely it was broken in the circumstances – 173 people dead and 400 more injured – but maybe it was holy, too. 'Maybe there's a God above' goes a verse that wasn't sung that day (the choir stuck to Cohen's 'official' version). Yes, and maybe there isn't. As with everything else about this song, it's hard to be sure. And perhaps that's the key to 'Hallelujah' for listeners in the early twenty-first century. The lyrics raise unanswerable questions – it is increasingly hard to be sure about anything – while the music comforts us. Doubt wrapped in consolation.

61

Music for a While

music by Henry Purcell
words by John Dryden

Music for a while
Shall all your cares beguile

PURCELL'S 'MUSIC FOR A WHILE' is a song that goes nowhere. It is the sonic balm the song itself promises: we listen – for a while – and our cares are beguiled. Yet what might induce in us feelings of relaxation was intended to have a dramatic function at the key point in a gory drama.

In 1660, a little over eleven years after his father, Charles I, was publicly beheaded on a specially built scaffold in Whitehall, Charles II ascended to the British throne. Oliver Cromwell's commonwealth was at an end and the monarchy restored. It is often believed that music and theatre were banned during the Interregnum, but in fact Cromwell was fond of music. If he could find a musical rationale for it, he was happy to allow theatrical performances at Hampton Court, where he lived as Lord Protector. There is evidence that on at least one occasion, Cromwell himself took part in such a pageant.

But this was behind closed doors. In London, the theatres were indeed shut down, so that when they opened again with the Restoration, there was a great flourishing of new plays, many of them comedic romps that poked fun at contemporary politics, but just as many violent, bloody tragedies.

The composer Henry Purcell (1659–1695) wrote a lot of incidental music for the London stage. Among his greatest songs was 'Music for a While', penned for a version of Sophocles' *Oedipus Rex* by the poet John Dryden and the playwright Nathaniel Lee. 'Music for a While' is sung in Act 3 by one of the priests who, together with the blind seer Tiresias, is attempting to conjure the ghost of King Laius so as to discover the identity of his murderer. That would, of course, be his son Oedipus. This is the whole poem:

> Music for a while
> Shall all your cares beguile:
> Wond'ring how your pains were eas'd
> And disdaining to be pleas'd
> Till Alecto free the dead
> From their eternal bands,
> Till the snakes drop from her head,
> And the whip from out her hands.

Alecto was a Fury, the spirit charged with inflicting punishment on those who kill their parents, and like Medusa, she had snakes for hair.

Purcell's setting of Dryden's words employs a ground bass – a bass line that repeats, while the melody above it changes and develops. Purcell used these basses in all manner of compositions, most famously in Dido's lament, 'When I Am Laid in Earth' from the opera *Dido and Aeneas*. There is in-built potential for the creation and resolution of harmonic tension when one element of a piece of music is fixed and repeating, while others are freely proliferating above or around it. In 'Music for a While', the ground bass is long and elaborate. It served a double function in the play, because in addition to providing the structural template of the song, it illustrated, in the purely instrumental introduction, the slow rising up of the dead king.

Not only was Purcell a musical dramatist, he was also a master word-setter. Listen only to how he sets the first word of this song, 'Music'. One of Purcell's greatest twentieth-century admirers, the composer Michael Tippett, pointed out the way in which the trochee (a strong syllable followed by a weak) is exaggerated in Purcell's setting. To begin, 'Mu–' is a dotted crotchet (a quarter note plus an eighth) on the beat, while '–sic' is a quaver (eighth note) off the beat. Then the composer goes one better. A fifth higher, he repeats the word, lengthening the first syllable – now it's a minim (half note) tied to a quaver, but leaving the '–sic' as an off-beat quaver. It might be slower in Purcell's song, but from a rhythmic point of view, this is how English is spoken.

Tippett compared Purcell's setting of the English language with Handel's. The German-born Handel didn't always get it right. In *Messiah*, for example, when he sets the words 'He shall feed his flock like a shepherd', Handel stresses 'shall', where Purcell would have stressed 'he' and 'feed'; Handel also places the second syllable of 'shepherd' (another trochee) on a strong beat, something the Londoner Purcell would never have done.

This is not to say that Purcell's word-setting is just like speech: it isn't. He paints words with the best of them. The first syllable of 'Wond'ring', for example, is given a melisma, as the word becomes momentarily lost in its own train of thought ('–ring', like '–sic', is a short offbeat tacked on to the end), and 'eas'd' is allocated easeful falling figures, first a semitone, then a tone, like a sigh.

And there are the snakes. Did any snakes before or since drop so unceremoniously to the floor, one after the other? It is a lovely moment because it is the antithesis of drama – these snakes seem to be dropping because they've fallen asleep or died. 'Drop' as in drop dead. But each 'drop' also seems to indicate the passing of time, like the steady ticking of a clock, so the snakes do double duty.

And then we're back where we started. The ground bass, from which, unusually, Purcell briefly departs in the song, is once more in its groove, the opening line returns (Purcell's idea, not Dryden's), and our cares – all of them – are again beguiled.

62

Night and Day

music and words by Cole Porter

AS SUNG BY FRED ASTAIRE, who introduced the song in the 1932 Broadway musical *Gay Divorce*, 'Night and Day' starts on a B flat: 'Like the beat beat beat of the tom-tom / When the jungle shadows fall / Like the tick tick tock of a stately clock / As it stands against the wall'. Four lines and thirty-three B flats later, he's still on that same note. This is minimalist, you might say literal word-painting: tom-toms and clocks don't change pitch.

In the verse's second stanza, he moves up a step to B natural on 'drip': 'Like the drip, drip, drip of the raindrops'. Then up another step to C on 'summer': 'When the summer shower is through'. Then he drops back via B natural to B flat again on 'voice': 'So a voice within me keeps repeating / You, you, you'. And with those repetitions of 'You', slow and insistent, one to a bar, the rhythm steadies and the chorus finally arrives, along with the song's title.

'Night and Day ...' Almost unbelievably, he continues to sing the B flat! It's only with the following line that the melody begins to unfold.

Porter's lyric describes an obsession. Guy Holden, Astaire's character in *Gay Divorce*, is besotted with Mimi Glossop and thinks about her 'night and day'. The 'longing' is with him not only in 'the roaring traffic's boom' but also 'the silence of [his] lonely room'. Porter wrote a number of songs about obsessive desire, including 'So in Love' and 'I've Got You Under My Skin', and 'Night and Day' gives the imagery of the latter a trial run: 'Night and Day / Under the hide of me, / There's an oh such a hungry / Yearning burning inside of me.'

Just as the verse's persistent B flat mirrored the sound of the drum and the clock, now it plays a vital role in the chorus. 'Night and Day' is in the key of E flat, so B flat is the fifth note of the scale, the dominant. It certainly dominates the melody of 'Night and Day'. The singer can't leave it alone.

As the tune drops away chromatically from the B flat, we may think we're going somewhere new, but the words tell us the truth: 'Whether near to me or far, / It's no matter, darling, where you are: / I think of you / Night and day.' Down the melodic line goes, step by step, all the way to the B flat an octave below ('I think of *you*'), only to bounce back up to the original B flat on 'Night and Day'.

The manner in which the melody of 'Night and Day' creeps around is typical Porter, whose songs are full of scalic lines. These contribute to a general perception of his music. Porter wrote major-key songs, but it's surprising how many of them seem to be in minor keys. The 'tragic major' is something Porter had in common with Schubert in his later music.

'Night and Day' is a good example. At the opening of the chorus, the third of those repeated B flats – the one on 'day' – sits on top of a chord of C flat major, the melodic B flat turning the chord into a seventh. It's a wonderfully strange and chromatic chord, the G flat hinting that the song is in E flat minor. None of this would matter very much, but it is harmonic ambiguities such as this that make Porter's songs so recognisable.

Structurally, the song is an oddity. Instead of the thirty-two bars that were fairly common among popular songs in the 1930s, 'Night and Day' has forty-eight, a structure we might label ABABCB – that's sixteen bars (AB), repeated with different words (the next AB), then varied (CB). In the C section, that G flat is reinforced because the music jumps, suddenly and memorably, to a chord of G flat major (this is at 'Night and day / Under the hide of me').

The final eight bars provide a further twist and the song's melodic climax. The lyrical payoff is Guy's declaration that his 'torment' will only be ended by Mimi's allowing him to make love to her for the rest of his life, an alarming prospect that was only slightly less alarming in 1932 when 'making love' meant sending flowers and holding hands. On the words 'this torment won't be through', Astaire begins the chromatic descent we've already heard twice in the earlier B sections, but this time he doesn't make it all the way down to the low B flat.

The line 'Till you let me spend my life making love to you' gets as far as E flat, but on the word 'making' arrests its descent, mid-phrase, to jump back up the octave and place 'love' on the high D. Then the line completes its journey down to B flat (on 'Day and night'), but it's the *original* B flat, which is now a springboard to E flat ('Night and day'), the song's highest note, its last and its tonic.

Gay Divorce was Astaire's final appearance in a Broadway musical, but two years later he starred in the RKO film *The Gay Divorcee* with Ginger Rogers. The Hays office, Hollywood's self-imposed moral enforcer, took the view that divorce should never be 'gay', and so insisted on the name change. Perhaps they heard in the new title an echo of *The Merry Widow*. It wasn't the only change the movie made to the stage show. All of Porter's songs were now gone, with the exception of 'Night and Day', because, by then, Astaire's recording with Leo Reisman's Orchestra was one of the decade's greatest hits.

63

Do Not Go Gentle into that Good Night

music by Andrea Keller
words by Dylan Thomas

MOST MUSICAL SETTINGS OF POETRY take into account the music already extant in the words, but in putting Dylan Thomas's famous poem to music, Andrea Keller (b. 1973) went further. Her starting point for turning his words into her song was to listen to a recording of the poet himself reading them.

'Do not go gentle into that good night' is a villanelle – the best-known villanelle in the English language – and any composer making a setting of it will have to decide what to do with its structure.

> Do not go gentle into that good night,
> Old age should burn and rave at close of day;
> Rage, rage against the dying of the light.

The first tercet (three-line stanza) of a villanelle is its key. The first and third lines, which must rhyme, function as alternating refrains as the final lines of the next four tercets. So, the poem's first line, turns up as the third line of the second stanza, and notice that the function of 'Do' is changed from the original imperative ('Do not go gentle') to the simple present tense ('they / Do not go gentle'):

> Though wise men at their end know dark is right,
> Because their words had forked no lightning they
> Do not go gentle into that good night.

The third stanza concludes with the poem's third line:

> Good men, the last wave by, crying how bright
> Their frail deeds might have danced in a green bay,
> Rage, rage against the dying of the light.

And so on with the next two stanzas, until the poem's final verse, which has four lines, the last two of which are our refrain lines placed next to each other for the first and only time:

> Do not go gentle into that good night.
> Rage, rage against the dying of the light.

When Thomas died in 1953, he was discussing ideas for a new opera with Igor Stravinsky, following the success of the composer's collaboration with W.H. Auden and Chester Kallman on *The Rake's Progress*. But following the poet's sudden death, Stravinsky set out to memorialise him in a setting of 'Do not go gentle' for tenor and string quartet, framed by wordless 'dirge canons' for the quartet with four trombones: *In memoriam Dylan Thomas*.

Stravinsky's lapidary setting of the poem makes its structure clear. The composer was becoming fascinated by the twelve-tone method of Arnold Schoenberg, and even more with that of Anton Webern, and there's much evidence of the technique – and Webern's aesthetic – in this piece, especially in the canons. But Stravinsky's regard for Thomas's structure appears to have held him back from following the Viennese composers' serial path to the bitter end, because the melodic line he created for that first tercet functions in precisely the same way the lines themselves function: 'Do not go gentle into that good night' and 'Rage, rage against the dying of the night' are always sung to the same notes.

In general Keller's approach is far freer, but her starting point – a transcription of both the rhythm and pitches of the poet's sing-songy reading – provided her with a vocal line that required little alteration. If you listen to Keller's setting and Thomas's reading in alternation, eventually the poet seems to be singing Keller's song. The one thing Keller added to the vocal line was the creation of a conventional refrain, so that each time, 'Rage, rage against the dying of the light' is sung – at the end of the first, third and fifth tercets – it is heard twice, and after the first tercet, the singer is joined by a backing vocalist. Finally, at the end of the song, the two lines are sung a total of four times, creating a chorus proper.

Keller is a jazz pianist and her song is part of a cycle about death and grief called *Still Night* (2016) that brings together poetry by Thomas, Keats, Yeats, Proust, Sara Teasdale and E.E. Cummings, the eleventh-century Japanese poet Izumi Shikibu and the contemporary Australian Richard James Allen. On the whole, the mood of the work is more accepting than despairing and in places there's an understated ecstasy. The Thomas setting is a good example.

Though Keller retains the poet's pitch and rhythm, the orotund tone of his voice is gone, his stagey reading replaced on the commercial recording by the infinitely more laid-back singing of Vince Jones, with Gian Slater in the refrains (the cycle as a whole is for two singers, each taking turns to sing lead and backing vocals). The effect is almost to domesticate the poem, to strip it of its portentousness and bring it within the experience of the listener. The father in Keller's song seems not so much 'there on the sad height' but at home in bed, and by the end of her song, the raging over, the final lines repeat consolingly.

64

Took the Children Away

music and words by Archie Roach

This story's right, this story's true.

ONCE YOU KNOW THE SONG and how it continues, that opening line is always heartbreaking. 'Took the Children Away' is said to be the first song Archie Roach ever wrote, and it remains his best known.

The principal melody is quite basic. It spans the first five notes of G major – G to D, with just a couple of reinforcing dips down to the E below and a single, expressive step up to the E above (the sixth note of the scale). The chords are equally simple: G major, C major and D major – that's I, IV and V. You could throw in a couple of D7s if you wanted to be fancy.

The song is like a child's picture book, and that's how it was meant to be. Roach was explaining, as simply and directly as possible, the forced removal of generations of Australian Aboriginal children from their parents and their placement with white foster families. If it sounds, at moments, as though he is addressing slow or reluctant learners, that's because he was.

Roach (b. 1956) wrote the song in 1988 and sang it on community radio stations in Melbourne. It came to the attention of the singer-songwriter Paul Kelly, who asked Roach to open a concert for him the following year. He sang 'Took the Children Away' to considerable acclaim from the large audience. In 1990, the song was released as a single and featured on Roach's first album, *Charcoal Lane*, which Kelly co-produced.

The simplicity of the song is reflected in its refusal to be dramatic – let alone melodramatic. The song's emotional power is in the story's slow unfolding, its occasional jump cuts and its moments of personal revelation. As we will learn in verse three, this is Roach's own story.

In 1960, the four-year-old Roach and his sisters were stolen from their parents at Framlingham Aboriginal reserve in south-western Victoria by Australian government agencies who doubtless believed, as his song says, that it was 'for the best'. He was eventually fostered by a Scottish couple in Melbourne. It was a musical household and Roach was introduced to the guitar. But at the age of fifteen, Roach was contacted by one of his natural sisters, who informed him that their birth mother had just died. Soon after, he left his foster family for a life on the street and more than a decade of alcohol abuse. During this period he met his future wife, Ruby Hunter, and with her help, got himself sober.

'Took the Children Away' opens with Roach's voice underpinned by soft organ chords, the whole thing bathed in reverb. We're in church. Roach sings that 'they' – authorities, missionaries – 'Taught us to read, to write and pray, / Then they took the children away'. It's the song's first emotional jolt. He sings the word so sweetly, but that high E on the first syllable of 'children' is a prick of pain.

Now the reverb recedes, Roach's voice comes into clearer focus, and the chorus repeats the words 'Took the children away' to just three notes – B, A, G, 'Three Blind Mice', the song more than ever now like a children's story. A picked electric guitar joins the organ in verse two, adding momentum, and we begin to learn details of these official abductions, of the parents' grief and of the humiliation and prejudice the children faced in their new white communities.

The organ and electric guitar continue in verse three, joined by bold, isolated twelve-string guitar chords. This is as dramatic as the song will get, and it draws our attention to a shift in the storytelling, because suddenly the song is about Roach himself: 'One dark day on Framingham / Came and didn't give a damn. / My mother cried: "Go, get their dad." / He came running, fighting mad'. And here is the first jump cut in the action. We're told that Roach's dad said, 'You touch my kids and you fight me', but the next line is 'Then they took us from our family'. Perhaps we don't need to hear what happened in between; perhaps it's more powerful with that ellipsis in the narrative.

'They took us away', the chorus continues, the words changed, the song now personalised. 'They took us away'. Then after a low, twangy guitar solo played by Steve Connolly (though it might almost be the work of the Shadows' Hank Marvin), the story continues in the final verse. The children ('we', 'us') are fostered, feeling 'alone' as they grow up, 'acting white / Yet feeling black', until – this time it's a giant jump cut – 'One sweet day all the children came back'.

Is this the happy ending to the children's story? In a way it is. Clearly it isn't exactly true. The children were not, for the most part, reunited with their parents; Roach certainly wasn't. But there were cultural returns, maybe spiritual returns. In many cases, the Stolen Generations at least learnt the truth and found their roots. So the song provides hope, and that's what children need at the ends of their stories. Roach once explained that when he visited schools to perform, children often asked him to play his song 'The Children Came Back'.

The hope is made palpable at the end of the song, which has an authentic coda: a whole new section, melodically unrelated to what has gone before. 'Back to their mother', Roach sings, 'Back to their father'. And each time he hits that top E, he converts pain to triumph: 'Back to their sister / Back to their brother'. At 'Back to their people / Back to their land' he sails up higher to top G, completing the octave. That sense of completion is also in the words to the final chorus, where 'The children came back' becomes 'Yes, I came back'.

The promise conveyed by Archie Roach's song had two tangible outcomes. First, the song that had always seemed to be a children's story was finally turned into a book, with illustrations by Ruby Hunter. And second, a new song, called 'The Children Came Back' appeared in 2014. Over the chorus of Roach's classic, sung by Dewayne Everettsmith, the rapper Briggs shouts out a litany of the names of successful Aboriginal Australians from music, from sport, from life, all of them children who came back.

65

Strange Fruit

music and words by Abel Meeropol

IN HER AUTOBIOGRAPHY, *Lady Sings the Blues*, Billie Holiday claimed that she wrote 'Strange Fruit'. She did not. But she certainly took it over – and in performance it took her over.

According to the journalist Dorian Lynskey, 'Strange Fruit' is 'the popular protest song's ground zero'. He points out that while such songs might have existed before it, they were best suited to chanting demonstrators and picket-line singalongs. This is debatable, but it's surely true that 'Strange Fruit' will never be a suitable vehicle for group singing. The disjunct melodic line and the necessarily slow tempo see to that, but so does the imagery in the lyrics, describing the violence meted out to African Americans by murderous white supremacists.

The song's author, in fact, was Abel Meeropol (1903–1986), a Jewish schoolteacher and Communist Party member from New York's Bronx district, who wrote under the somewhat less Semitic nom de plume Lewis Allan. And before 'Strange Fruit' was a song, it was a poem, 'Bitter Fruit', published under that pseudonym in 1937 in the magazine of the New York Teachers' Union.

Meeropol was also responsible for the tune. He didn't exactly compose it so much as cobble it together, and not terribly well. It took an arrangement of the music by the band leader at Café Society before Billie Holiday was interested in singing it, and to be honest the tune remains pretty undistinguished. Were it not for the shocking bluntness of the words, it's doubtful anyone would recall the song (just try humming it all the way through). In finding a tune for his words, Meeropol also transformed the rather obvious 'bitter fruit' into the more telling and more memorable 'strange fruit'. The phrase is not a euphemism; it is a horrifyingly exact metaphor for African American bodies: fruit bruises, fruit rots.

'Southern trees bear strange fruit / Blood on the leaves and blood at the root / Black bodies swinging in the southern breeze / Strange fruit hanging from the poplar trees'. Imagine Billie Holiday's bravery in singing that to a white audience. Eighty years after she first sang it, it remains a confronting lyric. The song directs our gaze to the hanging bodies and dares us to look away.

None of this makes the song an obvious addition to the set list of a jazz singer in a New York City club. But Café Society in Greenwich Village was no ordinary club. For one thing, the audience wasn't white – the club was integrated, unique in that at its opening in 1938. It was run by Barney Josephson, a New Jersey shoe salesman with a love of European political cabaret, helped by John Hammond, the record producer who discovered many of the club's performers. Holiday sang at the opening night in 1938, though she didn't perform 'Strange Fruit' until 1939.

Meeropol's lyrics are laced with irony. He contrasts the pastoral beauty of the former confederacy, the 'gallant south' portrayed in *Gone with the Wind* (the film of Margaret Mitchell's 1936 novel was also released in 1939), with the 'bulging eyes and twisted mouth' of the hanging bodies; the 'magnolias, sweet and fresh' are replaced in our nostrils by 'the sudden smell of burning flesh'. It's a vision of hell, and Josephson, who evidently had some theatrical flair, knew how to make the most of this 'strange and bitter crop'.

Josephson advised Holiday to sing 'Strange Fruit' at the very end of her Café Society set. The club's waiters had instructions to cease serving during the penultimate song and retreat to the back wall. When the room fell quiet, the houselights were suddenly extinguished and the singer's face was illuminated by a bare, white spot. Holiday stood stock still, her eyes shut as the band played the introduction. She opened her eyes at her first words, and then, at the song's conclusion, the spotlight was snapped out. There was no encore. What could follow 'Strange Fruit'?

Holiday's record producer at Columbia was Josephson's adviser, John Hammond. He had discovered Holiday and got her jobs singing with Benny Goodman and Teddy Wilson. Hammond was a political activist, an early supporter of civil rights, and he had connections to the Communist Party, but he was not ready to record 'Strange Fruit', fearing there would be financial implications for the label and its radio subsidiary CBS. Holiday, however, was committed to the song, so she took the Café Society Band to a small jazz label, Commodore Records, run by Milt Gabler, and recorded it for them. It was the label's biggest seller ever. Holiday's, too.

In 1956 she re-recorded the song for the album *Lady Sings the Blues*, released on Verve to coincide with the publication of her autobiography. The earlier account is more song-like; this late recording is slower and, apart from a couple of incongruous flamenco-like trumpet flourishes from Charlie Shavers, distinctly minimal. Like a harpsichordist in a baroque recitative, pianist Wynton Kelly plays a chord whenever the harmony changes, but he makes little attempt to fill out the accompaniment. The chords are only connected by the sustained notes from Aaron Bell's softly bowed bass. At the end of the song, guitarist Barney Kessel pops up for a single broken chord, and Lenny McBrowne finishes the song with a tom-tom stroke. The power of the song, as ever, is in the words and Holiday's unflinching delivery of them.

There have been numerous other versions of 'Strange Fruit'. Some, like Dee Dee Bridgewater's, have been as much tributes to Holiday as to the song; others have recast the song completely – UB40 did it as a reggae number; Siouxsie and the Banshees as a sort of folk song with a completely new tune. In 2013, the rapper and singer Kanye West sampled Nina Simone's recording in 'Blood on the Leaves', a song not about civil rights, but about Kanye and his relationship problems.

Simone's recording is almost as powerful as Holiday's second version. According to the co-founder of Atlantic Records, Ahmet Ertegun, 'Strange Fruit' was, in effect, 'the beginning of the civil rights movement', and 1965, the year of Simone's recording, was the year of the Selma to Montgomery march in support of black voter registration and of the Watts Rebellion in Los Angeles.

Even slower than Holiday's Verve recording, and accompanied only by her own piano, which is as sparing as Wynton Kelly's playing for Holiday, Simone makes every word tell and bite, and her ending is especially memorable. In fact, she sings a wrong word: instead of 'Here is a fruit … / … / For the sun to rot / For the tree to drop' she sings for the 'leaves to drop', which doesn't make sense. And she draws attention to it, with a long, slow, downward spiralling glissando on the word. No matter. It's the musical and dramatic high point in a tour de force of a performance.

66

Luka

music and words by Suzanne Vega

'LUKA' BEGINS WITH A BOUNCE, four syncopated synth-pop chords –
a sort of glassy marimba tone – leading to an acoustic guitar. But it didn't
always.

In the early 1980s, when Suzanne Vega (b. 1959) wrote and began singing the song that would become her greatest commercial success, it was
slower and more intense, befitting a work about domestic violence visited
upon a child. Luka was a real boy in an apartment block where Vega lived.
Vega didn't know him personally, and the boy was not, as far as she was
aware, mistreated. She simply borrowed his name.

'My name is Luka,' he announces through Vega, before going on to tell
us things about himself that reveal he is regularly abused. We never learn
the identity of his abuser – a parent, presumably, or an older sibling – just
that 'They only hit until you cry'.

It was Vega's manager, Rob Fierstein, who recognised the song's potential. The singer herself had doubts. Singing it in concert, she had noticed
that audiences tended to tune out. No one ever requested it. Did the subject matter make them uncomfortable or did the slow tempo and somewhat
monotonous melodic line leave them cold? Perhaps it was a combination
of the two. Either way, 'Luka' never seemed likely to be a hit. But Fierstein
insisted, Vega acquiesced and the producer, Steve Addabbo, knew what to
do next.

'Help' had also been a slow song when John Lennon first sang it to
George Martin, the tempo more in keeping with the depressed cry of the
lyrics. Martin saw that what was needed for it to join the Beatles' stream of
number one hits was a quicker tempo. As usual, Martin was correct, though
Lennon continued to bemoan the speeding up.

But Addabbo's instinct to increase the tempo of 'Luka' was not simply about making the song catchier, it also made it more real. The faster tempo brings an air of apparent insouciance to both Vega's lyric and her singing of it, and, paradoxically, adds poignancy. There's a defensiveness to Luka, as there might well be with a child who is being physically assaulted by a family member. Aided by the brightness and breeziness of the music, Luka brushes off his neighbour's concern: 'I walked into the door again'; 'It's not your business anyway'; 'Just don't ask me how I am'.

Addabbo was only responding to what was already in the song. As Vega once said, 'It's not a song about an issue; it's a song about a kid', and from the beginning she had known that a major key was required. In his apartment, Luka might be frightened some of the time, but when we meet him – when he tells us his name and that he lives upstairs – he's a chatty little boy.

There's no chorus in this song, just four verses. There's a guitar solo by Jon Gordon between the second and third verses, and a longer version of the same at the end of the song. The first three verses are each in two parts (AB), the fourth verse is extended (ABB). In fact, it's the first verse again, with the B part of verse two tacked on. The guitar solo and the final verse are particularly significant in terms of the surprisingly optimistic mood of the song.

Gordon seems to be emulating U2's guitarist the Edge, not only with his jangly tone, created by effects pedals and the use of first the high E string and then the B string as pedal points, but also in his strumming patterns and the way he frequently anticipates the beat.

Vega's vocal delivery is in character. She's the boy who would prefer not to meet your gaze, and the range of her melodic expression is appropriately narrow – chatty but downcast. At the beginning of verse four (the repeat of verse one), this is especially apparent. But then comes that extra half verse, the B section of verse two and perhaps the song's most arresting words: 'They only hit until you cry / After that, you don't ask why.'

The song is in the key of F sharp major, and the first time we heard that line, the melodic line to the words '[After] that you don't ask why' dropped through a minor seventh, from G sharp to A sharp before curling back up to place 'why' on B – the subdominant. But on this final appearance – the very end of the song – the line only descends as far as C sharp, climbing back up (on 'ask why') to E sharp and F sharp – the leading note and the tonic. It's a small moment, perhaps, but in a song that is all about reading between the lines, it's a moment of hope and even imminent triumph. Whatever is happening to Luka at home shouldn't be happening. He is being hurt until he cries. But that little upturn at the end of the song – whatever the words may say – reassures us that he will survive. Those two melodic notes – E sharp and F sharp – make the song bearable.

67

Last Kind Words Blues

music and words by Geeshie Wiley

WE DON'T KNOW VERY MUCH about Geeshie Wiley and, until recently, we knew nothing. All we had was three records – six sides – made in Grafton, Wisconsin, in 1930 with another singer and guitarist named Elvie Thomas. And we knew nothing of her, either. The two women had apparently come from nowhere, made their recordings, then vanished.

But in 2014, John Jeremiah Sullivan wrote up years of musical sleuthing for *The New York Times Magazine*, revealing the following: Elvie Thomas was really L.V. Thomas (she herself was unsure what the initials stood for), born L.V. Grant in Houston, Texas in 1891. She quit school at the age of eleven and supported herself by playing the guitar. By 1961, when she was found and interviewed back in Houston, by blues historian Mack McCormick, she had left her playing far behind her. The only singing she did by then was in the choir of her local Mount Pleasant Baptist church, long since having abandoned the 'sporting life'. She died in 1979.

L.V. Thomas told McCormick about the trip to Wisconsin with Geeshie Wiley, who she said was sixteen years younger than her. Geeshie's real name was Lillie May Wiley, and L.V. had given her the nickname, except that it was Geetchie – pronounced 'Gitchie'. We can hear L.V. calling to her in what sounds like rehearsed banter at the beginning of one of the recordings, 'Pick Poor Robin Clean'. L.V. insisted to McCormick that she'd neither seen nor heard from Geeshie Wiley since they last toured together in 1933, but she'd heard in the 1950s that Geeshie was living in West Texas. McCormick told Sullivan he felt sure L.V. was hiding something.

Sullivan's own investigations led him to conclude that Geeshie was born Lillie Mae Scott in Louisiana in 1908 and that she may have stabbed her husband, Thornton Wiley, to death in 1931. Taking into account family reminiscences of L.V. as unusual, masculine, deep voiced and trouser-wearing, the music critic Greil Marcus thinks it possible that the two women were a couple. We may never know. But we have their recordings.

On three of the recordings, L.V. sang and played lead guitar, with Geeshie on second guitar. On the others, including 'Last Kind Words Blues', their roles were reversed. 'Last Kind Words Blues' is the best known of the six recordings, and both the singing and guitar playing are remarkable. The song itself is more remarkable still.

First there's the structure. The song is like an eight-bar blues, but because Geeshie routinely adds two or three beats to the fourth bar and about six beats to the final bar, it's more like a nine- or ten- bar blues. And that's if it's a blues at all. The song is in A minor – blues are rarely in minor keys – each verse going to E major/minor and B major, before ending firmly in E minor.

Marcus stresses something L.V. Thomas told McCormick. She said she began playing the guitar in 1902 and that there was blues 'even back then'. Marcus suggests that we may conclude from this that L.V. recalled a time when there wasn't blues, a time before the blues, and that she carried this memory with her in her music. It's speculative – like everything else about these singers and this song – but given L.V.'s contribution to the recording as second guitar player, it's a perfectly reasonable explanation for the song as a *pre*-blues, which would explain its structure.

Then there's the words.

The last kind words I heard my daddy say
Lord, the last kind words I heard my daddy say

If I die, if I die in the German war
I want you to send my body, send it to my mother in law

If I get killed, if I get killed, please don't bury my soul
I prefer just leave me out, let the buzzards eat me whole

When you see me comin' look 'cross the rich man's field
If I don't bring you flour, I'll bring you bolted meal

I went to the depot, I looked up at the sun
Cried, some train don't come, there'll be some walkin' done

My mama told me, just before she died
Lord, precious daughter, don't you be so wild

The Mississippi river, you know it's deep and wide
I can stand right here, see my face from the other side

What you do to me baby it never gets outta me
I may not see you after I cross the deep blue sea

Marcus has taken a considerable interest in this song, writing about it more than once and at length in his book *Three Songs, Three Singers, Three Nations*. He points out, in particular, the oddness of the lyrics. That first verse, for instance, goes nowhere. What *are* the singer's father's 'last kind words'? Are we to assume they consist of the following verses? There is nothing especially kind about these words. The 'German war' is presumably World War I, but why does the father (if it is the father) want his body sent to his mother-in-law? How can you bury a soul? What and where is the 'rich man's field'? Why did the singer at the depot look 'up at the sun'? How can you see your face from the other side of the Mississippi river?

Some of these questions have been answered over the years by simply changing the words. It's not 'the rich man's field' it's 'the Richmonds' field'; when you go to the depot – the railway station – of course you look up at the sign, not at the sun; you can't see your face from the other side of the Mississippi, but you can see your baby. And so on. These and other rationalisations have been included in later performances of the song in an attempt to iron out the oddness. But Marcus, quite rightly, insists upon that oddness. Wiley clearly sings 'rich man', 'sun' and 'face', and she sings them fiercely.

Hers in an impassioned performance. Unlikely words are stressed, drawn out, exaggerated. 'If I die, if I die in THE German war', Geeshie sings, placing the definite article on the melody's highest note and holding it.

In each verse, the first word of the second line is held. Four times the word is 'I': 'IIIIIIIII want you to send my body.' And all this is accompanied by Geeshie and Elvie's thrillingly percussive guitar playing.

Impassioned yet inscrutable: the song might almost be a metaphor for Geeshie and Elvie themselves. But while we may never learn any more about these remarkable performers, their recording of 'Last Kind Words Blues' will continue to prick the curiosity of all who hear it.

68

Pon de Replay

music and words by Alisha Brooks,
Vada Nobles, Carl Sturken and Evan Rogers

If music be the food of love, play on;
Give me excess of it

THIS, IN A NUTSHELL, is the song. Rihanna is 'on the dance floor wanting some more' music, pleading with the DJ to turn up the volume and put that song *upon the* replay. In contrast to Shakespeare's Orsino, who reasons that if he consumes enough of love's food he will finally lose his appetite for it, Rihanna's musical needs seem insatiable.

'Put another nickel in / In the nickelodeon / All I want is loving you and music, music, music,' sang Teresa Brewer half a century before her, but for Rihanna, loving barely comes into it: music and dancing will be enough.

The song was the first track on Rihanna's first album, *Music of the Sun*, in 2005, and it was her first hit single. It was the work of a team of writers, but far from the beige blandness that so often emerges from committee work, this song created a vivid musical personality for its singer, obvious from its title alone, which is Barbadian or Bajan Creole.

There were several versions of the song: the radio edit, the album version, the internet version and numerous remixes and dub versions in the style of Caribbean dance hall. Some of the recordings had a kind of male hip-hop chorus, some just featured Rihanna herself. What they all shared was a distinctive beat – an up-tempo shuffle with a lazy dotted rhythm – and a striking use of the aeolian mode.

The aeolian mode is perfectly common. It's the scale behind many folk songs (including, as we've seen, the tune that Vaughan Williams borrowed for his hymn, 'O God of Earth and Altar'), and its uses in pop music include everything from REM's 'Losing My Religion' to Nirvana's 'Smells Like Teen Spirit'. But it is also close to the so-called 'Hindu mode', which is an aeolian without the flattened third – a sort of major aeolian.

It comes to mind in 'Pon de Replay' partly because of Rihanna's use of elaborate ornamentation, especially around that flattened fifth and sixth, complete with quarter-tone inflections that are strongly suggestive of Indian music. With the swinging rhythm of the drumming and the song's moderately fast tempo, 'Pon de Replay' has many of the hallmarks of a Bollywood dance song. Is this deliberate? Perhaps it's related to the Indian influence on Caribbean culture, dating back to colonial times.

Another possible explanation for the rhythm is entirely local. The tuk bands of Barbados, playing tuk (or rukatuk) music, date back to the seventeenth century, when African slaves adopted the percussion instruments of the British army's marching bands in their own music. These included the bass drum, side drum and triangle, but with the double-headed bass drum central to the music. Tuk drumming typically employs the lazy, swinging dotted rhythm heard in 'Pon de Replay'.

Who knows for sure what went into the writing of the song? It was made in America, not Barbados. Four writer-producers were involved and they knew how to fashion a hit. Just as 'Pon de Replay' is a song about music, it is also about musical style.

Songs about music abound – they always have – and there are also a good many, a subgenre if you like, that deal with the *need* for music. But 'Pon de Replay' belongs to a subgenre of a subgenre, because it's addressed to the provider of the music at one remove. It's a surprisingly large category, because the DJ is a powerful figure: out on the dance floor, the DJ is in charge. As Pink posited, 'If God is a DJ, life is a dance floor'.

'I am the Lord thy God' we read in the Book of Isaiah. 'I am a DJ / I am what I play,' sang David Bowie ('DJ' rhymes with 'play' in these songs as surely as 'moon' once rhymed with 'June' and 'baby' with 'maybe'). But even the most devout believers can feel anger with their god.

'I get tired of DJs / Why's it always what he plays?' Joe Jackson demands to know on 'Slow Song', before deciding to 'push right through' to insist on something he and his friend can dance to at the end of a busy day. But the typical DJ song is supplicatory, a kind of prayer to the DJ God.

'Hey Mr DJ / Why don't you slow this party down,' asked R. Kelly in 1992. 'Hey Mr DJ,' sang Van Morrison in 2002, 'I'm in a sad mood tonight / … / Won't you make everything all right?' A DJ can make things better. A DJ, as Indeep reminds us, can even save your life. The more usual manner of salvation is not to slow the music down, but pump it up.

'Hey Mr DJ,' sang Zahné in 1994, 'Everybody's ready to party / All night, all night.' 'Hey Mr DJ,' sang Madonna in 2000, 'Put a record on / I want to dance with my baby / … / I never want to stop.' 'Hey Mr DJ,' sang Rihanna in 2005, 'Song pon de replay.'

69

Too Much Monkey Business

music and words by Chuck Berry

SKELTONICS IS A POETIC FORM that takes its name from the work of John Skelton (1460–1529) of Diss in Norfolk. It's all short lines, often with just two stresses and tightly rhymed. Here's an example from Skelton's poem, 'To Mistress Margaret Hussey'.

Merry Margaret,
As midsummer flower,
Gentle as falcon
Or hawk of the tower:
With solace and gladness,
Much mirth and no madness,
All good and no badness;
So joyously,
So maidenly,
So womanly
Her demeaning
In every thing,
Far, far passing
That I can indite,
Or suffice to write
Of Merry Margaret
As midsummer flower,
Gentle as falcon
Or hawk of the tower.

Now consider the following:

> Runnin' to-and-fro,
> Hard workin' at the mill
> Never fail
> In the mail,
> Yeah, come a rotten bill

Chuck Berry (1926–2017) is so famous for his guitar playing, for his licks (which his piano player, Johnnie Johnson, said he taught him), his solos, his ebullient style, for his blending of country music with rhythm and blues, for having hit after hit after hit, and for his duck walk, that it is possible to forget he was the pre-eminent lyricist of classic rock'n'roll.

The well-turned phrase ('As I was motorvatin' over the hill / I saw Maybelline in a Coupe de Ville'), the telling simile ('he could play a guitar just like a-ringin' a bell'), the surprising metaphor ('I've got the rockin' pneumonia, / I need a shot of rhythm and blues'), the sophistication ('"C'est la vie", say the old folks, it goes to show you never can tell'): these were not qualities one discovered in the songs of Little Richard or Jerry Lee Lewis.

And this is not to mention his control of rhythm, rhyme and form. In 'Too Much Monkey Business' the three are interlinked. The song was released in 1956. It was his fifth single, and he'd already demonstrated a rather wide stylistic palette with the cheery, up-tempo blues of 'Maybelline', the rockabilly of 'Thirty Days', the talking blues of 'No Money Down' and the musical and lyrical ebullience of 'Roll over Beethoven'. 'Too Much Monkey Business' was harder to categorise.

The song is a fusion of twelve-bar blues and fast rockabilly, but the fabulous rhythmic variety comes from its lyrics. It's a poet's art. Take this verse, which consists of two bars of clipped quavers/eighth notes (the first four lines), followed by two bars of fast running semiquavers/sixteenth notes:

> Same thing,
> Ev'ry day,
> Gettin' up,

Goin' to school.
No need of me complaining
My objection's overruled.

Skelton never did that!

Tudor poets aside, 'Too Much Monkey Business' was a genre unto itself. Yet if there was nothing quite like it before 1956, plenty came after. Bob Dylan's 'Subterranean Homesick Blues' owes a clear debt to the song, but in a general sense there's an air of proto-rap about it, the verses not so much sung as chanted monotonically, the rhythm driving the song, the rhyming insistent. Perhaps we can't hear Chuck Berry in Public Enemy, but we can hear Chuck D in 'Too Much Monkey Business'. And it's not only the rhythm and rhyme, or even the tone of voice, it's also the subject matter.

'Too Much Money Business' opens, as Berry's records generally did, with a guitar lick, but rather than the generous, boogie-woogie riff that opened 'Roll over Beethoven' and would open plenty more Berry songs, this one obsessively repeats the same note, before giving way to Johnson's piano and Willie Dixon's slap bass. Because the tempo is fast and the lines are mostly brief, we're about to get through a lot in a short time. In under three minutes, Berry holds a range of occupations including working in a factory, going to school, fighting with the US army in Japan and serving in a filling station. And he does all this while being hassled by a salesman ('You can buy, / Go on, try, / You can pay me next week'), a prospective bride who wants him to 'Settle down / Write a book', and a telephone operator whose poor advice results in his losing his coins in a pay phone. That's too much monkey business for *anyone* to be involved in.

It's a portrait of life for the working man in postwar America (Springsteen was heavily influenced by Berry); this working man is evidently a returned soldier (that's not a random reference to Yokohama); and he's African American, the 'Brown-eyed Handsome Man', as the song on the B side of this single referred to him. On top of everything else, you could call 'Too Much Monkey Business' a protest song. Public Enemy may never have captured the levity and wit of Berry's music, but in other respects they have carried on his work.

70

It Happened in Monterey

music by Mabel Wayne
words by Billy Rose

FIRST THERE'S THE MISSPELLING. Monterey is in California, Monterrey in Mexico. But this is 'Monterey' 'in old Mexico': that's where 'it happened'. Then there's the fact that the song, which most people know from Frank Sinatra's 1956 album *Songs for Swingin' Lovers!*, had been composed more than a quarter of a century earlier. The spelling hardly matters, but the vintage of the song is interesting.

Sinatra's golden age was the mid-1950s, defined by a sequence of great albums for Capitol Records – four in 1957 alone – with band leaders Axel Stordahl, Nelson Riddle and Billy May, but mostly and most famously Riddle.

The singer's success was doubly against the odds. In the decade up to 1953, Sinatra, who had enjoyed great popularity during the war years, experienced the sort of career slump from which few popular artists recover. The public had stopped buying his records. He turned to acting, at first without much success, but then came *From Here to Eternity*. Suddenly, Sinatra was back, and with a recording contract to boot.

The other unlikely aspect of Sinatra's renaissance was that it coincided with the advent of rock'n'roll, a form of music for which Sinatra had undisguised contempt. In a 1957 interview with the *New York Post*, he described it as 'a rancid smelling aphrodisiac ... martial music of every delinquent on the face of the earth'. Not only were Sinatra's new albums for Capitol a long way stylistically from Little Richard and Elvis Presley, but they were also full of songs from the 1930s.

Gus Kahn and Walter Donaldson's 'Makin' Whoopee' had first been a hit for Eddie Cantor in 1928; Harold Arlen and Ted Koehler wrote 'I've Got the World on a String' in 1932; Cole Porter's 'I Get a Kick Out of You' was from 1934, and 'I've Got You under My Skin' from 1936; the Gershwins wrote 'They Can't Take that Away from Me' and 'A Foggy Day (in London Town)' in 1937, both for movies starring Fred Astaire; two years later, Jimmy Kennedy and Michael Carr penned 'South of the Border' for a Gene Autry film of the same name. All these songs are now popularly associated with Sinatra. His albums of the 1950s contained original songs too, but overwhelmingly the singer revived works from the pre-war era.

It would be wrong, however, to assume that Sinatra was purveying nostalgia. With Riddle's help, he was remaking these songs in his own image: Sinatra the man of the world, the voice of experience, the survivor. With perfect diction and impeccable timing, he sang these songs as though they were life lessons, while Riddle's arrangements – dynamic, earthy, sensual – suggested the singer had plenty more life in him.

Mabel Wayne (1890–1978) composed 'It Happened in Monterey' as a waltz, and that's how it was first heard in the 1930 film *The King of Jazz*, starring the Paul Whiteman Orchestra. On screen, it is sung by John Boles in a cod-Italian accent (Boles was actually from Texas), together with Jeanette Loff, and the song sounds as though it has escaped from a Rudolf Friml operetta. Sinatra's version is a far cry from this.

Songs for Swingin' Lovers! is arguably the high-water mark of Sinatra's Capitol years and features some of Riddle's greatest arrangements. Probably the most famous of them all is 'I've Got You under My Skin', with its raunchy bass clarinet and baritone sax, and an emphasis on low brass and high strings, allowing Sinatra an octave or two in between. The big band crescendo at the heart of the song is the recording's most celebrated moment, the violins soaring, the Latin-influenced brass syncopations pushing relentlessly to a trumpet climax that sets up Milt Bernhart's blistering trombone solo.

It was natural that these Latin influences should carry over into a song set 'in old Mexico', so consequently Mabel Wayne's waltz gains one extra beat per bar and becomes something like a samba. Following an introduction with splashes of Spanish colour from hectic muted trumpets, piano and violins, the song settles into its groove. As was his wont on these Capitol recordings, Sinatra ignores the verse, a wise decision in this instance ('In my imagination / I'm finding consolation / Somewhere along the Rio Grande …'). Many a pop song of the era featured a chorus that changed somewhat on each appearance, advancing the story. But not here. Billy Rose only wrote one version of his chorus, so Sinatra, singing it twice, must inject some variety of his own.

'It happened in Monterey, a long time ago / I met her in Monterey, in old Mexico': even in these opening lines, the record bears the singer's hallmarks. The tight syncopation of Riddle's orchestra is freely elaborated by Sinatra's tendency to sing before, after and around the beat. In that first line, it is really only the first syllable of 'happened' and the second syllable of 'ago' that are on the beat; everything else is fluid. It's much the same with pitch, Sinatra scooping up to notes starting a minor second lower on the final syllables of 'ago' and 'Mexico'. No one did this better than Sinatra.

Rose's chorus continues with some stock Mexican imagery: 'Stars and steel guitars / And luscious lips as red as wine / Broke somebody's heart, / And I'm afraid that it was mine.' The last couplet is cute, but this is hardly Rose – the lyricist of 'Paper Moon' – enjoying his finest hour. Fortunately, Sinatra and Riddle can uncover sophistication in the most unpromising places, and the second time through the chorus, they show us how it's done.

Sinatra begins by adding a long, lazy sigh to the front of the chorus: 'Ahhh, it happened in Monterey …' Then he holds back the second line to isolate the syllables of 'I met her in Monterey', placing each one squarely after the beat. Next, he begins leaving words out. It's almost as though he's bored and can no longer be bothered singing the song properly: 'Stars … guitars … / Lips … red as wine …' Finally, when he replaces the common phrase 'I'm afraid that' with the more mannered 'I *fear* that it was mine' he appears to be sending the song up.

Changing the words of a song was another Sinatra trademark. On *Songs for Young Lovers*, he'd done it to George and Ira Gershwin's 'A Foggy Day (in London Town)' adding the word 'much' in the line 'I viewed the morning with *much* alarm'. In that case, the singer weakened the lyric because his insertion negated Ira's play on words, subtracting from the richness of the song. The original line suggests the secondary image of an alarm clock; 'with *much* alarm' does not. But in 'It Happened in Monterey', Sinatra's 'I fear that it was mine' doesn't subtract, it adds. It adds character. Sinatra's character, to be precise. His first time through the chorus was all about the song; the second time through, it's all about the singer. He's affecting insouciance. He is Frank Sinatra: man of the world, voice of experience, survivor.

71

Mad about the Boy

music and words by Noël Coward

ALTHOUGH IT IS OFTEN SUNG as a love song, not least in Dinah Washington's famous, smouldering recording, 'Mad about the Boy' is really anything but. The boy in question is a matinee idol, as the first verse makes plain, and it's not one person who's mad about him, it's at least four.

Noël Coward (1899–1973) wrote the song for the satirical revue, *Words and Music*, which opened at the Adelphi Theatre in London in September 1932 and, in addition to 'Mad about the Boy', introduced 'Mad Dogs and Englishmen' to English audiences, the latter having been heard in New York the previous year. In 1939, *Words and Music* itself went to Broadway, now called *Set to Music* and starring Beatrice Lilley.

Revues – a mixture of sketch and song – were ensemble pieces, and it followed that so were some of the musical numbers. 'Mad about the Boy' is very much in this mode, its four verses and choruses sung by a society woman (Joyce Barbour), a school girl (Steffi Duna), a 'cockney' (Norah Howard) and a 'tart' (Doris Hare), queuing outside a cinema to see a movie starring the boy they're all 'mad about'. Talking pictures were only five years old in 1932.

'On the Silver Screen / He melts my heart in every single scene,' sings the society woman; 'When I do the rooms / I see 'is face in all the brushes and the brooms' sings the cockney, evidently a domestic maid. The tart sees him in the faces of her clients, though she admits 'I'm hardly sentimental: / Love isn't so sublime. / I have to pay the rental / And I can't afford to waste much time.'

For Broadway, Coward added a fifth character, a closeted business man, who has undergone psychoanalysis but nevertheless still finds himself 'mad about the boy'. Among his best lines are: 'When I told my wife, / She said,

"I've never heard such nonsense in my life!"' and 'People I employ / Have the impertinence to call me Myrna Loy'. The verse was never used.

Both Coward's humour and pathos depend, rather like Cole Porter's, on rhymes, and here he finds a raft of them for the opening line of his chorus, which is the song's title. The society woman admits the sleepless nights she's 'had about the boy', even though she finds 'traces of the cad about the boy'. (Five years later, in Rodgers and Hart's 'The Lady Is a Tramp', Ginger Rogers would sing that she'd 'never been to a party where they honoured Noël Ca'ad'.) The schoolgirl, who has traced a photograph of the boy's profile and finds a 'slight / Effect of Galahad about the boy' is also convinced that A.E. Housman 'wrote the *Shropshire Lad* about the boy'. The cockney maid has 'got it bad about the boy' and ''ad a row with Dad about the boy'. The tart, who thinks 'there may be something sad about the boy', is 'in some strange way … glad about the boy'.

The song was recorded at least five times in its first year and found success beyond its theatrical rationale. In performances by individual singers it was truncated and has been ever since. Over the years, recordings have tended to include the first verse and chorus, sometimes with the final chorus, sometimes the two choruses without the verse, though Beatrice Lillie recorded the schoolgirl's verse and chorus without the others.

The song's success is doubtless as much to do with the lovely, bluesy melody, as with the words. The chorus begins not in the tonic (C major), but with a half diminished seventh on the supertonic. We don't reach the home key until the fifth bar, and even then C major seems to want to be C minor as the melody rises through an E flat, its effect immediately undermined by an A natural. In the very next bar, the music lands on an especially bluesy F sharp diminished chord (on the word 'sleepless' in the first chorus). So there's a delicious unease about the song, a musical ambiguity matching the lyrical ambiguity. It was always possible to hear the lyrics of the first and last choruses as those of a reasonably straightforward love song – you could, after all, walk 'down the street' without being a prostitute – but if you knew the song's theatrical context, there were deeper levels of meaning.

From the beginning the song has carried with it the suggestion of homo-eroticism. The word 'gay' in this context might not have been in common parlance in 1932, but for those in the know that line in the fourth chorus, 'he has a gay appeal', meant only one thing. And then there were rumours about the subject of the song, about the boy himself. Was he Douglas Fairbanks Jr, Cary Grant, Tyrone Power or James Cagney? There's little evidence that Coward had anyone in particular in mind.

More than two decades after Coward's death, a recording was found of him singing 'Mad about the Boy' with piano accompaniment. Perhaps it was a demo, but he does it well. In a high tenor voice merging seamlessly into an expressive falsetto, he sings the society woman's verse and chorus and the tart's chorus with its line about the boy's 'gay appeal'. Stylistically, it's very much of its time, Coward making use of a swooning portamento, slowing down to make the most of these moments, for example, the vertiginous dive down a fifth (complete with vibrato), at the end of the first verse on the words 'like a silly fool *I fell*'. At the start of the chorus, he sharpens some of the thirds we're used to hearing as flat and bluesy. It's a beautiful performance, both funny and touching, a combination of 'pose and poise', as *Time* magazine once wrote of the man himself.

The recording seems to have been made for His Master's Voice in 1932, the year of the song's first performance. This was the year that Phyllis Robins, Anona Winn, Cecile Petrie, Elsie Carlisle and Gertrude Lawrence all recorded it, and Ray Noble's orchestra made their instrumental version; it was also the year Coward recorded several other songs from *Words and Music* with Noble's orchestra. But HMV would appear to have rejected his recording of 'Mad about the Boy'. It had its first release in 2002.

72

Waterloo Sunset

music and words by Ray Davies

IT'S 25 JANUARY 1979, and the Kinks are at St George's Hall, Bradford, in the north of England, playing their hits. You can tick them off: 'You Really Got Me', 'All Day and All of the Night', 'Sunny Afternoon', 'Lola', 'Days'. And then there's the one everybody's waiting for.

'Waterloo Sunset', the crowd keeps calling out. 'Waterloo Sunset.' And from the stage, the Kinks' lead singer, Ray Davies, joins in: 'Waterloo Sunset. Waterloo Sunset.'

Eventually, he leans casually into the microphone and sings, unaccompanied, the song's first words, 'Dirty old river', before breaking off: 'I'm sorry, that's it'.

'Waterloo Sunset' was one of the Kinks' biggest hits, reaching number two in the British charts in May 1967. But twelve years later, as Davies admitted in an interview, it had become a bit of an albatross. The song was eclipsing the band's other achievements – of which there were plenty – and for a while they couldn't bear to play it.

It's a dream of a song, the music and lyrics together creating a sonic oasis that suited the mind-altered zeitgeist of the mid-1960s. The pop charts that 'Waterloo Sunset' entered had only weeks earlier been host to the Beatles' 'Strawberry Fields Forever' and the Move's 'I Can Hear the Grass Grow' and would shortly welcome Jimi Hendrix's 'The Wind Cries Mary' and Procol Harum's 'A Whiter Shade of Pale'. May 1967 was the spring before the Summer of Love.

The song has one of those instantly recognisable beginnings. As Ray's guitarist brother Dave repeatedly picks on a B, the bass descends stepwise down an E major scale (beginning and ending on the dominant B), and the tune is launched, its first phrase played on Dave's guitar before Ray begins to sing: 'Dirty old river, must you keep rolling, rolling into the night? / People so busy, make me feel dizzy, taxi light shines so bright / But I don't need no friends / As long as I gaze on Waterloo sunset, I am in paradise.'

It's a funny sort of paradise, when you think about it. The lyrics are cobbled together and a little confused. There's a hint of 'Ol' Man River' in the Thames's tendency to 'keep rolling', but Davies seems to want it to stop, asking '*must* you keep rolling?' And busy people make him 'feel dizzy', the implication being that everything – river and people – ought to slow down. He doesn't 'need no friends', that's clear. But why the 'but'? Still, if the lyrics alone don't make complete sense, the music is another matter.

Dave Davies' guitar sound is rather old-fashioned – and maybe that's the point – the surf-rock echo seemingly at odds with the 'dirty old' Thames, but together with Ray's vulnerable singing voice (also laden with echo), and the floaty backing vocals that include his then wife, Rasa Didzpetris, it adds up to something unique. The sound of the song is out of this world, despite the imagery in the lyrics being quotidian: the 'dirty old river', 'Waterloo Station', and 'people swarming like flies round Waterloo Underground' are not the stuff that dreams are made on. Even 'Terry' and 'Julie', who meet at the station 'every Friday night', don't have names to conjure with.

From the moment of its release, people taken with the sound of the song have attempted to make full sense of it. 'Terry and Julie'? Well, that has to have been the actors Terence Stamp and Julie Christie, London's 1960s glamour couple and the stars of the hit film *Far from the Madding Crowd*. Except that the film wasn't released until six months after the song. It was the music at work again, transfiguring two common names and making them part of this peculiar contemporary paradise.

Ray Davies never liked giving interviews, which perhaps explains his contradictory answers to questions about the song. Terry and Julie are his sister and her boyfriend, ordinary people with dreams. Terry is his nephew, whom he always felt close to. The song recalls his sickly childhood, looking out of a hospital bedroom window at the Thames. It's about walking alongside the river with Rasa. It's really a song about Liverpool, a place he's always loved. Both the song and its writer have been hard to pin down. In an interview for the British *Telegraph*, just before Davies sang 'Waterloo Sunset' at the closing ceremony of the London Olympics in 2012, he described himself as 'the George Smiley of songwriters', comparing himself to John le Carré's reclusive hero.

There's no reason that Davies himself should be able to say – or even know – what his song is about. Like any musical work, a song is primarily about itself, and often will dictate its own terms. A song is a self-contained world and the world of 'Waterloo Sunset' is in the sound it makes. The gentle tempo, the descending bass line, the echoey guitar, the sha-la-las, and per-haps above all, the melody.

The melodic line of 'Waterloo Sunset' is surprisingly wide-ranging, covering nearly two octaves. We barely notice this because of the orderly manner in which it is laid out. The long first line stretches from the tonic E above middle C to the B an octave and a half below. Each of the three phrases includes a big step up: a perfect fourth between the second syllable of 'dirty' and 'old', another fourth from 'you' up to 'keep' and then a major sixth from the second syllable of 'rolling' to the first syllable of 'into'. Around these large melodic steps, smaller steps fill in the gaps. The first, second and fourth lines of the song are the same, but the third line is different. As we move away from chords of E, B and A (I–V–IV) to F sharp minor and C sharp major, the melody soars.

'But I don't need no friends'; 'But I don't feel afraid': the phrase has long C sharps – first on 'don't', then on 'friends'/'-fraid' – curling up, in between, to a high falsetto G sharp on 'need'/'feel'. That 'ee' sound produces a very special colour on a high note, thin and piercing, especially after the long-held 'oh' of 'don't', and it presents Davies' voice at its most vulnerable and beautiful. The return to the octave below, and the familiar opening melodic line ('As long as I gaze on Waterloo Sunset'), offers musical as well as lyri-cal solace.

Looking at the words on the page, we might wonder how the sunset over Waterloo Station could be anyone's idea of paradise, but in the musical con-text of the Kinks' song, there's little room for doubt.

73

Malaika

*music and words by Adam Salim
or Fadhili William Mdawida*

WHEN PETE SEEGER SANG 'MALAIKA' at the 1964 Newport Folk Festival it was fresh in his memory from a visit to Kenya. 'It's not an ancient folk song,' he explained to his audience, 'it's a pop song sung on the radio.' And so it was, though over the years, as sung by Miriam Makeba, with and without Harry Belafonte, and later recorded by Boney M and Angélique Kidjo, it came to seem more like a folk song, at least outside Africa.

Like those other singers, Seeger presented 'Malaika' to his Newport audience in its original Swahili – 'a real pretty language' – but, being Seeger, he paused, mid-performance, to inform his listeners what the lyrics mean: 'Angel, I love you, angel. But I am defeated, because I haven't got enough money and can't afford to buy you to make you my wife.' It's a good summary of the first verse, and the songwriter's financial concerns return in the later verses.

There is considerable dispute about the authorship of 'Malaika'. Makeba always introduced it as a song from Tanzania, and the claim of Tanzanian Adam Salim (1916–?) to have composed the song in 1945 is strong. It was, apparently, written from personal experience. Salim had been in love with a woman, Halima, but couldn't afford the dowry. Sadly, he also couldn't afford to record the song. The first recording of 'Malaika', made in 1963 or perhaps a little earlier, was the one Seeger heard on the radio. It was sung by Fadhili William (1938–2001) of Taita-Taveta in Kenya. Salim said William bought the song from him. William claimed to have written it in 1959, also from his own personal experience. He had been in love with a girl named Fanny while at school in Nairobi and her parents didn't approve. In Kenya and Tanzania, the authorship of the song remains a matter of controversy.

What is beyond dispute is that the song, far from being folkloric, is, as Seeger said, a pop song. In fact it is more than that. It is an urban song that celebrates progress, symbolised by its rhythmic structure, which is a rumba. In 1950s East Africa, 'rumba' was a generic term for any Afro-Cuban rhythm, but as recorded by Fadhili William and the Jambo Boys, 'Malaika' really is a rumba, complete with maracas. The American musician and academic Ian Eagleson has pointed out that the use of these rhythms would have made the song seem outward-looking and forward-looking. Probably for this reason, Miriam Makeba was invited to sing 'Malaika' with Belafonte in Kenya during the country's independence celebrations in late 1963, and the song went on to become something of a talisman for her in her American exile.

Becoming increasingly famous internationally at this time, Makeba had been unable to return to her native South Africa since the cancellation of her passport by the Verwoerd government in 1960. As 'Mama Africa', she carried quite some responsibility. Audiences who went to hear her wanted to experience something that might be authentically African, and her version of 'Malaika' – slower than the Kenyan recording (and devoid of maracas) – sounded traditional enough. So, as Eagleson notes, while for East Africans 'Malaika' was symbolic of the future, for Western audiences the song was exotic.

'Malaika' is one of just a handful of African songs to have become popular in the West. Another is 'Mbube' (or 'Wimoweh' or 'The Lion Sleeps Tonight'), and on Boney M's recording of 'Malaika', the song is accompanied by the repeated refrain 'Wimoweh, wimoweh', notwithstanding the fact that 'Wimoweh' is Zulu, not Swahili.

The success of 'Malaika' in the West raises a number of issues. There is, for instance, the whole business of hearing a song in a language you don't understand. Opera-goers who prefer their Verdi in Italian, Wagner in German and Musorgsky in Russian will argue, convincingly, that the meaning is in the music, and that the sound of the original language is part of that music. The same argument might be applied to hearing 'Malaika' in the 'real pretty language' of Swahili. Something might be gained from hearing the song in English, but arguably more would be lost.

But there's also the thornier issue of the cultural meaning of the music, and of finding something exotic in the first place. It's related to the 1990s 'world music' craze, where gypsy music or Qawwali singing or township jive or Argentinian tango became fashionable for a short time, generally with very little knowledge or acknowledgment of the context in which the music was created or what was intended by their creators. We liked the sound of the music without understanding the first thing about it.

But what is musical 'understanding'? How many people who love the music of Bach or Charlie Parker would claim to understand that? What does any of us understand from music? Can we separate the sound of a song from its cultural appurtenances? Should we?

All music consists of pitch, rhythm, tempo and timbre, and we can talk about these things on a technical level by pulling the music apart to see how it works, like stripping down a car engine. It might help us to understand the differences between pieces of music, but it won't account for why we might prefer one piece to the other – at least, not entirely. For that, we will probably need some cultural references, and if we don't have a grasp of the cultures that produced the music, we must rely on our own. It's not wrong to do this, but it's worth bearing in mind.

The cultural significance of a song such as 'Malaika' might elude us – even in Kenya and Tanzania, its significance depends, in large part, on who you believe wrote it – but we can still fall for its well-made, beautifully proportioned, diatonic melody, simple and gorgeous in its cascading phrases, especially when sung slowly by Makeba or Kidjo.

74

Finishing the Hat

music and words by Stephen Sondheim

THE WORDS AND MUSIC come out of the mouth of the French painter Georges Seurat in Stephen Sondheim's musical collaboration with James Lapine, *Sunday in the Park with George* (1984). The park is the island of La Grande Jatte in the river Seine, and Seurat is there painting his most famous work, *A Sunday Afternoon on the Island of La Grande Jatte* (1884). It depicts about thirty Parisians from different walks of life and of varying ages enjoying the sunshine and the river view. All but two of them are wearing hats.

In fact, the artist's song is not about finishing one of these hats, but 'how you *have* to finish the hat'. It is a song about being an artist, about the compulsion to work – to paint, to sculpt, to write, to compose – even when it's socially inconvenient, even when it is deleterious to a relationship. The act of sharing a vision might be essentially generous, but the work is solitary and the way of life selfish, because 'however you live / There's a part of you always standing by'. 'They have never understood,' George sings about his women, 'And no reason that they should', before allowing himself a moment of yearning for companionship: 'But if anybody could ...'

'Finishing the Hat' is unique. There are dozens of songs about writing songs. 'Why do I find it hard to write the next line?' asks Gary Kemp in Spandau Ballet's 'True' (it's the best line of his entire lyric). But there is no other song that deals with the irresistible nature of the creative urge, the itch that must be scratched, and with how scratching it makes you antisocial. And 'Finishing the Hat' doesn't just sing about it, it embodies it.

Melodically, the song is as obsessive as its subject. As sung by Mandy Patinkin, the first George, it's in the key of G flat, the phrase 'Finishing the hat' fitted to a pentatonic figure that rises from D flat to D flat (via E flat and

G flat), before dropping on to B flat for the word 'hat'. This never changes. 'Finishing the hat', 'Studying the hat', 'Starting on a hat', 'Look I made a hat' and, finally, the triumphant 'Where there never was a hat': they are all the same, and 'hat' is always B flat. It's the same with 'sky' and 'face' in the phrases 'Mapping out a sky', 'Studying a face'. This pentatonic pattern represents George (engrossed, devoted, possessed) and his work (repetitious, disciplined, never-ending).

But there are the interruptions. The first is the word 'window'. Here's the opening verse of the song proper:

> Finishing the hat.
> How you have to finish the hat.
> How you watch the rest of the world
> From a window
> While you finish the hat.

That entire verse follows the pentatonic pattern described above, except for the word 'window' which is sung to C flat. This note doesn't belong in the pentatonic scale the song has established. It distracts from it, it's disruptive, just like whatever is happening through the window. There's also something seductive about it. The C flat glints enticingly as Sondheim's song pauses for a moment. And it's not only the vocal line that pauses, but also the accompaniment.

Stephen Sondheim (b. 1930) knows a lot of music and cheerfully acknowledges its influence on him. In *A Little Night Music*, based on Ingmar Bergman's film *Smiles of a Summer Night*, every song is a waltz. The influence here is not Johann Strauss II or even Schubert, but Ravel's twentieth-century reimagining of their Vienna, especially in his piece *Valses nobles et sentimentales*. 'You Must Meet My Wife', 'A Weekend in the Country', 'Liaisons': they're all waltzes. 'Send in the Clowns' is a slow waltz.

There's a model, too, for 'Finishing the Hat' and it relates strongly to Seurat's art. Georges Seurat (1859–1891) was a post-impressionist, but more than that he was a pointillist, his images emerging from an ocean of coloured dots. In Sondheim's musical, George's girlfriend, whose jilting of him provokes the singing of 'Finishing the Hat', is called Dot, art and life colliding everywhere.

Step back from *Sunday Afternoon on the Island of la Grande Jatte*, which hangs in the Art Institute of Chicago, and you see the scene, the sunshine, the parasols, the people, the hats. But walk right up to it and you see only dots. It's like a pre-digital television set. When you consider the technique of applying hundreds of thousands of these dots to what is quite a large canvas, there's an obvious musical correlative. It is not from Seurat's time and place, but from Sondheim's. It's the music of Sondheim's contemporary, Steve Reich, specifically Reich's *Music for Mallet Instruments, Voices and Organ* (1973). It provides both the tone and texture of the accompaniment, an obsessive continuum of repeating phrases that chugs away so long as the painter applies his dots. When the painter pauses – either because he is glancing out of the window or 'stepping back to look at a face' – the accompaniment pauses; when he returns to his dots, the musical dots return. 'Finishing the Hat' is Broadway's work song.

75

Look What They've Done
to My Song, Ma

music and words by Melanie Safka

THE SONG IN THIS SONG is a metaphor for life – perhaps all songs are. But look what they've done to it!

In August 1969, aged twenty-two and not in the least bit famous, Melanie Safka – known simply as Melanie – played at the opening night of Woodstock (between Ravi Shankar and Arlo Guthrie). She only sang two songs, but the experience of performing to half a million people sitting in the rain and the dark, many of them holding candles, provided her with the inspiration for her first hit, 'Lay Down (Candles in the Rain)'. This would become the title track of an album, released the following year, that also included 'What Have They Done to My Song, Ma', as it was called on the record cover. In fact, the song's title has never been formally settled, but on her website in 2019 Melanie herself was referring to it as 'Look What They've Done to My Song, Ma'.

Melanie's actual ma was Polly Altomare, an actor and jazz singer, and it was through her that her daughter discovered a love of Lotte Lenya, Bessie Smith and Edith Piaf. The influence of the last is especially clear in 'Look What They've Done', from the accordion at the start of the song to the oom-pah/singalong style (not unlike that of Piaf's 'Milord') to the verse in French to the raspy, world-weary voice. Safka's songwriting would always be stylistically eclectic: compare this song to 'Lay Down (Candles in the Rain)' and 'Brand New Key'.

She recorded 'Look What They've Done' in London with some of that city's finest session musicians, the song proving an opportunity for them to show off their multiple skills. From verse to verse, instruments are added to the initial accordion and bass: a tambourine, a cymbal, a guitar, a honky-tonk piano, a glockenspiel, the colour always changing. The record might have been called 'Look What I Can Do to My Song'.

The song has sometimes been thought of as a protest against the record industry, where a big label will take singers and their material, remaking them to suit the label's needs. In the first verse Melanie complains that her song was the only thing she 'could do half right / And it's turning out all wrong'. The later French verse takes things farther: 'Ils ont changé ma chanson' ('They've *changed* my song'). In between, she's more melodramatic, claiming her brain has been 'picked like a chicken bone' and now she's 'half insane', but that one day she might be rich if 'the people are buying tears'.

The song was quite successful, though not in Melanie's own version. It was a hit for Daliah Lavi (in German) and the New Seekers (in English), and when a song you've written is performed by artists as different as Ray Charles and Ray Coniff, Nina Simone and Jack Wild, Miley Cyrus and Arthur Fiedler with the Boston Pops, you can't really complain about what they do to it. Admittedly there was a certain dark irony in the regular use of the song to advertise products from cars to porridge oats.

But songs are like children. They have lives of their own and you can't protect them forever. The more successful a song – and this is true for any piece of music, and any work of art – the less the artist controls it. If you paint a picture of a woman with an enigmatic smile and eyes that follow you around the room, and it becomes the world's most famous painting, sooner or later someone will draw a moustache on her.

There are those who find it a violation of a song to subject it to analysis in order to see how it works, though if any of them started reading the present book, they won't have made it this far. Some people think we should let songs wash over us, reducing critical commentary to a thumbs-up or thumbs-down. Perhaps they want songs to retain their mystery. But this book has not been about liking or disliking individual songs. And we don't imagine anything we've written here will affect the mystery we all feel on hearing a great song. Knowledge doesn't destroy our ability to feel wonderment. On the contrary, the more we know – about the natural world, about the universe, about cookery or cricket – the more we are likely to feel amazed and enthralled.

Oddly, the concern that our appreciation of music will be ruined by close attention only seems to apply to pop music. Classical music and jazz have long been regarded as 'proper' subjects for analytical enquiry, but in academic circles pop music remains largely the domain of sociologists. In many university music departments, still, pop songs can be looked down upon. But the biggest objections to applying musical analysis to pop music always seems to come from the musicians themselves. John Lennon used to scoff at the London *Times* critic William Mann's musical jargon as applied to Beatles songs. Lennon seems to have believed that because *he* didn't know what a pandiatonic cluster or an aeolian cadence was, he couldn't have used them in his songs. But he had.

In writing the present book, we've tried to avoid jargon wherever possible, but there really is nothing you can call a diminished chord except a diminished chord, and if you haven't yet discovered it, you'll find a glossary containing some explanations of terms like this just over the page.

Songs are all around us – we can't avoid them. Most of us know hundreds of songs and can recognise thousands more. Knowing a little about their workings and something of the stories behind them, we believe, helps us better to appreciate these small parcels of music and words. But whatever we may have done to the seventy-five songs in this book – and it's true that some of them, as Melanie complained, have been turned upside down – now is the time to put the book down, listen to them, sing them, and live them again.

Glossary

Aeolian mode Modes are scales, and the aeolian mode is a scale with a flattened (minor) third, sixth and seventh. It may be found on a keyboard by playing the white notes from A to A.

Atonal, atonality Literally the absence of tonality or of a tonal centre. Since some would argue that tonal centres are in the ear of the beholder, atonality may exist more in the composer's intent than in the listener's experience.

Bridge In classical music a bridge is a transitional passage. In pop music, however, where it is often called the 'middle eight' (because it comes in the middle of a song and surprisingly often consists of eight bars), it is a contrasting part of the song. It usually has new words, a new melody, and often sits on a chord that the song hasn't previously used. In the Lennon–McCartney song 'We Can Work It Out', which is in D major, the bridge begins in B minor at the words 'Life is very short', before leading back (as bridges generally do) to the chorus.

Cadence Cadences in harmony are a bit like punctuation marks: full stops, commas, colons. A perfect cadence (V–I) brings with it a sense of finality. A plagal cadence (IV–I) brings a gentler close, most commonly associated with settings of the word 'Amen'. Imperfect cadences are incomplete, they lead the music on (I–V or I–IV).

Chorus or refrain The part of a song that returns, generally with the same words. Broadway songs tend to use the word differently. See *Verse*.

Chromatic, chromaticism A chromatic scale moves by semitones. Chromatic harmony, therefore, in using these close intervals, tends to be richer, more complex and more dissonant than diatonic harmony.

Coda The tailpiece of a song – or any piece of music. It often contains new material.

Diatonic, diatonicism Diatonic scales are the common major and minor scales – also modes – consisting of seven notes including the intervals of five whole tones and two semitones. Diatonic harmony, then, is generally simpler and clearer than chromatic harmony, relating strongly to the system of keys.

Diminished chord A chord made of minor thirds. An example might be C, E flat, G flat (or F sharp), A. The chord consists of two interlocking tritones (C/G flat and E flat/A). It can both disrupt and enrich diatonic harmony.

Dominant note or chord The fifth note of a scale and the chord that is built on it, often represented as chord V. In the key of C, the dominant note is G.

Drone A single tone, generally low, sustained against a moving melodic line.

Enharmonic The 'spelling' of a pitch. F sharp and G flat, for example, are the same note on a piano, its nomenclature dependent upon the other notes around it.

Expressionism The style and ambience of much art – especially post-Romantic Germanic art – at the beginning of the twentieth century, often nightmarish.

Glissando A smooth slide from one pitch to another.

Ground bass A repeating bass line above which a song or other musical composition is elaborated.

Leading note As its name suggests, a leading note leads to the note above it or sometimes below, usually resolving a dissonance in the process. Most commonly, however, the term refers to the seventh note of a major scale (the note B in C major), which often plays a role in leading the harmony back to the tonic.

Mediant The third note of the scale or the chord built on it (chord III).

Melisma In singing, this is when more than one note (and usually several) is allocated to a single syllable.

Middle eight See *Bridge*.

Mixolydian mode A scale with a major third and sixth, but a flattened seventh, found on a keyboard by playing the white notes from G to G.

Obbligato Originally, this referred to part of a score that must be played (that was obligatory). Now it usually means a prominent, soloistic, instrumental line. Some baroque arias, for example, have an obbligato part for oboe, say, or violin, that acts as a decorative counter-melody to the vocal line.

Passacaglia A musical composition above a repeating bass line (or ground bass). Originally, it would have been in the form of a triple-time dance metre.

Pedal point A sort of temporary drone, in which a note (usually in the bass) is sustained creating an expressive dissonance with the next chord or chords, or the vocal line.

Pentatonic Pentatonic scales have five notes including three whole-tone intervals and two intervals of a minor third. You can find them by playing the black notes on a keyboard. These scales are most closely related to the naturally occurring harmonic series.

Portamento A scoop from one note to another, especially in singing and string playing. It is not quite a glissando – which is an even slide from note to note.

Relative minor Every major scale has a relative minor, which shares its key signature (the same number of sharps or flats) and every minor scale a relative major. B minor is the relative minor of D major, and both have two sharps in the key signature.

Sfogato A female singer with a low voice (mezzo-soprano or alto) who nevertheless can hit the high notes of a coloratura soprano.

Subdominant The fourth degree of the scale, or the chord (chord IV) built upon it.

Submediant The sixth degree of the scale, or the chord (chord VI) built upon it.

Tonic note or chord The first (root) note of a scale, or the chord based on that note. Also known as chord I or the 'home key'.

Tritone An interval consisting of three whole tones, also known as augmented fourth or a diminished fifth; for example, C to F sharp. In medieval music, this interval was associated with the Devil.

Verse In a song, the verses, with changing words, often advance the story or change the point of view, while the words of the chorus tend to be fixed. In the classic Broadway song, the verse often came as a preamble, a sort of rationale for the chorus, which generally had changing lyrics, like the verses in a folk song. Jazz singers performing show tunes as standards typically leave out the verse.

Acknowledgements

Four of our chapters (6, 25, 34 and 41) first appeared in *Meanjin*. Some of the ideas and a few sentences from chapters 7, 60 and 63 were tried out by Andrew Ford in *Inside Story*, and parts of chapter 39 are adapted from an article about national anthems he wrote for *The Monthly*. Grateful acknowledgement is made to the editors of these three publications, Jonathan Green, Peter Browne and Nick Feik.

Hugh Riminton and Andrew Ford discussed many of these songs in a segment called 'The Song Remains the Same' on ABC Radio National's *Sunday Extra* throughout 2019. Our thanks to Hugh and to the program's producers, Chris Bullock, Skye Docherty and Amruta Slee.

Over a lifetime, the authors have discussed these songs and hundreds of others with family and friends, editors and producers, as well as each other, but for specific illumination regarding the songs in this book we would like to thank Zane Banks, Felix Cross, Robert Davidson, Graham Devlin, Kate Fagan, Rhiannon Giddens, Rosa Gollan, Heidi Heino, Andrea Keller, Paul Kelly, Seija Lappalainen, Maria Lurighi, Greil Marcus, David McCooey, Brian Ritchie, Daniel Rojas, Vesa Sirén and Andy Vores.

Our thanks go to La Trobe University Press and Chris Feik of Black Inc. for commissioning the book, to Michael Dunn for his close reading of the text and to Dion Kagan for editing the book with enthusiasm, good humour and an eagle eye.

Bibliography

The principal research for this book has consisted of listening to and analysing the songs. In some cases, we listened to more than a dozen recordings of the same song. In the case of the classical songs we studied the scores. For background, we also consulted a wide range of books and articles, and these are some of them.

Block, Geoffrey, ed. *The Richard Rodgers Reader*. New York: Oxford University Press, 2002.

Booth, Mark W. *The Experience of Songs*. New Haven: Yale University Press, 1981.

Branch, Taylor. *Parting the Waters: America in the King years, 1954–63*. New York: Simon & Schuster, 1988.

Bush, Kate. *How to Be Invisible*. London: Faber & Faber, 2018.

Carmichael, Hoagy. *The Stardust Road*. New York: Rinehart and Company, 1946.

Cohen, Leonard. *Stranger Music: Selected poems and songs*. London: Jonathan Cape 1993.

Coleman, Nick. *Voices: How a great singer can change your life*. London: Penguin, 2018.

Daub, Adrian and Charles Kronengold. *The James Bond Songs: Pop anthems of late capitalism*. Oxford: Oxford University Press, 2015.

Day, Aidan. *Jokerman: Reading the lyrics of Bob Dylan*. Oxford: Basil Blackwell, 1988.

Debussy, Claude. Trans. and ed. Richard Langham Smith. *Debussy on Music*. London: Secker & Warburg, 1977.

Dibble, Jeremy. *C. Hubert H. Parry: His life and music*. Oxford: Oxford University Press, 1992.

Dylan, Bob. *The Lyrics: 1961–2012*. New York: Simon & Schuster, 2016.

Eagleson, Ian. 'The Global History of African Music: the Kenyan song "Malaika"', in Toyin Falola and Christian Jennings (eds). *Africanizing Knowledge: African studies across the disciplines*. New Brunswick, NJ: Transaction Publishers, 2002.

Feinstein, Michael. *Nice Work if You Can Get It: My life in rhythm and rhyme*. New York: Hyperion, 1995.

Forte, Allen. *Listening to Classic American Popular Songs*. New Haven: Yale University Press, 2001.

Gottlieb, Robert and Robert Kimball, eds. *Reading Lyrics*. New York: Pantheon, 2000.

Heino, Anni, ed. *Talking to Kinky and Karlheinz: 170 musicians get vocal on The Music Show*. Sydney: ABC Books, 2008.

Holiday, Billie and William Duffy. *Lady Sings the Blues*. New York: Doubleday, 1956.

Kidson, Frank. *Traditional Tunes: A collection of ballad airs*. Oxford: Chas. Taphouse & Son, 1891.

Kramer, Lawrence. *Music and Poetry: The nineteenth century and after*. Berkeley: University of California Press, 1984.

____. *Song Acts: Writings on words and music*. Boston: Brill, 2017.

Lewisohn, Mark. *The Complete Beatles Recording Sessions: The official story of the Abbey Road years 1962–1970*. London: Octopus, 1988.

Lynskey, Dorian. *33 Revolutions per Minute: A history of protest songs*. London: Faber & Faber, 2010.

Maddocks, Fiona. *Hildegard of Bingen: The woman of her age*. London: Faber & Faber, 2013.

Marcus, Greil. *Invisible Republic: Bob Dylan's Basement Tapes*. New York: Henry Holt, 1997.

___. *Three Songs, Three Singers, Three Nations*. Cambridge, MA: Harvard University Press, 2015.

Margolick, David. *Strange Fruit: Billie Holiday, cafe society and an early cry for civil rights*. New York: Running Press, 2000.

Mitchell, Donald. *Gustav Mahler: The Wunderhorn years: Chronicles and commentaries (Volume 2)*. London: Faber, 1975.

Oliver, Paul. *Blues Fell This Morning*. London: Cassell, 1960.

Peterson, Gilles and Stuart Baker, eds. *Bossa Nova: The rise of Brazilian music in the 1960s*. London: Soul Jazz, 2011.

Petkov, Steven and Leonard Mustazza, eds. *The Frank Sinatra Reader*. New York: Oxford University Press, 1995

Potter, Keith. *Vocal Authority: Singing style and ideology*. Cambridge: Cambridge University Press, 1998.

Ricks, Christopher. *Dylan's Visions of Sin*. London: Viking, 2003.

Roach, Archie. Illust. Ruby Hunter and Peter Hudson. *Took the Children Away*. Melbourne: One Day Hill, 2010.

Robine, Marc. *Grand Jacques: Le roman de Jacques Brel*, Paris: Editions Anne Carrière/ Editions du Verbe (Chorus), 1998.

Sams, Eric. *The Songs of Robert Schumann*. London: Methuen, 1969.

Schiff, David. *The Music of Elliott Carter*. London: Ernst Eulenburg Ltd, 1983.

Sirén, Vesa. *Aina poltti sikaria: Jean Sibelius aikalaisten silmin*. Helsinki: Otava, 2012.

Sondheim, Stephen. *Finishing the Hat: Collected lyrics (1954–1981), with attendant comments, principles, heresies, grudges, whines, and anecdotes*. New York: Virgin, 2010.

___. *Look I Made a Hat: Collected lyrics (1981–2011), with attendant comments, amplifications, dogmas, harangues, digressions, anecdotes and miscellany*. New York: Virgin, 2011.

Springsteen, Bruce. *Born to Run*. New York: Simon & Schuster, 2016.

Sudhalter, Richard M. *Stardust Melody: The life and music of Hoagy Carmichael*. Oxford: Oxford University Press, 2002.

Swafford, Jan. *Johannes Brahms: A biography*. New York; Vintage, 1997.

Tippett, Michael. Ed. Meiron Bowen. *Music of the Angels: Essays and Sketchbooks of Michael Tippett*. London: Ernst Eulenburg, 1980.

Vaughan Williams, Ralph. *National Music*. Oxford: Oxford University Press, 1934.

Weller, Sheila. *Girls Like Us: Carole King, Joni Mitchell, Carly Simon – and the journey of a generation*. New York: Simon & Schuster, 2008.

Index

ANDREW FORD is a composer, writer and broadcaster. His award-winning music, performed in more than forty countries around the world, is known particularly for its settings of poetry. A former academic at the University of Wollongong, he has written nine previous books on a wide range of musical topics, and has, since 1995, presented *The Music Show* on ABC Radio National.

ANNI HEINO studied singing, musicology and journalism in her native Finland. Since moving to Australia in 2001, she has written on topics as diverse as politics, wine and music for a variety of publications in both countries. She works as an editor at the Australian Music Centre and was the editor of *Talking to Kinky and Karlheinz*, a book of interviews from *The Music Show*.